Saṁvidullāsaḥ

Manifestation of Divine Consciousness

Swami Lakshman Joo

– A Centenary Tribute –

Swami Lakshman Joo's Birthday (c. 1970s).

संविदुल्लासः

Saṁvidullāsaḥ

Manifestation of Divine Consciousness

Swami Lakshman Joo

Saint-Scholar of Kashmir Śaivism

– A Centenary Tribute –

Edited by

Bettina Bäumer

Sarla Kumar

D.K. Printworld (P) Ltd.

Publishers of Indian Traditions

Cataloging in Publication Data — DK
[Courtesy: D.K. Agencies (P) Ltd. <docinfo@dkagencies.com>]

Saṁvidullāsaḥ = Saṁvidullāsa: manifestation of divine consciousness: Swami Lakshman Joo, saint-scholar of Kashmir Śaivism: a centenary tribute/edited by Bettina Bäumer, Sarla Kumar.

p.; 25 cm.

Includes passages in Sanskrit (roman).

On the life and achievements of Swami Lakshman Joo, 1907-1991, saint-scholar of Kashmir Saivism; contributed articles.

Includes bibliographical references.

ISBN 13: 9788124605882

1. Lakshman Joo, Swami, 1907–1991. 2. Śaivites — India — Jammu and Kashmir — Biography. 3. Kashmir Śaivism. I. Lakshman Joo, Swami, 1907–1991. II. Bäumer, Bettina, 1940– III. Kumar, Sarla, 1928– IV. Title: Saṁvidullāsaḥ.

DDC 294.551 309 2 22

ISBN 13: 978-81-246-0414-4 **Hardbound** **ISBN 10: 81-246-0414-2**
ISBN 13: 978-81-246-0588-2 **Paperback** **ISBN 10: 81-246-0588-2**
First published in India in 2007
Second Revised edition, 2011

Published and printed by:
D.K. Printworld (P) Ltd.
Regd. Office: 'Srikunj," F-52, Bali Nagar
Ramesh Nagar Metro Station
New Delhi-110 015
Phones: (011) 2545-3975; 2546-6019; *Fax*: (011) 2546-5926
E-mail: indology@dkprintworld.com
Website: www.dkprintworld.com

स्वमुक्तिमात्रे कस्यापि यावद्विश्वविमोचने ।
प्रतिबोधेति खद्योतरत्नतारेन्दु सूर्यवत् ॥

svamuktimātre kasyāpi yāvadviśvavimocane,
pratibodheti khadyota-ratna-tārendu-sūryavat.

Enlightenment dawns in some
only for their own salvation, but in others
for the liberation of the entire universe —
just as a firefly, a jewel, a star, the moon
(reflect the light in differing degrees),
but the Sun (enlightens everything).

— Abhinavagupta, *Tantrāloka* 13.159

Saints are broad-minded like the ocean.

— Swami Lakshman Joo

संवित् वपुषे नमः

परम पावन गुरुवर्य के प्रत्यक्ष सान्निध्य से विलग रह कर सोलह वर्षीय काल यापन को हम सभों ने विवश होकर अति धैर्य के साथ बिताया। इस अवधि में न जाने कितनी कठिनाइयों का हमने सामना किया। इन सब विघ्नों के उपस्थित होने पर भी परोक्ष में गुरुदेव का वरद हस्त हम सबों पर रहा तभी हम संकटापन्न परिस्थितियों से अछूते आगे निकल गये ।

गुरुदेव की जन्म-शताब्दी के उपलक्ष में सभी भक्त-जन संवित् उल्लास नामक ग्रन्थ का उन्मोचन कर रहे हैं। इस में कई ऐसे महानुभावों के लेख हैं जिन्हे गुरुदेव का सान्निध्य प्रत्यक्ष रूप से प्राप्त था और कई ऐसे भी हैं, जिन्होंने गुरुदेव के भौतिक कलेवर का दर्शन तक भी नहीं किया है, किन्तु शक्तिपात वश उन्होंने भी अपने लेख लिखे हैं। सभी गुरुदेव के प्रसाद पात्र हैं।

गुरुबहिन बेत्तीना जी तथा सरला जी के कठिन प्रयास का फल साकार रुप में पुस्तक द्वारा हम सबों के समक्ष प्रतिफलित हुआ है। इन दोनों शिष्याओं ने गुरुदेव के प्रति लिखे गये सभी लेखों को जहां एकत्रित किया वहां लेखों के अनुकूल स्मृति दिलाने वाले गुरुदेव के मनोहर चित्रों को भी इस पुस्तक में स्थान दिया है, जिससे ग्रन्थ की महिमा द्विगुणित हो गई है। सभी गुरु-भक्तों के प्रति साधुवाद देते हुए हमें प्रसन्नता हो रही है। भक्तों की चिरकालीन पिपासा को यह ग्रन्थ गुरुदेव से भली-भाँति परिचित करा के शान्त करेगा, ऐसी आशा है। यह निश्चित है, गुरुवर्य का आशीर्वाद ही प्रत्यक्ष तथा परोक्ष रूप से हम सभों का मार्ग-दर्शक है। पुस्तक का मूल्यांकन पाठकजन तो स्वयं कर सकते हैं।

सबों को हार्दिक आशीर्वाद देते हुए,

गुरुकृपावगाहिनी,

प्रभादेवी

Preface

Sixteen years have elapsed since we have been separated from the physical presence of His Holiness Swami Lakshman Joo, our revered Master. It has been a difficult period of our lives when we had to summon all our faculties of fortitude to come to terms with our loss. However, it was only because of the unseen hand of our Master that we realized that he was always with us. It is only due to his powerful grace that we have emerged untouched by the troubled circumstances.

On the occasion of Gurudeva's Birth Centenary which falls on 9th May 2007,[1] we, his devotees and disciples, are bringing out a collection of essays in his memory, titled *Saṁvidullāsaḥ*, or "joyful manifestation of Divine Consciousness." It contains contributions by great scholars and spiritual people who have had direct experience of Gurudeva, but also by those who have not had the *darśana* of his physical form, but who have been touched by his grace.

My Guru sisters Bettinaji and Sarlaji have undertaken this difficult task to bring out this book, the fruit of their effort, to present to the readers Gurudeva's greatness. These two disciples have collected these articles on Gurudeva, and they have also illustrated them with beautiful photos which evoke his memory, and which have enhanced the importance of this volume. I am very happy and I express my gratitude and blessing on all the devotees of Gurudeva. The long-standing desire of the devotees to know about their Gurudeva will be fulfilled, and thus Gurudeva will bestow peace on the readers. One thing is certain, that Gurudeva's blessing is with all of us, whether directly or indirectly, and that he is guiding us from within. The readers of this volume can experience this themselves.

With blessings and asking for Guru's grace,

Prabha Devi

---

1. According to the calendar, the *tithi* falling on 14th April 2007.

Contents

संवित् वपुषे नमः
प्रभादेवी vii

Preface
PRABHA DEVI viii

Key to Transliteration xii

List of Photographs xiii

Introduction 1
BETTINA BÄUMER

1.
Gurustuti — Verses in Praise of the Master 29
ĀCĀRYA RAMESHVAR JHA

I. Life

2.
A Yogī of Kashmir 43
JAIDEVA SINGH

3.
The Sage of Ishber 48
JANKINATH KAUL "KAMAL"

4.
Śrī Guru Īśvara Svarūpa — His Way of Life 58
PRABHA DEVI

5.
Guru-Paramparā: Three Generations of Śaiva Saints 68
RAM CHANDRA RAINA

II. The Ācārya of Kashmir Śaivism

6.
Lilian Silburn and Swami Lakshman Joo — A Fertile Relationship 89
JACQUELINE CHAMBRON

7.
Swami Lakshman Joo and His Place in the Kashmirian Śaiva Tradition 93
ALEXIS SANDERSON

8.
Tribute to the Sage of Kashmir 129
KAPILA VATSYAYAN

9.
The Power of Pure Awareness 133
BETTINA BÄUMER

III. The Enlightening Master

10.
The Making of a Yoginī 157
MOHAN LAL SOPORY

11.
The Ascent to the Lord 162
SARLA KUMAR

12.
The Scientist and the Saint 167
SUDHIR K. SOPORY

13.
My Gurudeva 178
Motilal Sopory

14.
I saw Śiva in Him 184
Arunditi Raina

15.
In Search of Myself 187
Rajan Khosa

16.
Sitting under a Mighty Chinar Tree 193
Sharad Chandra

IV. The Presence Continues

17.
A Transforming Meeting 219
Ernst Fürlinger

18.
The "Icon" of the Divine 224
Borghild Baldauf

19.
Love-song to the Master 233
Ariane Hentsch Cisneros

Appendix 241
Published Works of Swami Lakshman Joo

The Contributors 243

Glossary of Sanskrit Terms 251

Index 257

Key to Transliteration

VOWELS

अ *a*	आ *ā*	इ *i*	ई *ī*	उ *u*	ऊ *ū*
(but)	(palm)	(it)	(beet)	(put)	(pool)
ऋ *ṛ*	ए *e*	ऐ *ai*	ओ *o*	औ *au*	
(rhythm)	(play)	(air)	(toe)	(loud)	

CONSONANTS

Guttural	क *ka*	ख* *kha*	ग *ga*	घ *gha*	ङ *ṅa*
	(skate)	(blockhead)	(gate)	(ghost)	(sing)
Palatal	च *ca*	छ* *cha*	ज *ja*	झ *jha*	ञ *ña*
	(chunk)	(catch him)	(john)	(hedgehog)	(bunch)
Cerebral	ट *ṭa*	ठ* *ṭha*	ड *ḍa*	ढ* *ḍha*	ण* *ṇa*
	(start)	(anthill)	(dart)	(godhead)	(under)
Dental	त *ta*	थ *tha*	द *da*	ध* *dha*	न *na*
	(path)	(thunder)	(that)	(breathe)	(numb)
Labial	प *pa*	फ* *pha*	ब *ba*	भ *bha*	म *ma*
	(spin)	(philosophy)	(bin)	(abhor)	(much)
Semi-	य *ya*	र *ra*	ल *la*	व *va*	
vowels	(young)	(drama)	(luck)	(vile)	
Sibilants	श *śa*	ष *ṣa*	स *sa*	ह *ha*	
	(shove)	(bushel)	(so)	(hum)	
Others	क्ष *kṣa*	त्र *tra*	ज्ञ *jña*	ळ* *ḷ*	ॠ* *ṝ*
(*kṣatriya*)	(*triśūla*)	(*jñānī*)	(*play*)		

अं (ं) *ṁ anusvāra* (nasalisation of preceding vowel) like *saṁskṛti*

अः *visarga* = *ḥ* (aspiration of preceding vowel) like (*prātaḥ*)

ऽ *Avagraha* consonant #'consonant (like:- *ime 'vasthitā*)

Anusvāra at the end of a line is presented by m (म्) and not ṁ

List of Photographs

Frontispiece Birthday (c. 1970s). Courtesy: Rajni Rai.

Plate 1. Sri Narainadas Ràina and Smt. Aranimali, Swamiji's parents, with their Guru, Swami Rāma Joo. Courtesy: P.N. Raina.

Plate 2. Lakshman Joo's birth place. Courtesy P.N. Raina.

Plate 3. An early portrait (1933). From *Srimad Bhagavad-Gita* with Commentary by Abhinavagupta (see Bibliography).

Plate 4. Swami Lakshman Joo's parents. Courtesy: P.N. Raina.

Plate 5. Swami Rāma Joo with his disciples. Courtesy: Motilal Sopory.

Plate 6. *Upanayanasaṁskāra* (initiation with the sacred thread) of the three brothers, with their mother and family (1914). Courtesy: P.N. Raina.

Plate 7. Swami Rāma Joo. Courtesy: N.K. Raina.

Plate 8. Swami Mahtab Kak. Courtesy: N.K. Raina.

Plate 9. Swami Mahtab Kak with disciples. Swami Lakshman Joo is sitting second from the right. Courtesy: P.N. Raina.

Plate 10. Swamiji in his teens. Courtesy: P.N. Raina.

Plate 11. The young saint. Courtesy: P.N. Raina.

Plate 12. Swami Lakshman Joo at the feet of Sri Ramaṇa Maharshi (E.P. Noye in the middle), Tiruvannamalai, 1936. Printed with kind permission from The President, Sri Ramanasramam, Tiruvannamalai.

Plate 13. Swami Lakshman Joo with Sri Ramaṇa Maharshi and his devotees on Arunachala, 1936. Printed with kind permission from The President, Sri Ramanasramam, Tiruvannamalai.

Plate 14. An early portrait. Courtesy: P.N. Raina.

Plate 15. Swamiji in his first ashram. Courtesy: Prabha Devi.

Plate 16. On pilgrimage to Amarnath. Courtesy: Motilal Sopory.

Plate 17. Khir Bhavani Temple complex. Photo credit: Kapil Kaul.

Plate 18. Lilian Silburn with Swami Lakshman Joo, 1975. Courtesy: Jacqueline Chambron.

Plate 19. Lilian Silburn studying with Swamiji, 1975. Courtesy: Jacqueline Chambron.

Plate 20. Alexis Sanderson with Swami Lakshman Joo (c. 1975). Courtesy: Prof. Alexis Sanderson.

Plate 21. Tantra Sammelanam at Vārāṇaseya Saṁskṛta Viśvavidyālaya, 1965. Swami Lakshman Joo is sitting in the front row, fourth from left. Courtesy: Prabha Devi.

Plate 22. Thakur Jaideva Singh with his Master (*c*. 1980s). Courtesy: Jaideva Singh.

Plate 23. Teaching in the Guptaganga Hall. Courtesy: P.N. Raina.

Plate 24. Pandit Jankinath Kaul 'Kamal' with his Master (*c*. 1985).

Plates 24-34: Photo credit Kapil Kaul.

Plates 25-34. Teaching Tantrāloka under the Chinar Tree, 1985.

Plate 35. Swamiji in *samādhi* on his Birthday. (*c*. early 1980s). Courtesy: N.K. Raina.

Plate 36. Swamiji with Devis Sharika and Prabha in Iśvara Āśrama. Courtesy: Prabha Devi.

Plate 37. Swamiji with Sharika Devi in the verandah on their usual *āsana*. Courtesy: Prabha Devi.

Plate 38. Swamiji with devotees in Nishat Bagh. Courtesy: P.N. Raina.

Plate 39. Deep concentration. Courtesy: Rajan Khosa.

Plate 40. In his natural *āsana*. Photo credit: Sarla Kumar.

Plate 41. Teaching under the Chinar tree, 1989. Photo credit: Bettina Bäumer.

Plate 42. In a relaxed mood, 1989. Photo credit: Bettina Bäumer.

Plate 43. Sharika Devi, 1989. Photo credit: Bettina Bäumer.

Plate 44. Devi Sharika at the feet of her Master in the upper ashram (*c*. 1930s). Courtesy: Rajni Rai.

Plate 45. Sharika Devi with Swamiji. Courtesy: Prabha Devi.

Plate 46. The Yoginī. Courtesy: Prabha Devi.

Plate 47. Iśvara Svarūpa. Courtesy: M.L. Kokiloo.

Plate 48. In absorption. Courtesy: M.L. Kokiloo.

Plate 49. In *samādhi* on his Birthday (c. late 1970s). Courtesy: N.K. Raina.

Plate 50. Emerging from *samādhi*, 1985 (still from a video of Swamiji's Birthday, received from P.N. Raina).

Plate 51. Absorbed in study. Courtesy: L. Silburn

Plate 52. Iśvara Āśrama, Nishat, Srinagar. Photo credit: Bettina Bäumer.

Introduction

सर्वदा सर्वभावेषु युगपत्सर्वरूपिणम् ।
त्वामर्चयन्त्यविश्रान्तं ये ममैतेऽधिदेवताः ॥
— शिवस्तोत्रावली १७.३

sarvadā sarvabhāveṣu yugapat-sarva-rūpiṇam ।
tvāmarcayantyaviśrāntaṁ ye mamaite'dhidevatāḥ ॥
— *Śivastotrāvalī* 17.3

Those who in every state worship you always
as having assumed the form of all things —
they indeed
are my chosen deities.

Introduction

By Bettina Bäumer

THE twentieth century has seen great saints in India, some of whom became universally regarded without any attempt at propagating their message, or even without ever leaving their native places. Others have remained hidden and their influence became perceptible only after they left their physical bodies.[1] Some saints became spontaneously enlightened, or seemed to have been in a divine state from childhood onwards; others came to embody a specific spiritual tradition which they not only revived but also carried forward into our age. A sage like Ramaṇa Maharshi attained enlightenment at the age of sixteen and, one might add, without any preparation or seeming effort. It was only later that he tallied his experience with the scriptures, especially of Vedānta. Swami Lakshman Joo Raina,[2] on the other hand, is said to have been in a divine state from early childhood, but he grew up in the context of the Advaita Śaiva tradition of Kashmir. His parents were devotees of the greatest living Śaiva saint of their time, Swami Ram Joo (1853-1915). In his case, actual spiritual experience preceded a later phase of learning and knowledge of the Śaiva tradition and its scriptures.

Swami Lakshman Joo's greatness remained hidden beyond Kashmir and still remains largely so. This may be because of two main reasons: firstly, the geographical and political situation of Kashmir in pre- and post-Independence India, given the context of the reduced number of Kashmiri Hindus in a place of Muslim majority;

1. For the saints of Kashmir, see Bhushanlal Kaul, *Kaśmīr kī Santa-Paramparā* (in Hindi), published by Bhagavan Gopinath Trust, Jammu, 2005.
2. He preferred to call himself "Brahmacārī," also in many of his publications. The suffix *"Joo"* corresponds to Hindi *ji* (or *-jee*), expressing an address of respect. In Sanskrit publications his title is given as *Rājānaka*.

secondly, Swami Lakshman Joo's own reluctance for any kind of publicity or attention. This was due to an innate reticence in his personality, but perhaps more importantly, it may be ascribed to a state of immersion in his spiritual experience which continued throughout his life. Swami Lakshman Joo had an inborn attraction for, and a lifelong engagement with, what he called, as a child, *Baḍe Bod* — in Kashmiri — "the greatest of the great." Significantly, he never gave "It" any name during his childhood. He considered any external activity as a distraction from that "one-pointedness" which he successfully preserved throughout his life. The radiance of his divine personality came totally from within, and it was paired by an equal neglect of any pursuit of fame.

Swami Lakshman Joo only felt drawn to study Sanskrit and the Śaiva scriptures after he had actually undergone some powerful inner experiences and attained unimaginable states of absorption. Interestingly, it was his father's recitation of Utpaladeva's mystical Hymn, the *Śivastotrāvalī*, which awakened a desire to study Sanskrit. Even more significant, perhaps, is the fact that despite his sharpness of intellect and philosophical understanding of *Pratyabhijñā*, it was this *stotra* and its expression of *bhakti* that accompanied him throughout his life. No wonder that he edited and translated this text into Hindi and shared it with his devotees. Advaitic, or non-dualist, *bhakti* remained the undercurrent of his spirituality. For him there was no contradiction between intense devotion and non-duality. Whenever the *Saṁgrahastotra* (his favourite 13th *stotra* of the *Śivastotrāvalī*) was recited, he would break into tears when uttering the verse: *śaktipātasamaye vicāraṇaṁ*.[3] This despite the fact that he was in an uninterrupted state of *śaktipāta* or grace. The following verse of the *Vijñāna Bhairava* — the most important Tantra for practice — is the only verse on *bhakti* and indeed is a complete expression of Swamiji's state:

> *bhaktyudrekād-viraktasya yādṛśī jāyate matiḥ* ।
> *sā śaktiḥ śāṅkarī nityaṁ bhāvayet-tāṁ tataḥ śivaḥ* ॥

> The intuitive insight which is born from intense devotion in one who is detached is the very Energy of Śaṅkara; then one becomes Śiva himself. — v. 121

3. 13.11: "At the time of bestowing grace, O Lord, it is fitting that you should consider (whether I am worthy) but you never do this. What has happened to me now that you delay in revealing your glory?"

It is impossible to fathom the depth of such an experience. Only somebody who could share the same state of consciousness would have been able to receive it. According to his own assertion, there was only one disciple who was so perfectly attuned to her Master — Devi Sharika — and it was she who could fathom and share in the same experience. Others could only receive it in the form of grace. As Swami Lakshman Joo himself expressed it:

> By realizing the state of Universal consciousness, one enters and is established in the Kingdom of Parama Śiva, the Transcendental Being. So the one who is completely established in the transcendental consciousness is no longer a disciple (*śiṣya*), but becomes *jagadguru*, master and our guide and enlightens the whole Universe. Just as the poisonous effect of a venomous cobra is transmitted to a person from a distance, in the same way a mere glance of the one who has attained the state of Universal consciousness, makes one enter the kingdom of transcendental bliss, or just as with an unintentional touch of the flame of a candle another candle burns with the same splendour and glory, in the same way the intentional touch of the great master sends the seeker into the same state of Universal consciousness without making the least difference between the master and the disciple.[4]

This beautiful passage is revealing on different levels: the reality attained by such a *yogī* is universal, and it can be communicated to a worthy disciple. It is a sharing in the power of a supremely blissful state.

But what was unique in Swami Lakshman Joo was the perfection not only at the human and spiritual levels, but in the knowledge of the texts and teachings of the tradition which he inherited from his gurus, which for the sake of brevity and precision we will call Trika from now on.

His Gurus

Even though he was too young to receive any śāstric knowledge from his first Guru, Swami Ram Joo, he was blessed by him at his birth. Swami Ram Joo was an extraordinary saint who not only remained immersed in *samādhi*, but who also

---

4. *Shraddharcan*, p. 202, "Krama system."

possessed knowledge of the scriptures and composed verses in Sanskrit, such as the following:

> *mohaḥ śānto guruvaramukhāmnāyatattvopalabhāt*
> *magnaṁ cetaḥ samarasasamāsvādalolaṁ cidabdhau* ।
>
> *bhāvavrātaḥ praśamamagamāt nirvikalpe samādhau*
> *siddhābhāsaḥ sa bhavatu hi me ko 'pi saṁvit vikāsaḥ* ॥

> My delusion has ceased, having received the ultimate reality of the tradition from the mouth of my Guru.
> My mind, eagerly desirous to taste the same flavour is merged in the ocean of the ultimate consciousness.
> The multitude of thoughts has been subsumed in that ultimate state of *samādhi*.
> May I experience the manifestation of that awareness which is experienced by the perfect beings.[5]

A few years after Swami Ram's death which occurred in 1915, when Lakshman Joo was just seven years old, he became the disciple of his successor, Swami Mahtab Kak.[6] It was from Swami Mahtab Kak that he took formal initiation at the age of sixteen. He studied the *Bhagvad-Gītā* with him, but Mahtab Kak was not really a *Śāstraguru*, rather he was the one who bestowed a powerful *śaktipāta*. Lakshman Joo served him as a devoted disciple, although their personal habits were quite dissimilar. Swami Mahtab Kak lived in a state of *śāmbhavāveśa*,[7] and was a *tāntrika* in the classic sense — he ate meat, drank wine and smoked the *cilam* (water pipe). Swami Lakshman Joo, however, had an innate instinct of non-violence, he was a strict vegetarian, and abhorred alcohol. Still, he used to cook meat for his Guru and serve him alcohol. Later, he described his Master as a *yogī* who could combine the ordinary and the extraordinary:

> The thing that everybody does, the *jñānī*, the realized person also does the same thing. My master used to wake up at 1 a.m. and he

5. Published in *Sāmarasya: Studies in Indian Arts, Philosophy and Interreligious Dialogue (in Honour of Bettina Bäumer)*, ed. S. Das, E. Fürlinger, New Delhi: D.K. Printworld, 2005, motto.

6. He died in 1942.

7. The state of absorption in the Divine (Śambhu).

> would go to the bathroom. Then he would wash his face and then he would call me to give him a cup of tea . . . he would take tea with *kulcā* (Kashmiri bread) and then meditate up to 5 or 6. And then he would smoke hubble-bubble . . . The things you were doing in the period of ignorance, you have to do the same thing in the period of knowledge, in the period when you are realized . . . Activity remains the same, everything remains the same, but the fruit is unique. The fruit of that action is liberation from the pangs of repeated births and deaths.[8]

This extraordinary ordinariness — without meat and wine — was a characteristic also of Swamiji. To casual visitors he would appear simply as a human being performing human actions — such people were unable to perceive the divinity in him.

Swamiji's relationship with his Guru was intense and left a lasting impression — even decades after his *mahāsamādhi*, he would break into tears when performing the annual *śrāddha* ceremony for him. Despite this strong bond, however, he never did ask permission or informed his Master when he left his home in search of solitude. The spirit of independence (*svātantrya*) was indomitable.

The transmission he received from Mahtab Kak was direct and powerful — it was along the lines of Abhinavagupta's description of *śaktipāta*.[9] In the context of the "wayless way," *anupāya*, in his *Tantrāloka* (ch. II) Abhinavagupta says that the mere presence or vision (*darśana*) of a realized Guru can induce the same state in the disciple. Years later, in a conversation with Mother Alice Christensen, an American Yoga teacher, Swamiji described a *kuṇḍalinī* experience which he had had in the proximity of his Master. Here, he speaks of him as a *yogī* of the highest order, one who was "filled with God consciousness." When Mahtab Kak was in meditation — or rather *samādhi* — Swamiji revealed: "The same thing happened to me, by his touch, by his nearness." It was not a physical touch, but "it hit me also," as he expressed it in the briefest possible way. He was not prepared to contain such a powerful experience, and he became unconscious. But the result was, "I

---

8. *Bhagavad-Gītā*, Abhinavagupta's *Saṁgraha Ślokas*, tr. by Swami Lakshman Joo (transcribed from a tape), circulated 2006, p.11.

9. Cp. *Tantrāloka* XIII.

was overjoyed, I was intoxicated," and this intoxication continued: "I am intoxicated now also!" he exclaimed.

In fact, this extraordinary experience with his Guru was later repeated with many of his own disciples: a sharing of the experience by the mere nearness and by the *darśana* of his *samādhi*, a transmission of the power of the divine state — neither by touch nor by word, but by the mere presence.

Despite the power and force of his spiritual masters, however, one should not underestimate the importance of his teacher of the scriptures or *Śāstraguru*, Paṇḍit Maheshvar Razdan. This great scholar of Sanskrit and of the Śaiva texts was employed as a Paṇḍit in the Research Department of the Kashmir State. It was this very Department which did a great service by publishing the "Kashmir Series of Texts and Studies" in the first decades of the twentieth century, and made this great tradition known for the first time outside Kashmir. Paṇḍit Maheshvar Razdan had lost his wife at an early age, and he lived in a kind of *gurukula* with his pupils. Although his name rarely appears as an editor in the Kashmir Series, his contribution must have been noteworthy. His knowledge of the texts of the tradition and his firm grounding in Sanskrit grammar was a powerful attraction as a teacher for Swami Lakshman Joo; eager to match his experience with the original texts, Swamiji dived into learning with all his sharp intelligence.

We do not have any written account by Swamiji about his learned teacher. The only acknowledgement are the concluding *śloka*s of two of his works — the *Gītārthasaṁgraha* and his edition (with Hindi translation) of the *Śivastotrāvalī* with Kṣemarāja's commentary. In the first work he pays tribute to his *Śaivaśāstraguru* thus:

> *sāṁkhyayogādiśāstrajñaḥ pāṇinīye kṛtaśramaḥ* ।
> *śivārkaraśmisaṁpātavyakoṣahṛdayāmbujaḥ* ॥
>
> *mahāmaheśvaraḥ śrīmānrājānakamaheśvaraḥ* ।
> *śaivaśāstraguruḥ sa me vāgpuṣpairastu pūjitaḥ* ॥
>
> I offer worship to my Master in Śaiva Śāstra, Mahāmaheśvara Rājānaka Maheśvara, with the flowers of my speech, he who knows the philosophical systems like Sāṁkhya, Yoga and others, who has

> exerted himself in Sanskrit grammar, and the lotus of whose heart has blossomed because the rays of Śiva's sun have fallen on it.[10]

At the end of the *Śivastotrāvalī* he offers the greatest respects to Maheshvar Razdan.[11] In the style of Abhinavagupta he also mentions there his two chief disciples, Sharika and Prabha, whose devotion has prompted him to do this work.[12] Surely, it was the encouragement from his Paṇḍit that inspired him to edit Abhinavagupta's *Gītārthasaṁgraha* at an extraordinarily young age of 26 (in 1933). Here, he began with an English introduction which already shows his universal outlook. He writes: "In the *Gītārthasaṁgraha* Abhinavagupta has tried to discuss and solve the problem of Life in the Light of the Lord's Song. What is the main purpose of our life here? Why is our mind torn by conflicting duties and loyalties? These are the very questions which he sets out to solve in his commentary. The freedom from all our miseries, he very boldly and emphatically declares, can neither be obtained through the renunciation of the world, nor in hatred towards this world, but by feeling the presence of God everywhere, Who is the inmost centre of each and every object." (p. 6)

The Śaivācārya

For Swami Lakshman Joo there was no dichotomy between experience and learning, between practice and the knowledge of the texts. These were in perfect unity and harmony in his person, so that the one would throw light on the other. Every *śloka* or *sūtra* taught by him would be replete with the living experience contained in it; every, even ordinary action or speech would remind one of the experience described in the texts. One could apply the *biṁba-pratibiṁba* theory to these two aspects: they reflected each other. But clearly, for Swamiji, the priority lay with practice and experience. He would say sometimes that Guru-*bhakti*, devotion to the Guru, was the "master key" for understanding the Śāstras.

What was the tradition which Swamiji received from his masters, which he made known to a wider world, and carried forward? Alexis Sanderson points out

---

10. Abhinavagupta Commentary on the *Bhagavad-Gītā*, p. 187.

11. *Śivastotrāvalī*, p. 356.

12. *śārikāprabhayorbhaktyā tuṣyata jñaptaye tayoḥ* ।
rājānakalakṣmaṇeneyaṁ bhāṣāṭīkā mayā kṛtā ॥ — v. 2

in his contribution that it was only the spiritual and metaphysical side of what came to be known as "Kashmir Śaivism," the ritual and other textual traditions having been lost for some centuries, due to the historical circumstances. Swamiji saw himself in a direct line of succession from Abhinavagupta, and it did not seem that a millennium separated them. Many of his visitors, disciples, and students, were struck by the impression when they met Swamiji that they were in the presence of Abhinavagupta. Lilian Silburn writes in her *Hymns of Abhinavagupta*:

> These hymns are almost unknown in India, only Swami Lakshman Joo and his disciples have the habit of reciting these verses for which they have a great admiration. It is thanks to him that the oral tradition had been solidly renewed, after an apparent eclipse, because the Swami, who is a very learned Paṇḍit as well as a true *yogin* and *jñānin*, has lived and experienced mystically what the ancient Śaiva masters of Kashmir, Abhinavagupta in particular, have expounded. At an early age he decided to devote his life to Trika; he studied texts and manuscripts with two of the best Paṇḍits of his time: Hara Bhatta Shastrin[13] and Rājānaka Maheshvara. From them he acquired a deep and extensive knowledge of all the branches of the philosophy and mysticism of Kashmir Śaivism. It is with him that I have read and re-read these hymns of Abhinavagupta during my stays in Srinagar. During more than twenty years I have profited from his vast knowledge of the *Tantrāloka* which he helped me to translate. He may find here the expression of my profound gratitude.
>
> — p. 1

In a footnote she adds:

> Swami Lakshman Joo has this impression (i.e. that Abhinavagupta remained a *brahmacārin*). One can imagine what Abhinavagupta must have been by living near that Swami.[14]

And in her translation of the *Paramārthasāra* she adds:

---

13. According to the information received from Prabha Devi, he did not receive instruction from this Paṇḍit.

14. *Hymnes de Abhinavagupta*, Paris, ed. De Boccard, 1970, p. 3, fn. 2.

> Lakshman Brahmacārin of Srinagar is a distant but fervent disciple of Abhinavagupta.[15]

Whenever Swami Lakshman Joo referred to his great predecessor, he equated him with Śiva. On my request he composed a dedication to the *Parātrīśikā Vivaraṇa* as translated by his disciple Jaideva Singh (with the double meaning):

> *abhinavacamatkārātmane śivāya namaḥ* ।
>
> Homage to Śiva in the form of the wonderful Abhinava, or
> Homage to Śiva who is ever a new wonder!

In the Preface to his Hindi *Ṭīkā* to the *Tantrāloka* (which unfortunately has remained a fragment) he compares Abhinavagupta with his "chosen deity (*iṣṭadeva*), the embodiment of Śiva (*śivasvarūpa*), who has entered the state of Bhairava."[16]

Historical differences and temporal distance apart, there was a deep inner link with that greatest *ācārya* of Trika. Whatever traditions were lost (as described by Sanderson), it is indeed a great good fortune that in Swamiji's person so much was preserved.

The fact that he was the last living exponent of the ancient Śaiva tradition attracted scholars from all over the world to study with him. They came to learn the principal scriptures and exegetical literature of the Trika school. These scholars seemed to be impelled only by personal contact and chance discovery; this was a time without internet and there were few means of communication or propaganda of any kind. When Swamiji was still living in his first ashram on the hillside above Ishber village in total isolation, he was discovered by scholars like Lilian Silburn, spiritual seekers (a woman from Poland, among others!), and by Paul Reps, a Zen practitioner. The latter mentions his meeting with Swamiji in his book *Zen Flesh Zen Bones*:

> Wandering in the ineffable beauty of Kashmir, above Srinagar I came upon the hermitage of Lakshman Joo.

---

15. *Le Paramarthasara de Abhinavagupta*, Paris, ed. De Boccard, 1979, p. 6, fn. 1.
16. *Śrī Tantrāloka* with Commentary (in Hindi) by Īśvarasvarūpa Svami Laksmana Joo, Ishvar Ashram Trust, Ishber, Nishat, 1995, *Pūrvavaktavya*.

> It overlooks green rice fields, the gardens of Shalimar and Nishat Bagh, lakes fringed with lotus. Water streams down from a mountaintop.
>
> Here Lakshman Joo — tall, full-bodied, shining — welcomes me. He shares with me this ancient teaching from the Vigyan Bhairava . . . It presents 112 ways to open the invisible door of consciousness. I see Lakshman Joo gives his life to its practice.[17]

His period in the upper ashram was certainly a period of intense *sādhanā*, shared only by his chief disciple Sharika Devi, and later by her sister Prabha. This was a time when he was withdrawn from any external contacts into complete silence for months on end, and he even covered his face when moving outside. The inner radiance was too strong. This was also a time of consolidation, and involved imposing a strict discipline on his few close disciples. Thus they were not even allowed to touch him or to do *praṇāma* at his feet.[18] It was only after being completely established in the inner state of God consciousness, and externally, after moving down the hill into the new (and present) Īśvara Āśrama, that he became more accessible and free in relation to his devotees.

Disciples

Lilian Silburn of Paris came to Swamiji when she was already a great scholar in Sanskrit and was a spiritual practitioner. She was in a position to receive Swamiji's teaching of the texts and to make the best possible use of it, as all her translations and commentaries show. She was ready to undergo any hardship and to tolerate external difficulties in order to study with Swamiji, and he was happy to share his knowledge with such an advanced pupil. There was nothing to distract them, not even the crowds of devotees who came to flock the ashram in later years. Lilian only regretted that Swamiji did not give her as much time as she wanted, because he was sometimes busy supervising the construction of his new ashram.

17. Zen Flesh, Zen Bones, compiled by Paul Reps (Penguin Books), first published 1957, several reprints. It has to be said also critically that Paul Reps' version of the *Vijñānabhairava* is a new and highly abridged version of the text and far from the original.
18. This detail was kindly communicated to me by his nephew, Sri P.N. Raina, who was a witness.

In the early 1970s a bright young student from Oxford came to study the texts with Swami Lakshman Joo — Alexis Sanderson (see his article). He has now become the leading scholar in the field of the various schools and texts of non-dualist Kashmir Śaivism. To mention other scholars from Europe who came to study with him at different times: André Padoux from Paris, an authority on the *Mantraśāstra*; and Mark Dyczkowski who worked extensively on the Spanda school.

Two other important scholars who became his disciples were both from Varanasi (or Kāśī), the city of Sanskrit learning. Both were older than Swamiji in years, but they assumed the most humble role of disciples: Ācārya Rameshvar Jha, a great Sanskrit grammarian who became, so to say, "converted" to Trika or Pratyabhijñā, and Thakur Jaideva Singh who was primarily a scholar of musicology and philosophy, but had a good grounding in Sanskrit language. Their role in spreading the tradition of Kashmir Śaivism was different, but equally important. Rameshvar Jha composed Sanskrit *śloka*s in praise of his Guru, a collection of which has been published as *Gurustuti* and is regularly recited by devotees.[19] He also wrote an independent Sanskrit text on the Pratyabhijñā philosophy: *Pūrṇatāpratyabhijñā*. He was a source of reference in teaching the texts back in Varanasi. In fact, Paṇḍit Gopinath Kaviraj and he were the greatest authorities on the school in Kāśī, where they made it known to a number of scholars. Both were in intimate contact with Swamiji, and there was a mutual respect and recognition which united them.

Jaideva Singh, of whom Swamiji remarked "he was very faithful," had the great merit of bringing out the first English translations of some of the most important texts which he had studied with Swamiji. He was engaged with this work until the ripe age of 92, when he was still working on the translation of the *Parātrīśikā Vivaraṇa*. After having studied a number of systems of Indian philosophy — including Vedānta and Buddhist Mādhyamaka — Jaideva Singh used to say: "Kashmir Śaivism is the culmination of Indian philosophy."[20]

---

19. Several editions and collections have been brought out by Ishvar Ashram Trust; to mention only an early one: *Śrīrāmeśvarācāryaviracita Śrī Gurustutiḥ*, ed. Prabha Devi with a Hindi Ṭīkā, Srinagar, 1968.

20. It is not possible in this Introduction to mention other disciples who contributed to the study and spread of Kashmir Śaivism. Among Kashmiri Paṇḍits who studied at his feet we may mention Paṇḍit Jankinath Kaul 'Kamal' (see his article), Paṇḍit Nilkanth Gurtoo, and Paṇḍit M.L. Kokiloo.

Tantra Sammelanam

In 1965 Swamiji was invited to an important scholarly event in Varanasi, the purport of which was to give an authentic presentation of Tantra, a much misunderstood spiritual and philosophical current in Hinduism as well as Buddhism (see plate 21 on p. 81). The gathering of scholars and practitioners at the conference was important, and Gopinath Kaviraj was the key person. Ācārya Rameshvar Jha and Jaideva Singh were present and, as seen on the group photo, there were also Tibetan Lamas of the Vajrayāna tradition. Gopinath Kaviraj requested Swamiji to bring his two disciples, Sharika and Prabha, who were also very learned in the scriptures, but Sharikaji refused to go to such a conference, being too much immersed in her inner state and *sādhanā*.

Swami Lakshman Joo's visit to Varanasi, and specially the presentation of his Sanskrit lecture on *Kuṇḍalinīvijñānarahasya* ("The Secret Knowledge of Kuṇḍalinī")[21] made a great impact. One outcome of this impression made on the scholars of Varanasi was that he was awarded an Honorary D.Litt. by the Varanaseya Sanskrit University! Upon receiving this news back in his ashram in Srinagar, he simply smiled and commented: "I am now a Doctor!"

His contact with Gopinath Kaviraj was deep and mutually enlightening. Probably it was he who spoke to Mā Ānandamayī about Swamiji, and she came herself to meet him. It must have been an extraordinary meeting of the two saints, but we have no record of it.

Kuṇḍalinī

Swamiji was very reserved when speaking about his own experience of awakening; he rather used to give hints about it and, of course, it could be directly fathomed in his presence, if one was attuned to it, or was, in traditional terms, a *pātra*, a worthy receiving vessel.[22] He hints at his awakening of the *kuṇḍalinī*, which was

21. This paper was originally published along with the other papers of the conference in: *Sarasvatī Suṣamā* (*Vārānaseyasaṁskṛtaviśvavidyālayapatrikā*) 20/1, Saṁvat 2022 (1965), pp. 57-62. It has been republished and translated several times, without mentioning the source.

22. According to double meaning of *pātra*: vessel, person, especially worthy person and disciple.

so powerful that he could stand it for only a few seconds: "It remains only for three or four seconds and the rest of your life is intoxicated with that . . . you cannot tolerate that intensity of joy in the limited body."[23] He often remarked that if it had lasted longer he would have had to leave the body. The greatest grace was that he remained in the body as a *jīvanmukta*, showing the integration of that highest experience with ordinary life in total naturalness.

Comparable to the *bodhisattva* ideal of Mahāyāna Buddhism, the Śaiva *yogī* who remains in the body after enlightenment does so for the sole purpose of helping others. In this sense Swamiji explains the following *sūtra* from the *Śivasūtras*:

> *dānamātmajñānam* — III.28
>
> His only purpose for remaining in his body is to impart his knowledge to others. (Sūtra)
> During the remainder of his life, his reason for living is giving his real knowledge of God consciousness to others.
>
> — *Śivasūtra Vimarśinī*, p. 197

And the quotation given by Kṣemarāja from an unknown Tantra applies to himself:

> Those yogic heroes who are established in the Kula system reveal the reality of God consciousness to others by merely looking (*darśana*) or touching. By this revelation, all of their disciples cross over to the other side of the bondage (*saṁsāra*) of repeated births and deaths and are liberated.
>
> In fact, only that person who has become just like Śiva, being always busy in his daily routine with internal recitation (*ajapa*) and ruling his own wheel of energies, can be helpful in illuminating others.
>
> — *Śivasūtra Vimarśinī*, pp. 197-98

We find another hint at his enlightenment in a poem which he composed. In this poem he tries to describe another form of *kuṇḍalinī* experience, one that has happened spontaneously at the moment of waking up, or rather at the juncture point between sleep and waking.[24] Such an experience or *dhāraṇā* is described in

23. Interview with Mother Alice, p. 11.
24. Poem published in *Swami Lakshman Joo, Kashmir Saivism — The Secret Supreme*, p. 120.

the *Vijñāna Bhairava* which, in its brevity, sheds light on Swamiji's own spiritual states.[25]

In the Sanskrit lecture on *kuṇḍalinī* he also stresses the fact that this is based on his own experience:

> Here also I want to express something on the basis of my own experience. When the vital airs (*prāṇa*) of a Śiva-*yogī*, who is endowed with grace of extreme intensity (*tīvra śaktipāta*) get entrance into the Royal Road (*suṣumnā mārga*) then his vital power (*prāṇa-śakti*) without touching the course of piercing the *ṣaṭ-cakra*s in the system of its rising through the middle path, reaches the aperture of *Brahman* (*brahmarandhra*, the prāṇic centre at the top of head — the *sahasrāra cakra*) towards being-consciousness-bliss itself. In this way that *yogī* abides in *krama-mudrā*.[26]

His reluctance to speak about this and to share it only with advanced disciples, was also due to the fact that so much misuse and misunderstanding of the practice and experience of *kuṇḍalinī* was — and is — prevalent, both, in India, and more so in Western countries. He attributed most of the claims of people having the *kuṇḍalinī* experience to imagination or self-deception. According to Swamiji, the dangers involved in practising without guidance by an experienced Guru are many, reaching from physical to mental disorders and spiritual perversion. Above all, the important factor missing in many who attempt to "practice *kuṇḍalinī yoga*" are the basic disciplines of *yama* and *niyama* (the first two steps of *yoga*). These are indispensable according to Swamiji and give a firm moral and ethical ground to spiritual practice.

Besides, a practice without devotion to God is in danger of becoming a search for self-satisfaction. His two lectures given to disciples of Mahesh Yogi and published in his book *Kashmir Śaivism — The Secret Supreme*, are brief but enlightening. Whatever he expresses in general terms is in fact his own experience:

> When a *yogin* has an intense desire and longing for achieving the

25. Cp. *Vijñānabhairava*, v. 75 which, interestingly, refers to the intermediary state between waking and sleep.

26. Translated by Jankinath Kaul "Kamal" in *The Awakening of the Supreme Consciousness*, pp. 95-96.

> recognition of Supreme "I" through the *mantra 'aham,'* "I am," then because of this desire and longing, his breath becomes full of bliss, joy, and ecstasy. . . . This is because the blissful force of breath is transformed into energy. This is the rise of energy in *prāṇa kuṇḍalinī.* He feels that energy is being developed and that he is becoming the embodiment of energy. — pp. 129, 131

What better illustration but his own radiance as an embodiment of divine energy? He said himself that this experience of God consciousness is a "fountain of excessive joy" which "continues for a long time and it flows in each and every vein of your body." (Interview with Mother Alice, p. 11)

The introductory verse to his Sanskrit lecture on *kuṇḍalinī,* in the form of a *maṅgala śloka,* reveals in a nutshell his *kuṇḍalinī* experience:

> The Primal Energy —
> flashing from her Divine innate source,
> with sublime illumination perceived by her radiance,
> piercing the six wheels of Energy,
> arousing awareness of Self,
> producing a sweet resonant note while in upright course,
> and, imparting bliss
> as She attains union with her Lord
> in the lotus of thousand petals,
> centered in consciousness that pervades the universe;
> May that Kaulikī *kuṇḍalinī*—
> The Power of Śiva that manifests the universe —
> Bestow on you all
> The spontaneous flow of cosmic ecstasy.[27]

Advaita in Practice

Swamiji loved to begin every reading of the *Tantrāloka* or any other lecture with the introductory verse by Somānanda to his *Śivadṛṣṭi.* When he started the Journal *Mālinī* (of which only one issue came out during his lifetime), he also introduces it with this verse, and his interpretation:

---

27. Translated by Jankinath Kaul in *The Awakening of the Supreme Consciousness,* p. 87.

asmadrūpasamāviṣṭaḥ svātmanātmanivāraṇe ı
śivaḥ karotu nijayā namaḥ śaktyā tatātmane ıı

Spiritual writings mostly begin with salutation to God. Generally speaking, these salutations are offered in the first person, e.g. "I offer salutations to God, and pray that all obstacles may be removed so that I may attain my real nature." In Śaivism the manner of salutation is not only different but also unique in that here the one who offers homage to Śiva is not other than Śiva, nor are the obstacles (for the removal of which the prayer is offered) other than Śiva; and even the media, through which homage is offered, are one with Śiva. In the above *śloka,* therefore, Somānanda substitutes the first person by third person saying: "Let Śiva, who has taken the form of my individual being, offer salutation to His Universal Being — Śiva, through media, which are, indeed, one with Śiva, for the removal of obstacles which are indeed, one with Śiva." The purpose of this salutation is too obvious to need explanation, namely to unite the individual being with the Universal Being.

— *Mālinī,* June 1970

Advaita, non-duality, is not merely a philosophical doctrine, it is a practice, called *advaitācāra,* or *paramādvaita,* "supreme non-duality," "such an elevated viewpoint that it does not fear what is different from itself."[28]

The practical implications of Advaita could be seen in Swamiji's life. As he comments on the following *dhāraṇā* of *Vijñāna Bhairava*:

sarvatra bhairavo bhāvaḥ sāmānyeṣvapi gocaraḥ ı
na ca tad-vyatirekeṇa paro 'stīyadvayā gatiḥ ıı — V. 124

The reality of Bhairava is present everywhere, even in common people. He who knows that nothing exists apart from Him, attains the non-dual state.

And Swamiji comments on this verse:

God is realized by everybody. He is perceived by everybody. God is

28. R. Torella, *The Īśvarapratyabhijñākārikā*, p. xxi.

> realized by ignorant people. God is realized by those who have nothing to do with God. They have also realized God. And those who are only engrossed in household activities, those women carrying water from the river, who know nothing else, they have also realized God. So, *dṛṣṭaḥ:* he is realized, from all sides he is realized, let Him elevate us.[29]

Universality

The natural consequence of a living practice of Advaita is universality which implies openness of this spiritual path to all people irrespective of race, religion, gender and caste.[30] This universality is based, first of all, on the all-pervasiveness of the Divine consciousness, which is not limited to living beings but equally present in the whole of reality:

> "Knowledge, will, etc. are not only found within me, they are present in jars and other objects." Meditating in this way on the omnipresent (Reality), one becomes all-pervading.
>
> — *Vijñāna Bhairava* v. 105, p. 126[31]

For Swamiji this truth was not only a theory but a practical reality. He was open to all and received people from different castes and religions. Muslims used to come to him for help and blessing even in the worst times of terrorism and expulsion of Hindus from the Valley. He would never encourage any negative comments about Muslims, which are common among other Kashmiri Hindus, due to the persecution they have suffered. Many simple people came to him for blessing and healing, and they were not treated differently from the great, such as Indira Gandhi. Nobody would go away empty-handed.

Although he respected the feelings of the orthodox Paṇḍits and fulfilled their rules and expectations, orthodoxy or the pure-impure dichotomy did not concern him personally.[32]

---

29. *Vijñāna Bhairava, The Practice of Centring Awareness*, p. 146.
30. This equality has also been laid down by Swamiji in his Final Will, para 8.08 (printed by the Ishwar Ashram Trust, p. 5).
31. See Swamiji's commentary on the same.
32. Cp. *Vijñāna Bhairava* v. 123 (p. 145f.).

Swamiji's openness to other religions also included a respect for the masters of other traditions, be they Buddhist, Christian, or Muslim. He always spoke with deep respect and reverence about Christ,[33] or about Buddhist masters. He would never ask any disciple coming from a different religious background to give up his or her original faith when taking Śaiva initiation. The initiation was given on a purely spiritual level and did not carry any sectarian implications.

Universality meant for Swamiji also the significance of Kashmir Śaivism for a spirituality of our present age. In the Preface to the first issue of the *Mālinī*, he writes:

> There is a real case for consideration of Kashmir Śaivism, the spirit of the present age being conducive to the appreciation of all such attempts as are made to know the truth of things. Kashmir Śaivism is basically an enquiry into the truth of human experience. It is a venture at discovering permanence in changefulness and universality in individuality. It, therefore, affirms the spirit of modern science. Studied in the right way, Kashmir Śaivism is bound to reveal its utility and charm to the modern world.
>
> Kashmir Śaivism is one of the systems of Indian spiritual thought; there is a purposeful uniqueness in its outlook. Here one is not required to strive for the attainment of universal consciousness as it is already there, but the difficulty is that there is lack of awareness because of which one feels its absence: once there is awareness there is no question of forgetting one's true nature.
>
> — *Mālinī*, June 1970

Ascending and Descending

Following the expression of the Trika tradition, Swamiji stressed that the individual must rise to universality — the texts speak of the spiritual aspirants as *āruruksụ*, those desirous of ascending. It is significant that Abhinavagupta presents the three — or four — spiritual ways (*upāya*) in his *Tantrāloka* in descending order. The inner logic of this apparent contradiction was resolved by Swamiji. As long as we are at the level of individuality, ascension to a higher level of consciousness is

33. In a video interview with Mother Alice, for instance, published in *Malini*, September 2006, p. 13.

essential. However, when one dwells at the Divine level, such as was true for Swamiji, it is rather a descent, in order to help others, the disciples, to ascend. The same applies to the four levels of speech: *parā, paśyantī, madhyamā* and *vaikharī*:

> When the aspirant resides in the *śāmbhava* state[34] in complete universal I-ness (*pūrṇāhantā*), he is travelling in the kingdom of *vāk*, 'speech,' Here he resides in the principal and supreme speech which is called *parāvāk*. And not only does this aspirant reside in that state of *parāvāk*, but he travels in other sounds also. He comes out and he goes in. He has the ability of travelling from the supreme to the gross and from the gross to the supreme. He can ascend and descend without varying his consciousness. His consciousness will remain the same in each and every state.[35]

In Swamiji's presence, one could actually feel the difficulty he had in coming down from the highest level of consciousness. What Vishvanatha Swami writes about Ramaṇa Maharshi was equally true of Swamiji: "When he spoke, the words seemed to come out of an abyss."[36] In terms of Kashmir Śaivism, one could say that his words descended from the level of *parā*, the Supreme Word, down to *vaikharī*, the expressed. Every word emerged as it were from deep silence. When the *Vijñāna Bhairava* describes a practice to keep awareness between words or even syllables, this is what is meant.[37] The background of real speech is silence. That is why Swamiji abhorred gossip and superficial talk which was sometimes prevalent among devotees.

Descending has to do with compassion, and Swamiji's coming down to our level was sheer compassion.

Simplicity

For Swamiji, silence and simplicity were like protective shields around the state of God consciousness in which he always bathed. Simplicity was a lifestyle, from the

34. The highest of the three states of union or pervasion with the Divine (Śambhu).
35. *Kashmir Saivism — The Secret Supreme*, p. 45.
36. First Meetings with Ramaṇa Maharshi, p. 1.
37. Cp. *Vijñāna Bhairava* v. 40, it speaks actually about *varṇa*, phonemes.

ashram buildings and its daily routine such as food, to the way of dealing with devotees and visitors.[38] Swamiji would sit in the open verandah or in the *maṇḍapa* in the garden, preferably in the garden itself in an easy chair. There was no *siṁhāsana* or golden throne as in some ashrams and for some Gurus. The devotees spread out on the lawn in the garden. There were no formal *darśanas*. Swamiji's spontaneity was a true expression of *svātantrya*, the freedom taught by the tradition. There was no question of any donation and no money involved. He shared everything freely with his devotees, and if anybody brought fruit or sweets or almonds, these were immediately distributed. The simplicity and purity of the ashram was guarded by the absence of telephone, radio, television or even newspaper. Telepathic communication was more direct than any phone or e-mail. Anything artificial like plastic or even soap was avoided, instead pure earth and ash was used for washing hands and cleaning vessels. Without any expressed ecological ideology it was Swamiji's love for nature which dominated life in the ashram and on excursions. He insisted so much on vegetarianism out of love for all living beings and a deep-rooted sense of non-violence. Kashmiris, even Paṇḍits, are mostly meat-eaters, and it took much persuasion to turn them into vegetarians.

Meeting Saints

Swamiji believed in a kind of spiritual network and a communication between saints, including, of course, those from different traditions. He would personally visit them; and they came to have his *darśana*. The most memorable meeting was in early 1936 when he travelled from Kashmir to the far South, to Tiruvannamalai, to meet the sage Śrī Ramaṇa Maharshi. He was just 28 and had already reached a high stage of realization. Still, he felt the need of confirmation by a living saint or *jīvanmukta*. Ramaṇa's fame had reached as far as Kashmir, and, of course, Western countries through his Western disciples. With characteristic brevity, Swamiji only described what happened when he reached the ashram at the foot of Arunachala, and entered the meditation hall where Ramaṇa would sit, give *darśana* and answer questions of seekers. He did *praṇāma* before the Maharshi, and as soon as Ramaṇa's eyes fell on him he entered a state of *samādhi* which lasted for a long time. It must have been a moment of recognition — *pratyabhijñā*, even mutual recognition of their state of self-realization. For the young Kashmiri saint, it was also an immediate

38. See the article by Prabha Devi in this volume.

initiation by look: *dṛṣṭidīkṣā,* one of the ways of transmission which does not need any words.

He remembered that during his stay of a few weeks that he spent in the nearness of the Maharshi, these were blissful days in the divine presence. Ramaṇa would invite him every morning early at 4 or 5 to climb up on the holy Hill, Arunachala. His surrender and devotion is visible on the photos taken at the time (see plates 12 and 13 on p. 40).

In the *Talks with Sri Ramaṇa Maharshi* we find two entries of Lakshman Joo Brahmachārī asking questions.[39] Brief as they are, they show his occupation with the central theme of both, Kashmir Śaivism and Ramaṇa Maharshi's approach to self-enquiry, the central question concerning the I, *aham.*

> Lakshman Brahmachārī asked: Enquiry of "Who am I?" or of the I-thought being itself a thought, how can it be destroyed in the process?
>
> Maharshi: When Sītā was asked who was her husband among the *ṛṣi*s (Rāma himself being present there as a *ṛṣi*) in the forest by the wives of the *ṛṣis*, she denied each one as he was pointed out to her, but simply hung down her head when Rāma was pointed out. Her silence was eloquent.
>
> Similarly, the Vedas also are eloquent in *neti neti* (not this, not this) and they remain silent. Their silence is the Real State. This is the meaning of exposition by silence. When the source of the I-thought is reached it vanishes and what remains over is the Self.
>
> Lakshman Joo: *Pātañjala Yogasūtras* speak of identification.
>
> Maharshi: Identification with the Supreme is only the other name for the destruction of the ego. — 6th January 1936[40]

There we find a subtle hint at the difference of the two schools of spirituality, Vedānta and Trika or Pratyabhijñā, the latter speaking not only of Recognition of the Lord, but of union (*samāveśa*).

---

39. There he is wrongly identified as belonging to the Sri Ramakrishna Mission, and no mention is made that he has come from Kashmir (see pp. 115 and 121)

40. Talks with Śrī Ramaṇa Maharshi, Tiruvannamalai, Sri Ramanasramam, 6th edn., 1978, p. 115.

A similar question was asked a few days later on 15th January, 1936:

> Lakshman Brahmachārī asked: "Can one imagine oneself as witness of the thoughts?"
>
> Maharshi: It is not the natural state. It is only an idea (*bhāvanā*) — an aid to stilling the mind. The Self is ever the witness, whether so imagined or not. There is no need to so imagine except for that purpose. But it is best to remain as one's Self.[41]

But no doubt the deepest communication and also clarification happened in silence.

It is the spiritual bond which unites India from North to South in spite of the differences in languages and customs. What happened at the time of Abhinavagupta when a monk from Madurai travelled all the way to Kashmir to become a disciple of the great Śaiva *ācārya*, was, so to say, repeated in reverse with Lakshman Joo coming to Ramaṇa Maharshi. Madhurāja composed the wonderful *Gurunāthaparāmarśa*. Swamiji composed Sanskrit *śloka*s in praise of the Maharshi which he titled *Ramaṇastutiḥ*. To quote only two verses:

> *maunena mandasmitabhūṣitena*
> *sadbhaktalokasya namo nudantam* ।
>
> *apārakāruṇyasudhātaraṅgair-*
> *apāṅgapātairavalokayantam* ॥ 3 ॥
>
> *adrakṣamakṣīṇadayānidhānam*
> *yatkṣetrabhāge ramaṇam maheśvaram* ।
>
> *upāsakānām yadupāsanīyam*
> *aruṇācalaṁ taṁ śirasā namāmi* ॥ 4 ॥
>
> I bow my head to Ramaṇa, the great Lord, who in silence is adorned with a slight smile, and who removes the darkness from the true devotees by waves of nectar from the ocean of compassion, looking with a side glance. In the sacred place I got a direct vision of the treasure of indestructible mercy. The one who is the object of worship for the spiritual seekers — to Arunachala (I bow).

---

41. Talks with Śrī Ramaṇa Maharshi, p. 121.

It is difficult to know from outside what really happens when two saints meet. We can only mention some such meetings, without going into further details. In Kashmir itself there were some saints with whom Swamiji kept in contact, whether of his own tradition, of other Hindu traditions, Vedānta or *bhakti*; or Sufis. Swami Atmaram was a great saint as well as a scholar and a benefactor of the poor and suppressed people, and Swamiji met him often and stayed in his ashram (Gosani Gond Ashrama in Anantnag). He passed away in 1976. Sufi saints used to visit Swamiji and he felt close to them. One episode illustrates this relationship. Once Swamiji went on pilgrimage to Khīr Bhavānī, the famous Devī Shrine and spring, with a group of disciples. At the gate to the temple complex the priest met Swamiji, fell at his feet and stated a problem that he was facing. A Muslim wanted to enter the shrine, but he was not permitted to let him in. Swamiji knew him as a Sufi, he immediately solved the problem. He embraced the Sufi tightly and entered the temple with him, saying "we are one!." What objection could the priest have to such a spiritual unity? Another Sufi saint whom he visited specially was a famous Hindu Sufi in Kanpur who was the Sufi Master of Lilian Silburn who told Swamiji about him. Their meeting was brief but powerful.

Swamiji went several times to Rishikesh with a whole group of devotees, where he met Swami Śivānanda, stayed in his ashram, and gave a discourse on *yoga* in the Kashmir Śaiva tradition. Famous Gurus and spiritual personalities visited him in his own ashram, including Swami Muktananda of Ganeshpuri, and Mahesh Yogi who invited Swamiji to deliver lectures on Kashmir Śaivism to his disciples. J. Krishnamurti also visited him whenever he came to Kashmir. There is an interesting anecdote about the failed meeting with the famous miracle saint Meher Baba from Bombay. It was at the time when Swamiji lived in the upper ashram, and was still reluctant to receive visitors. He was in *samādhi* when a messenger came to request him to receive Meher Baba with about 60 disciples. Swamiji flatly refused to receive him! Meher Baba with all his followers were on their way back to their camp in Srinagar when Swamiji regretted his refusal and sent a messenger after them. But then Meher Baba was not ready to return. To make up for this missed meeting, Swamiji sent his two disciples, Sharika and Prabha, to Meher Baba's *satsaṅga*. The hall was full with hundreds of devotees. The two Devis placed themselves at the back of the hall. But Meher Baba spotted Sharika Devi and called her in front to sit by his side, to the surprise of the crowd of devotees. He thus acknowledged her high spiritual state.[42]

Sacred Places

One may argue that saints do not need to visit holy places, *tīrtha*s and temples, because they contain them in their own body which is a *tīrtha*. But in spite of this truth, they do feel the attraction of the sacred places where a special power is present. Kashmir is blessed by such powerful places, as Abhinavagupta acknowledges at the end of his *Tantrāloka*. It is after all the *siddha*s and *yoginī*s who have lived and practised at such places which have sanctified them. Swamiji was no exception. He used to visit these places either alone, in company of his two close disciples, Sharika and Prabha, or with a whole group of devotees. We may focus only on a few of his favourite pilgrimage sites.

Since his Guru, Mahtab Kak, was living in Chandpora, near Harwan, it was natural for him to meditate at the ancient Buddhist site dating from the fifth century CE and set in a splendid landscape, facing the Mahādeva Mountain, and overlooking the valley and the Dal Lake. He frequently returned to Harwan, mostly on foot from his ashram, and enjoyed the special atmosphere of the place where Buddhist monks had meditated for centuries, and which therefore emanates a deep stillness. Not very far from Harwan, in the valley and now located inside the Dachigam Wildlife Sanctuary, among leopards, deer and bears, is situated the large rock on which, according to legend, Vasudeva discovered the *Śivasūtras* inscribed, still called Shankarpal.[43] Swamiji frequently went there with his disciples, and bathed in the pure stream flowing beneath this legendary rock. He would often teach the *Śivasūtras* at the very place of their original revelation. Prabha Devi recalls that they sometimes spent several days there, cooking their picnic food outside, and studying the *Śivasūtras*.

On the other side of Harwan is the massive Mahādeva Parvat on which Vasugupta is supposed to have lived in the ninth century. The pilgrimage to that sacred mountain is arduous and takes three days. Swamiji did it at least once with his devotees.

---

42. As told by Prabha Devi who was a witness.

43. The reference is found in Kṣemarāja's commentary on the *Śivasūtras*, I.1.

A powerful *śaktipīṭha* in Srinagar itself, or rather on Hariparvat, is the self-manifested rock and temple of Shārikā Devī. Swamiji used to go there with his two disciples and often meditated at the foot of the rock for the whole night. His disciple Sharika would enter deep states of *samādhi*, and Swamiji once said that she was the human embodiment of the same Devī who was manifested in a rock. On such occasions he would dress up Sharika as a man, to avoid any misgivings.

The event related to the pilgrimage to Vaiṣṇavī Devī[44] recounted by Prabha Devi in this volume is revealing: on that occasion the Devī herself manifested in Swamiji, so that their physical pilgrimage became redundant.

* * *

These are some glimpses of the life of Swami Lakshman Joo. Neither this introduction nor the contributions in this volume pretend to give a biography which still needs to be written. The following contributions come from disciples, students, relatives and admirers of Swamiji, covering different aspects of the influence he exerted and continues to exert on different people. All of them acknowledge the inadequacy of language in describing the experiences with the Master. And yet, even inadequate accounts may throw some light on the presence of this great saint and scholar whose life and influence spanned nearly the whole of the twentieth century.

There are witnesses of the early times, relatives who have been present at important events of his life; occasional visitors, disciples and students, and some who have been attracted by his radiance even after his physical disappearance and without ever meeting him in the body. They witness to the fact that he is still present and guiding spiritual seekers on that extraordinary path.

Saint Thomas Aquinas already said that "whatever we receive, it is received in the mode of the receiver."[45] Therefore, obviously, the contributions in this volume reflect as much as the author could receive from Swamiji's infinite store of consciousness, and it is also natural that they do this in the light of their own experience and expression. In Swamiji's own words, we all "have only touched the

44. Swamiji corrected the spelling of the name of this famous Devī shrine, which is wrongly called "Vaishno Devī."

45. In Latin *quodquod recipitur ad modum recipientis recipitur.*

shores of that great ocean of God consciousness." Few have really dived in it, as he had.

A spontaneous way of approaching the life of a saint is always directed at the beginnings — therefore several articles focus on Swamiji's birth, early experiences, flight from home and initiation. But, in fact, when Swamiji was once asked in an interview: "What was the turning point in your life?," he answered briefly: "No turning point. Everything was already there." This is the true expression of *pratyabhijñā* — whatever experience we have, it is only a reminder of that very divine state that was always there. For the same reason, the most important event in our relation to the Master is always the overwhelming impression of the first meeting. The editor of the inspiring book *First Meetings with Ramaṇa Maharshi*[46] writes in the Introduction: "The first meeting stands apart. When we record what happened then it comes straight from the heart unpolluted by thought. It has the aroma of eternity."

The Title

This volume is intended as a tribute on the Birth Centenary of Swami Lakshman Joo and is a kind of commemoration volume (*Smr̥tigrantha*). However, the title *Saṁvidullāsaḥ* suggests that it is a reflection, albeit imperfect, of that joyful and overwhelming manifestation (*ullāsa*) of Divine consciousness (*saṁvid*) as it was embodied in Swamiji.

46. Ed. A. R. Natarajan, Bangalore (Ramana Maharshi Centre for Learning), 3rd edn., 2000, p. iv.

1

Gurustuti
Verses in Praise of the Master

Ācārya Rameshvar Jha

सर्वज्ञो यो गुरुः साक्षात् शिवो लक्ष्मण एष सः ।
यत्पादरजसा पूतो मादृशोऽपि शिवायते ॥ १ ॥

sarvajño yo guruḥ sākṣāt śivo lakṣmaṇa eṣa saḥ ।
yat-pādarajasā pūto mādr̥śo'pi śivāyate ॥ 1 ॥

The omniscient Guru who is Śiva Himself

he is Lakṣmaṇa.

Purified by the dust of his feet

he transforms even a person like me into Śiva.

अपीन्द्रवज्रादपि विष्णुचक्रतो न हन्यते यो भवदोषविप्लवः।
तदादिदोषक्षणन्नैक हेतवो जयन्ति मत् श्री गुरुपादपांसवः ॥ २ ॥

apīndravajrād api viṣṇucakrato
na hanyate yo bhavadoṣa-viplavaḥ ।
tadādi doṣa kṣaṇannaika hetavo
jayanti mat śrī guru-pāda pāṁsavaḥ ॥ 2 ॥

Neither the thunderbolt of Indra nor Viṣṇu's discus

can destroy the misery of the defect of worldly existence.

(But) the dust of the feet of the glorious Guru

is victorious in defeating the causes of this defect

in a moment.

अनन्तरूपेण भयप्रदेन विभासमानेन जगद्ग्रहेण ।
गृहीत आसं नितरां विपन्नः कृतः प्रवृद्धो भवता समृद्धः ॥ ३ ॥

anantarūpeṇa bhayapradena
vibhāsamānena jagad-graheṇa ।
gṛhīta āsaṁ nitarāṁ vipannaḥ
kṛtaḥ pravṛddho bhavatā samṛddhaḥ ॥ 3 ॥

I was completely caught by unending worldly troubles

creating fear —

but you have drawn me out and given me fulfilment.

विहाय देवं सकलं परोक्षं समक्षभूतं गुरुदेवमेकम् ।
नमामि सोऽहं फलदं समक्षं श्रीलक्ष्मणं लक्ष्मणयौगिकार्थम् ॥ ४ ॥

vihāya devaṁ sakalaṁ parokṣaṁ
samakṣabhūtaṁ gurudevam ekam ।
namāmi so'haṁ phaladaṁ samakṣaṁ
śrī lakṣmaṇaṁ lakṣmaṇa-yaugikārtham ॥ 4 ॥

Abandoning the entire group of the invisible gods

I offer obeisance to the one visible God in the form of the Guru, to him who is none than myself, who is Śrī Lakṣmaṇa,

who is visible and present to us,

and whose name is true to its meaning.

भवन्तमासाद्य जनैर्विमुच्यते न यान्ति पारं यदि कोऽपि दुर्धियः।
सहस्रभानोर्महिमा न हीयते दिवा न पश्यन्ति च पेचका यदि॥ ५॥

bhavantamāsādya janair-vimucyate
na yānti pāraṁ yadi ko'pi durdhiyaḥ ।
sahasrabhānor-mahimā na hīyate
divā na paśyanti ca pecakā yadi ॥ 5 ॥

Having taken refuge in you, people are liberated,

but if any ignorant person

does not attain the other shore (of liberation)

(it is not your fault, for:)

it does not diminish the glory of the thousand-rayed sun

if the owl does not see by day !

विलोक्यते नाथ य एव कश्चित् प्रसाददृष्ट्या भवता भवेऽस्मिन्।
स एव मान्यो भवतीश वन्द्यो महान् यशस्वी भवभूतिमांश्च॥ ६॥

vilokyate nātha ya eva kaścid
prasāda-dṛṣṭyā bhavatā bhave'smin ।
sa eva mānyo bhavat-īśa vandyo
mahān yaśasvī bhavabhūtimāṁśca ॥ 6 ॥

O Lord! if anybody is blessed by your graceful glance

he is verily worthy of respect and praise,

he is great and full of glory and power.

सर्वाद्वैतपदासीनः सर्वद्वैतविभासकः ।
जयतात् श्रीगुरुर्लोके शिवाद्वैतप्रदो मम ॥ ७ ॥

sarvādvaita padāsīnaḥ sarvadvaita-vibhāsakaḥ ।
jayatāt śrī-gurur-loke śivādvaita-prado mama ॥ 7 ॥

The revered Guru is glorious in this world

who has attained the complete state of non-duality

and who (also) illumines all dualities.

It is he who bestows on me

non-duality with Śiva.

अगाधाय समुद्राय व्याप्तविश्वाय भानवे ।
दीयतेऽर्घः प्रदीपोऽपि तथेयं गुरवे स्तुतिः ॥ ८ ॥

agādhāya samudrāya vyāpta viśvāya bhānave ।
dīyate'rghaḥ pradīpo'pi tatheyaṁ gurave stutiḥ ॥ 8 ॥

As one offers a handful of water even to the fathomless ocean,

and as one offers an oil lamp to the sun

which pervades the whole universe,

in the same way (do I offer) this praise to the Master.

I.
Life

शब्दः कश्चन यो मुखादुदयते मन्त्रः स लोकोत्तरः
संस्थानं सुखदुःखजन्मवपुषो यत्कापि मुद्रैव सा।
प्राणस्य स्वरसेन यत्प्रवहणं योगः स एवाद्भुतः
शाक्तं धाम परं ममानुभवतः किन्नाम न भ्राजते ॥ ३॥

— अभिनवगुप्त, अनुभवनिवेदनम्

śabdaḥ kaścana yo mukhādudayate mantraḥ sa lokottaraḥ
saṁsthānaṁ sukha-duḥkha-janma-vapuṣo yatkāpi mudraiva sā ।
prāṇasya svarasena yatpravahaṇaṁ yogaḥ sa evādbhutaḥ
śāktaṁ dhāma paraṁ mamānubhavataḥ kim-nāma na bhrājate ॥3॥

— Abhinavagupta, *Anubhavanivedanam*

Each word from his mouth is a supernatural *mantra*, the
posture of his body, cause of joy and suffering,
is itself the mystic *mudrā*.
The spontaneous flow of his breath is truly the wonderful *yoga*.
When I realize the supreme light-filled domain of Divine Energy,
what is it that does not shine ?

1. Sri Narainadas Raina and Smt. Aranimali, Swamiji's parents, with their Guru, Swami Rāma Joo.

2. Lakshman Joo's birth place.

3. An early portrait (1933).

4. Swami Lakshman Joo's parents.

5. Swami Rāma Joo with his disciples.

6. *Upanayanasaṁskāra* (initiation with the sacred thread) of the three brothers, with their mother and family (1914).

7. Swami Rāma Joo.

8. Swami Mahtab Kak.

9. Swami Mahtab Kak with disciples. Swami Lakshman Joo is sitting second from the right.

10. Swamiji in his teens.

11. The young saint.

12. Swami Lakshman Joo at the feet of Sri Ramaṇa Maharshi (E.P. Noye in the middle), Tiruvannamalai, 1936.

13. Swami Lakshman Joo with Sri Ramaṇa Maharshi and his devotees on Arunachala, 1936.

14. An early portrait.

15. Swamiji in his first ashram.

16. On pilgrimage to Amarnath.

17. Khir Bhavani Temple complex.

2

Lakshman Joo — A Yogī of Kashmir

Jaideva Singh[1]

I HAD a great desire to study the Śaiva philosophy of Kashmir. I struggled with some texts, but found that I could not understand them without the help of a teacher who was brought up in the tradition of the school. All the great savants of the Śaiva philosophy of Kashmir are dead and gone. The sole surviving exponent of this system is Sri Lakshman Joo, also known as Swami Īśvara Svarūpa. He was kind enough to accept me as his pupil, and I learned much from him. As I came in contact with him, I found that he was not only a great scholar of Śaiva philosophy and could give a lucid exposition of the texts, but was also a great *yogī*.

He was born in 1907 in Srinagar, the capital of Kashmir. His father's name was Sri Narainadasa Raina, and mother's Shrimati Aranyamali. His father was the first man to introduce the house-boat in Kashmir. His family Guru was Śrī Rāma. Śrī Rāma was the greatest exponent of Śaiva Āgama, but more than that he was the greatest *yogī* that Kashmir had known at the time. In Srinagar, many stories are current about his *siddhis*. He had only to look at or touch a person, and he was bound to be a changed man. Such was the wonderful *śaktipāṭa* that he wielded. Narainadasa had built a separate house for him where he could carry out his *sādhanā* and teach the Āgama texts to his pupils. This is now known as Rāma-Trika-Śaivāśrama.

Narainadasa approached Swami Rāma to give a name to his child. Swamiji said, "I am called Rāma, let this child be called Lakshman." Lakshman's leaning towards the higher life were marked even in early childhood. When he was three

1. This article was written originally for *The Mountain Path*, Journal of Sri Ramanasramam, and it was handed over to the editor after his death by his daughter Smt Manjusri Singh.

years old, his play consisted in making a *Śiva-liṅga* out of clay and worshipping it. At the age of five, he would sit down for meditation, and while in this condition would now and then show signs of sudden surprise. His parents were puzzled by the abnormal condition of the child and took him to Swami Rāma. He said, "This boy was a great *yogī* in the last life. His *yoga* would be consummated in this life."

His *yajñopavīta saṁskāra* (sacred thread ceremony) was performed when he was a child of seven. Swami Rāma taught him the *japa* of Gāyatrī *mantra* with *prāṇāpāna*, and also certain *yoga* practices according to the Śaiva discipline.

He was now sent to school. There he used to go into *samādhi* now and then. He was considered to be an abnormal boy by his teachers. One of his inquisitive teachers put to him this question, "What do you notice in your state of absorption?" The boy replied in the Kashmiri language that he experienced *Baḍe Bod*, i.e. the Supreme.

One day his teacher asked him to do physical exercise. Instead of doing physical exercise, he formed a group of a few students and started singing *bhajana*s (devotional songs). His teacher grew furious and inflicted on him twenty-five strokes with a cane. He went back home, crying. Next day the teacher fell ill and had fever exactly for twenty-five days.

When he was thirteen years of age, his parents thought of arranging his matrimony. He came to know of it, and said to his parents politely but firmly, "Kindly don't arrange my marriage. I have decided to remain a celibate all my life." His parents proposed his marriage a number of times, but knowing his great resolve gave up the idea of getting him married for good.

His father fell seriously ill, and so he asked his son to look after his business. He was in the pre-matriculation class but had to give up his studies and look after his father's business.

As he was now free from the routine work of the school, he decided to study the Śaiva Śāstra. Swami Rāma, the greatest savant of Śaiva Śāstra was dead by now, but he had taught the Śāstra to his devoted pupil, Mahtab Kak. So he decided to start studying the Śāstra under the guidance of Mahtab Kak. But it was not only the theoretical side of this Śaiva system that he wanted to learn, he gave even much greater time to the practice of *yoga*. He used to get up at two in the night and practise *yoga* till dawn. When he was fifteen years old, he had the experience of self-realization for the first time. After this he used to go into *samādhi* even while he was in his workshop. He now lost all interest in the workshop and neglected his business. His father reprimanded him many a time for this.

This put him in a quandary. He began to cogitate within himself, "On the one hand, there is the duty of carrying out the desire of my father, on the other, there is the call of the Spirit. What am I to do?" The call of the spirit proved to be irresistible. He bowed to the inner Monitor. In 1926, he took a lion's skin for his seat and left home without taking anything else with him. His father used to take lunch with him. Finding him absent, he queried where he was. His mother thought that he might have gone to the house of his teacher, Mahtab Kak, to study the Śāstras. So a messenger was sent there, but the messenger returned with the news that he had not gone to his teacher at all. A number of people were sent to different quarters in the city to search him out, but he was nowhere to be found. His brothers began to rummage among his books and papers, and found on a piece of paper the following note left behind by the boy: "My dear brother, I am leaving in search of the Supreme. Take care of my parents."

The parents were in great mental anguish at the sudden departure of the son from the house, and sent frantic telegrams and telephonic messages to friends and relatives. A formal request was also made to the police to find out the whereabouts of the boy.

Next day his father received the following message from a relative in Sopore — "This morning I saw Lakshman going on foot to Sādhu-Gaṅgā Āśrama."

On receipt of this news, the parents went posthaste to Sopore, and after a few hours found the boy seated on the lion's skin in deep meditation near a spring in a jungle. They sat there with heavy heart without disturbing the boy. When he returned to normal consciousness, he found his parents seated before him. They requested him to go back home. He said in a grave and determined voice, "Now I cannot live at home." His father promised to build for him an ashram in an unfrequented place in Srinagar itself. His father went back to Srinagar, and started building a small house for him.

Lakshman Joo meanwhile came and began to live in a village, named Denhāmā in Harvan near Srinagar near his Guru Mahtab Kak. After four months, his ashram was completed, and he moved into it. Now he started learning Sanskrit grammar and Śaiva scriptures from the reputed scholar, Paṇḍit Maheshwar Razdan. He studied Śaiva scriptures under his guidance for seven years, and became thoroughly proficient in these.

At this time, Sharika Devi, the daughter of Shri Jiyalal of Srinagar felt deeply interested in *yoga* and approached Lakshman Joo to accept her as his pupil. Swamiji was prepared to teach her *yoga* on condition that she would remain unmarried throughout her life. Sharika Devi accepted his condition. She prastised *yoga* under his guidance from two in the night till six in the morning. After a few years, she was lucky enough to experience self-realization. But she was so overwhelmed by her experience that she lost her mental balance for quite a few years and had to be moved to her parents home. She became abnormal, would sob and weep. Her parents were greatly perturbed. Lakshman Joo went to see her, and gave her a grape to eat. After eating that grape, she started improving and regained her normal condition in due course.

In 1934, Lakshman Joo built an ashram for himself on a site between Nishat and Shalimar. It was named Īśvara Āśrama. Sharikaji's father also built a house for her on a plot of land nearby. Here Lakshman Joo taught her yogic practices and Śaiva scriptures systematically.

Now Lakshman Joo's father retired from business, divided his property equally among his sons, and came to live with him along with his wife.

Lakshman Joo taught *Sāmbapañcaśikā* and a few other books to Prabha, the younger sister of Sharika Devi. She was married in 1942, but her husband passed away in 1943. Since 1944, she also became a disciple of Sri Lakshman Joo who initiated her in yogic practices and also started teaching her Śaiva scriptures.

In 1946, his mother fell seriously ill. He nursed her assiduously for two years. She passed away in 1948. Six months later, his father also passed away. Lakshman Joo has always been devoted to his parents, and performs their *śrāddha* every year with great earnestness.

He has ungrudgingly taught the scriptures to many seekers after truth. He taught *Brahmasūtras* to Śrī Nīlakaṇṭhānanda Sarasvatī in 1954. The present writer had also the benefit of learning Śaiva Śāstra at his feet. He has taught Śaiva philosophy to Miss Lilian Silburn of Paris for a number of years. She has translated many books on Śaiva philosophy into French. The translations of *Paramārthasāra* and *Vijñānabhairava* have already been published. The present writer has translated *Pratyabhijñāhrdaya* into English. Swamiji has himself translated *Śivastotrāvalī* of Utpaladeva and *Sāmbapañcaśikā* into Hindi, and has edited Abhinavagupta's commentary on the *Bhagavad-Gītā*.

In 1959, Sri Lakshman Joo gave up his old ashram at Īśvaragrāma, and built a new smaller ashram near Nishat garden, and now resides here.

Mahārājā Karan Singh of Kashmir had no male issue. His mother expressed a keen desire to Sri Lakshman Joo that she should be blessed with a grandson. She had the blessing of the *yogīrāja*, and the Mahārājā is now a proud father. The Mahārājā in gratefulness has promised to open a Śaivāśrama in the Guptagaṅgā temple.[2]

Sri Lakshman Joo is a great scholar, a great man and a great *yogī*. As a man he is upright, humble and extremely generous and kind. Hundreds flock to him with their tales of woe every Sunday, and he tries to help everybody.

As a *yogī*, he is greatly advanced. He lives mostly in *pramātr-bhāva* (in the full state of a knower). He is a great admirer of Ramaṇa Maharshi and says he visited the ashram of the Maharshi once when he was alive.[3] His exposition of the Śaiva texts is backed by his personal experience and therefore comes home to the student as living, throbbing truth. We are really fortunate that there are *yogin*s like him still alive in our land.[4]

2. In fact, Dr Karan Singh's Dharmartha Trust opened there a Hall in which Swamiji used to give regular teachings on Sundays.

3. In the year 1936.

4. Jaideva Singh passed away in 1986, and he must have written this article a

3

The Sage of Ishber
A Brief Life-Sketch[1]

Jankinath Kaul 'Kamal'

Introduction

FATHERS of the Kashmiri monistic Śaiva thought, who flourished in the valley from the ninth to the thirteenth century CE, were erudite scholars and eminent saints. They recorded what they practised and accomplished thereby. Later, there were interruptions in this line of thought, and it was mostly the ritualistic faith that kept the tradition alive. After Śivopādhyāya, the eighteenth-century scholar-saint who wrote commentaries and books of the kind, there appeared saints of the order during the nineteenth century. But they only taught the lore and made no use of the pen. In the early twentieth century, the Kashmir of past glory was blessed with a son who not only practised and lived this wonderful philosophy — the Trika Śaiva of Kashmir named *Pratyabhijñā Darśana* — but also disseminated its postulates by teaching and writing among the seekers of the Truth in the country and among those from foreign lands.

Birth and Initiation

A luminary of the first magnitude on the spiritual firmament of modern times, Lakshman Raina was born at Namchibal in Srinagar (Kashmir) on May 9, 1907. He showed signs of spiritual fertility from his very birth. Finding the child far too precocious, his noble, God-fearing and devout parents put him in the tutelage of

1. Originally published in *The Awakening of Supreme Consciousness, Lectures of Swami Lakshman Joo*, ed. Jankinath Kaul "Kamal," Delhi Utpal Publ. and Ishwara Ashrama Trust, 1998, pp. vii-xx. Edited and republished with kind permission of Dr Advaitavadini Kaul.

Swami Rāma, who had been their family priest, later turned a saint of high order in the tradition of the refined Tantric Monism of Kashmir known as the Trika system. From his early childhood "Lāl Sāb"[2] cast a spell not only over his parents and relatives but also on Swami Rāma. At the age of sixteen, however, the boy was ripe enough for being initiated by Swami Mahtab Kak, who had been commissioned by his illustrious preceptor just before entering *mahāsamādhi*, when the promising Lakshman was only seven years old. The enterprising and well-to-do parents could not prevail upon the young boy to enter the life of a householder or even to take up a job.

Renunciation and Learning

It was typical of young Lakshman to take his own time to do things rather than act at the spur of the moment and force the pace. He had requested his loving parents to make a place available for him in solitude. But it took them some time to execute the promised plan. Yet the spiritual urge compelled the earnest aspirant to leave home for practising *yoga* at the famous forest ashram of Sādhu-malyun in Handawara District of Kashmir. He left no clue about himself at home except a line on a piece of paper requesting his brothers to give comfort to his parents. Getting the clue after a thorough and anxious search for the young Lakshman his father Paṇḍit Narainadasa[3] and his preceptor Swami Mahtab Kak[4] went there to meet him. They succeeded in persuading him to come to the city and accept to live in a newly built house in their factory premises as he had desired. Here the earnest scholar-saint devoted himself to the study of Kashmir Śaiva literature available at the Research Department of the Jammu and Kashmir Government started early by Sir Pratap Singh, the then Mahārājā of the state. Highly learned Paṇḍits had helped the Department in editing and publishing of a number of

2. Pet-name given by his parents.
3. The pioneer houseboat merchant of Kashmir had provided complimentary houseboats to Swami Vivekananda on his visit to Kashmir in 1897-98. It is understood that the great Swami had visited Swami Rāma, the grand-preceptor of Swami Lakshman Joo, at Fateh Kadal Ashrama.
4. The chief disciple of Swami Rāma and preceptor of Swami Lakshman Joo, Swami Mahtab Kak had also been the preceptor of my father Pt. Jagannath Kaul who could see only 32 summers till *c.* 1927.

books on Kashmir Śaivism,[5] discovered throughout the state. Lakshman Joo engaged the most efficient Paṇḍit, Rājānaka Maheśvara to teach him Śaiva Śāstra at home. He also studied the Sanskrit grammar and the allied schools of Indian philosophy at full length. He edited the *Bhagavad-Gītā* with its Sanskrit commentary by Abhinavagupta and appended important notes to it. This was published when he was about twenty-five years old.

Seclusion

During the year 1934-35 Brahmacārī Lakshman Joo chose a secluded place at the foothill above Ishber village in the vicinity of the famous Nishat garden. He loved the spot because his ideal preceptor Abhinavagupta, one of the most prominent authors of Kashmir Śaivism, had lived somewhere around the place in vineyards about nine centuries ago. A bungalow was constructed by his parents at the selected site. It had a spacious garden with multi-colour flower-beds, fruit-bearing trees and a vegetable garden. Adjacent to this spiritual abode Sri Jiyalal Sopory of Srinagar built a house for his daughter Sharika Devi, who, after taking a vow of leading a celibate life, had found her worthy preceptor in Brahmacārī Lakshman Joo. Deviji remained in utter penance for attaining perfection in the monistic Śaiva order by learning Āgama Śāstra from him and practising Śaiva *yoga* under his care. Devotees and seekers of Truth began to pour in now. It was about this time that the present author[6] was introduced to this holy soul of divine charm by his own master and

5. Sri Jagdish Chandra Chatterji, author of the book *Kashmir Śaivism* published by the State Government in 1914 as the opening volume of this series of publications, i.e. *The Kashmir Series of Texts and Studies*, with a group of enthusiastic and erudite scholars had done yeoman work in establishing the Research Department (of J&K Govt.) which was nurtured by Mahamahopadhyaya Mukundaram Shastri, Sri Ram Chandra Kak (who later rose to be the Prime Minister of the State), Paṇḍit Maheshvara Razdan, Paṇḍit Harabhatta Shastri and other scholars. Besides discovering works related to Kashmir Śaivism, some manuscripts of historical importance like the Gilgit Mss., etc. were also published by the Department.

6. One fine day probably in April 1935, Brahmacārī Nīlakaṇṭha (of Drabiyar) at whose lotus feet I studied *Śaṅkaranandī* then and who was a close friend of Brahmacārī Lakshman Joo, asked me if I desired to go to see the Mahatma at Ishber, Nishat. I readily agreed as I had already heard about his endeavour of holding fast to the virtues of renunciation. The Mahatma was performing →

was later recommended for the study of Utpaladeva's masterpiece *Śivastotrāvalī*. This marked the beginning of Sunday classes at the ashram that always remained increasingly surcharged with wonderful spiritual vibrations.

Meeting Ramaṇa Maharshi

Suddenly the young saint made a silent trip to certain places of his own choice in India. He wanted to confer with saints of high order perhaps to ascertain his attainments. He spent some time at Bombay beach to establish his power of spiritual perception. Then spending a short time with Mahatma Gandhi at Sevagram he rushed to have a glimpse of Sri Aurobindo at Pondicherry where the Mother evinced interest in him. Therefrom he found his way to Tiruvannamalai to meet Ramaṇa Maharshi at the Ramaṇashram. Bhagavān Ramaṇa looked at the young attractive saint graciously. It must have been the moment of *dṛṣṭidīkṣā* — initiation by mere sight. Swami Lakshman Joo spent some weeks in the presence of the Maharshi. He later said: "I felt those golden days were indeed divine."[7] Thus Swamiji revived the spiritual link in 1938 that united Madras and Kashmir when a monk of Madurai, named Madhurāja had travelled to Kashmir in the eleventh century to meet the great Abhinavagupta. Swamiji returned to Kashmir with greater spiritual radiance. Then he wrote a Hindi translation of the *Sāmbapañcāśikā*, adding important hints as footnotes to it. This was published in 1943.

Solitude

Swami Lakshman Joo took to strict seclusion in his own ashram premises for several months. During that period of "Aurobindavan solitude" he concentrated on the *Kramastotra* culled out from the *Tantrāloka*. Giving a wonderful exposition of the twelve forms of Śaiva *yoga* in lucid Hindi preceded by the original Sanskrit text,

→ *Puruṣcaraṇa Yajña* prior to *gṛha-praveśa* — entering to live in the new house. On being introduced as a poet-in-becoming, I was asked to read one of my compositions. Taking out a piece of paper I sang from it my latest poem in Hindi. When I looked up I saw pearl-like tears trickling down the smiling brilliant face of the Mahatma on whose left and right were Brahmacārī Nīlakaṇṭhaji and Swami Sarvanandaji, all sitting in chairs. I was all wet with sweat but soon held myself with his applause. This was my first blissful meeting with Swami Lakshman Joo.

7. Refer to the *Mountain Path* (*Tiruvannamalai*), April, 1985.

this small book of deep insight into the Reality of *Dvādaśakālī* was published in the year 1958. Along with his progress in spiritual attainments, Swamiji propagated the Śaiva faith so efficiently and effectively that scholars and seekers after Truth got drawn towards him, not only from his own country but also from abroad.

The Īśvara Āśrama

After India was declared a free country, she has virtually remained in shambles. A sense of insecurity increased day by day in everyone's mind and almost everywhere. In the uncertain circumstances, Swamiji disposed of his immovable property along with that of Sharika Deviji, about the year 1957 and started to live in a small house newly constructed at a stone's throw from the general road near Guptagaṅgā Temple in Ishber village. *Īśvara Āśrama* was the name given to the ashram and the disciples began to call Swamiji Īśvara Svarūpa.

Āśrama Activities

The ashram activities gathered momentum. Swamiji held regular Sunday class/ *satsaṅga*. On Mondays he observed silence (*maunam*) and spent his day in "God's House," the tiny cottage for meditation, built in a beautiful small garden near the previous ashram-place on the hill. A set programme was followed on other weekdays. A spacious lecture-hall with cupboards on one side for library and a *havana-śālā* for annual *yajña* were constructed in the premises of Śrī Raṇavīra Śiva Temple, Guptagaṅgā by the Dharmarth Trust of Jammu and Kashmir under the trusteeship of Dr Karan Singh, former Union Minister and ambassador. The complex was named "Kashmir Śaiva Pīṭhikā." Sunday discourses on *Tantrāloka* by Swamiji, lectures by eminent spiritualists and seminars were held there in an atmosphere of divinity. Swamiji, at certain occasions gave a series of lectures on spiritual topics for the elevation of common people, besides taking special classes and guiding scholars in their research work. A maiden translation with footnotes in Hindi of his favourite *stotra* the *Śivastotrāvalī* of Utpaladeva was published by the Chowkhamba Sanskrit Series Office, Varanasi in 1964. This, Swamiji taught with a new exposition each time.

Honours Received

Two saintly persons of Swamiji's calibre, who were his contemporaries were Paṇḍit Nīlakaṇṭha Jyotiṣī (later Swami Nīlakaṇṭhānanda Sarasvatī, Divine Life Society,

Rishikesh) and Paṇḍit Satram Bhat of Ishber. Although each had a different mode of thought yet the "spiritual trio" was destined to meet and corroborate on the *yoga-bhūmi* of Ishber. They met closely on *Brahma-Sūtra Śāṅkarabhāṣya* and *Yogavāsiṣṭha Mahārāmāyaṇa*. Scholars and professors came to Swamiji from the universities of Paris, Oxford, Rome and U.S.A. for guidance in *Pratyabhijñā* and *Tantrāloka*. To the scholars and his disciples from foreign lands he gave pithy and short lectures on abstruse topics in English. For Kashmiri disciples he explained the tenets of Śaivism in a literary style full of elegance and wit. To the general audience he spoke in lucid Hindi. Swami Lakshman Joo read his paper in Sanskrit on *Kuṇḍalinī-Vijñāna-Rahasyam* at the *All India Tantra Sammelanam* held under the auspices of the Varanaseya Sanskrit University at Varanasi in the year 1965.[8] His exposition of the subject was much applauded by the great luminary Mahāmahopādhyāya Gopīnātha Kavirāj and other scholars of great repute. After some years the Varanaseya Sanskrit University conferred upon Swami Lakshman Joo the degree of D.Lit., *honoris causa*, in recognition of his splendid and valuable services to the cause of Sanskrit. When Swamiji was informed about this, he simply gave an innocent smile and said in an expression of humour "I have become a doctor now!" The Jammu and Kashmir Akademi of Art, Culture and Languages presented the Robe of Honour to Swamiji at a special function while Mir Qasim was Chief Minister of the State.

Contribution

Swamiji's contribution to the promotion of the studies in Kashmir Śaivism, propagation of the *Trika* philosophy and growth of Kashmiri culture will be remembered for long. He helped considerably the revival of this philosophy and the way of life which had otherwise been fading away due to political changes in the valley. Swamiji, however, became known nationally and internationally as the best and luminous exponent of the mystical experiences in the texts, namely *Pratyabhijñāhrdaya*, *Śivasūtra*, *Vijñānabhairava* and *Parātriśikā-Vivaraṇa*, which also bear his elaborate introductions. Swamiji's immense erudition stimulated some more disciples and admirers to expound these Śaiva texts. Prof. Nilakanth Gurtoo

8. Published in the Proceedings of the Sammelana in *Sarasvatī Suṣamā* 20/1, Varanasi 1965. A paper in Sanskrit *Pūrṇahantā Vimarśa* by Jankinath Kaul "Kamal" was also read at the Sammelana.

wrote Hindi translations of *Parātriśikā* and *Spandakārikā*. The present writer wrote an independent Hindi commentary on *Śivasūtra* that was highly praised by the Master. Srimati Kamala Bawa translated the text of *Pratyabhijñāhrdayam* into Hindi. Sushri Prabha Devi translated into Hindi *Parāpraveśikā, Paramārthasāra, Gītārthasaṁgraha* of Abhinavagupta, and *Gurustuti* by Ācārya Rameshvar Jha. All these have been published. Dr Lilian Silburn of Paris translated some Śaiva hymns and many texts on Śaivism into French.[9] Alexis Sanderson, now Professor at Oxford, studied many texts with Swamiji. Thus Swamiji taught as well as spread with effective measure this unique philosophy of Kashmir in the country and abroad.

Birthday and Excursions

Swamiji's birthday was celebrated every year on such a grand scale that it turned out to be a great fair for common people and an auspicious day for his admirers and devotees who flocked from all parts of the country to have a glimpse of the sage sitting in long *samādhi*. Indian as well as foreign disciples attended to see this godman "living free" on this earth. Sri Dinanath Ganjoo, Smt. Kamla Bhagati, Sri Narayan Joo and Smt. Raj Dulari Kaul among many others sang Kashmiri poems of eulogy to their preceptor. This genial holy man of wisdom, wit and peace distributed *prasāda* all day long. The next day Swamiji spent in giving gifts to devotees and disciples. Once Swamiji remarked "If I have to celebrate my birthday twice a year I would finish up all my extra property by distributing it."[10]

Excursions to places of sanctity and natural scenery in the valley were occasionally arranged. *Kīrtana*s by disciples and discourses by Swamiji were usual features all along. Prominent places visited on large group excursions were: Verinag, Takshakanag, Karkutanag, Sadha-malyun, Uma Nagari, Hangalgund, Tangamarg, Narannag (Sindh Valley), Khir Bhavani, Dacchigam and Dara, etc. by bus and different places around and in Dal Lake by *dūṅgā* (houseboat) during summer besides longer trips to Hardwar and Rishikesh during winter.

Moments of bliss were experienced when saints and men of learning came to

9. Dr Raniero Gnoli of the University of Rome translated the *Tantrāloka* into Italian, but he was not a disciple of Swamiji (Ed.).

10. Refer to the last of the seven lecture series.

meet the sage of Ishber. Dr Karan Singh often visited the ashram to receive blessings. Smt. Indira Gandhi, the former Prime Minister of India, sought interview with the sage, whenever she came on a visit to the state. Swamiji had a meeting with J. Krishnamurti at Kotarkhana in the Dal Lake. Maharshi Mahesh Yogi visited the Īśvara Āśrama and invited Swamiji to his house-boats in the Dal Lake. Swamiji gave an interesting exposition of the *Vijñānabhairava*[11] to his devotees on request. Paul Reps, in his short introduction to the chapter "Centering,"[12] says: "It presents 112 ways to open the invisible door of consciousness. I see Lakshman Joo gives his life to its practice." Swami Ramdas (a *jīvanmukta*) of Kanhangarh, Mangalore, Swami Satyananda Sarasvati of Munger and Swami Muktananda of Ganeshpuri were happy to meet the Swami when they visited Srinagar. Swami Lakshman Joo himself attended and presided over spiritual meetings held occasionally in the valley and outside it. In 1976 Sri Ramakrishna Āśrama, Srinagar (Kashmir), organized a spiritual congregation in the ashram precincts. This was graced by the world-famous cultural ambassador of India, Swami Ranganathananda while the meeting was presided over by Swami Lakshman Joo, who described Sri Ramakrishna as a *siddha yogī*.

Another time Swami Ranganathananda was invited by Swamiji to address a special meting of scholars and devotees and declared the chief guest as "messenger of peace." Swamiji occasionally went to Hardwar and Rishikesh to meet saints especially Swami Śivānanda Sarasvatī of the Divine Life Society giving expositions to parallels in Kashmir Śaiva mysticism with the mysticism of Śāṅkara Vedānta.

Ecstasy

During his years of maturity, Swami Lakshman Joo was writing a comprehensive compendium of Kashmir Śaiva Darśana in lucid Hindi. It runs into several chapters. Excerpts from the manuscript were at times read out by him to the selected disciples among whom the present writer was fortunate to be one. It is understood that writing of the book remained incomplete but was published later in 1994 by Sushri Prabha Deviji. Prof. P.N. Pushpa, while writing his foreword to this book titled *Trikaśāstra-Rahasya-Prakriyā* has also observed the incompleteness of this work.

---

11. A page from the *Rudrayāmala Tantra*. Sanskrit commentary by Kṣemarāja and Śivopādhyāya.
12. A chapter from *Zen Flesh Zen Bones*, compiled by Paul Reps, 1957.

During his later days of ecstasy Swamiji only explained selected pithy verses from the Āgama Śāstras and *Yogavāsiṣṭha* and sang these along with his disciples in divine rapture. These continue to be sung by the devotees at the Sunday *satsaṅga* meeting with the wonderful *Gurustuti* composed early by one of Swamiji's illustrious disciples of Varanasi, Sri Rameshvar Jha, who having studied and practised Vedānta mysticism had found great interest in the Kashmir Śaiva mysticism and had accepted Lakshman Joo as his preceptor of the Faith.

Occult Power

Though Swamiji was a master of occult powers he never made a display of those powers. Swamiji was against their being used as he was convinced that the use of occult powers was an impediment on the spiritual path. He was a past master of self-control and compassion. However he appeared to have made use of his divine power sparingly and with great caution. Not only his close disciples but also unacquainted people of different beliefs, from far and near, some of whom had not even met the Swami in person, were convinced of his powers which he might have used unassumingly for their upliftment. Certain contemporary saints of the country expressed that Swami Lakshman Joo had been strictly guarding his earned treasure of powers and if at all, he used them scarcely. His awe-inspiring sight and proverbial sympathy drew people from all walks of life near him with their problems to which he was often sharp in giving decisions. It was also observed that he gave a healing touch to those who needed it. Common people believed him to be a redeemer from evils. Some persons of pure heart felt a current of mysterious joy running through their body while receiving his touch on bowing at his lotus feet.

Picture of Personality

Swamiji was disciplined, vigilant, and he was never found saying or doing a thing that was not in consonance with the Truth of his way of life. Only eight months before Swamiji chose to merge in the Infinite, his chief disciple Brahmavādinī Sharika Devi entered the Divine on February 2, 1991. He did wonderfully well what was befitting to his nature and practice. In fact, there were very high goals in the core of the Swamiji's very existence which was manifest in a happy combination of three elements:

(i) Simplicity, an expression of simplicity;

(ii) Enthusiasm, the vital push of the spirit within; and

(iii) Wisdom, the light of the soul as the portion of the Divine Himself.

Endowed with magnetic personality, divine charm and wide scholarship behind his spiritual attainments Śaivācārya Īśvara Svarūpa Sri Swami Lakshman Joo was an inextricable combination of life and religion. By years of study and contemplation, his practice of *yoga* had ripened to such an extent that his teachings contain the best solution to the problems that face humanity today. His very presence was solace to the depressed, hope to the forlorn, joy to the seeker, inspiration to the scholar and satisfaction to the soul striving for spiritual upliftment. The best in him was all-lovingness that attracted towards him people of all faiths and of different creeds. An embodiment of magnificent qualities, he was a faithful friend, a benefactor, brother, a fondling father, a true teacher, a noble neighbour, an instinctive instructor, an affirmed administrator, a congenial companion and above all the guide of all who came near him. His disciples and admirers sought to throng around his radiant personality as honey-bees hover about a fragrant lotus in bloom. Īśvara Svarūpa's sagacity made him into an exemplary sage. He looked simply divine, when he made a short tour to the United States in June-July, 1991.

Homage

The playful ways of the Master — the sage of Ishber — came to an end on this earth in Delhi in the early hours of the 27th September, 1991, in moments of calmness and tranquillity. He had verily been *yogabhraṣṭa* (fallen from *yoga* in his previous birth) for he was born in a house of pious as well as wealthy and respected parents — *sūcinām śrīmatam gehe yogabhraṣṭo vijayate.*[13] The present life of grace and glory was only the means for this Divine Being to merge into Supreme Śiva, the final beatitude of life. The powers of Truth and light may not be visible to the naked eye but they are there for the discerning. To pay homage to the beloved "Gurudeva" let us live for the Divine and let the Divine take control of our life to fulfil his purpose.

13. *Bhāgavad-Gītā*, VI. 41.

4

Śrī Guru Īśvara Svarūpa
His Way of Life

Prabha Devi

GREAT souls who are seeped in spirituality have a unique way of life. Their behaviour and the manner in which they perform even ordinary acts of daily life are quite unlike that of worldly people. How extraordinary is the life of one who like Śukadeva was immersed in spirituality right from childhood. The life of such saints has to be written in letters of gold. It was only through the grace of my master that my whole life was spent at his lotus feet and everyday life acquired a state which was far removed from that of ordinary people.

Even from childhood our Gurudeva led a life which was unparalleled. His parents said that when Gurudeva was five years old, he would take his bath and then sit in a cross-legged position for hours in meditation. He had to be shaken for taking breakfast. After partaking his breakfast he would make *Śivaliṅga*s out of mud and worship them with flowers, etc. His brothers and sisters would join him in this play of divine worship.

At one o'clock he would have his vegetarian meal which was specially prepared for him as his parents were non-vegetarians. After resting for one hour, he would again play with other children. The games consisted of preparation for worship, such as gathering flowers, soaking rice for offering to Lord Śiva, collecting incense, etc. Then he would again sit for meditation for an hour. His parents looked upon these activities as child's play. Little did they know that this play would gather strength and he would become a great saint who uplifted humanity.

When the child was seven years old his father performed the sacred thread ceremony with great enthusiasm. His grand master Swami Rāma himself put the sacred thread on the child Lakshman. This was in the year 1914 when the budding saint spent the entire day and the evening in prayer reciting the Gāyatrī and various other *mantras*.

Now he was sent to school. He studied most assiduously both at school and at home. He was always placed first in class. While going to school he would carry a mat to sit for his prayers. While the other pupils would stand and pray this child would sit in the lotus-pose. One day his teacher asked him as to what he saw when he sat with his eyes closed. The child replied simply in Kashmiri: "I see *Baḍe Bod*," "The Greatest of the great." On hearing this the teacher was so pleased that he embraced him.

When Lakshman arrived at the threshold of youth, his father became very ill. It seemed that he would not survive. Seeing his deteriorating health his father persuaded him to leave school. He had just passed the eighth class obtaining first degree marks. Obeying his father he left school. In a way he felt that he had been freed from an obligation. Now he was absolutely free. After breakfast he would go to the houseboat workshop and supervised the skilled labour, but while he sat on the chair he would watch his spiritual awareness. In this way his day was spent blissfully. In the meantime his father's health improved, and finding an appropriate moment he said to his father: "I would like to be initiated by a worthy Guru." His father was very pleased and took him to Swami Rāma's ashram where Swami Mahtab Kak had taken the place of Swami Rāma who had passed away. In the year 1920 Gurudeva was initiated by Swami Mahtab Kak in the traditional manner. As a result he became absorbed in meditation day and night without any obstacle. Each day brought fresh experiences. Swami Mahtab Kak encouraged him in his *sādhanā*. Now Gurudeva's mind delved deep into his self and he became weary of worldly activities. He spent more and more time with his master rather than in his father's workshop. He would study the *Gītā* with his Guru and on returning home he would spend hours in his *pūjā* room in silence. He neglected the workshop and earned his father's ire. Naturally he was caught between doubt and dejection. He expressed his helplessness to his Guru who consoled him and advised him to remain aware and spiritually absorbed even while he was busy with worldly affairs. He reassured him saying that he had already been blessed.

Even as Gurudeva listened to his master, in his heart of hearts he sought only deep concentrated oneness with the Lord. He became disinterested in his work. Consequently one morning he left home at the break of dawn without informing anyone. His family was terribly upset at his disappearance from home. After one week they found out that he had reached a forest in Sādhu-Gaṅgā which lies beyond Sopore. There he spent all the time only in meditation. In those days there was a beautiful ashram nearby, and so he had the facility of taking his food there. After breakfast Gurudeva would sit at the bank of a natural spring, totally lost to the outside world. People would see his divine glowing appearance and found themselves blessed. No one dared to speak in his presence. After one week his parents also reached the place of his hiding. They pleaded with their son to return home but he made it clear to them that he would not do so and asked them to make a separate house for him where he could live independently. His father accepted the son's wishes and promised that the house would be ready in three months. He asked him to stay in the meantime at some place near his master Swami Mahtab Kak. Gurudeva assured his father that he would return himself to Srinagar and stay at Rāma Trika Āśrama.

Exactly after one week Gurudeva returned and stayed at Harvan under the guidance and care of Swami Mahtab Kak. After some time the separate house was ready and his father asked him to move in on an auspicious day. All facilities were provided in the house. Now Gurudeva started living in his new hermitage without any hindrance to his spiritual practice. His meals were sent by his mother. It was in this house that Sharika Devi became his disciple.

Gurudeva remained absorbed in meditation all through the day and night.

He now wanted to verify his spiritual experiences through the scriptures. He fulfilled his desire by studying Sanskrit grammar for three years from Paṇḍit Maheshvar Razdan, who was the Chief Paṇḍit at the Kashmir Śaivism Research Institute.[1] With him he studied the most important scriptures of Trika according to the traditional methodology.

His daily life also changed accordingly. At five in the morning Sharika Devi accompanied by her younger brother Mohan Lal would come to him to study the *Gītā* and then sit for meditation for one hour. Thus till 9 o'clock he assumed the role of the Guru. At 5 o'clock he would study the scriptures with Paṇḍit Maheshvar Razdan as a student. He would be merged in meditation from three o'clock in the night till morning. This was in the early 1920s.

After staying in this house in the city for many years, studying and experiencing the Trika texts, he was somewhat disillusioned with the city atmosphere and wished

1. The Department which has brought out the texts of the tradition in the "Kashmir Series of Texts and Studies."

to stay in the solitude of the countryside. Now Sharika Devi was also getting detached from worldly life. As a consequence the respective parents had two beautiful cottages, facing each other, constructed at the top of a hill above Nishat garden. Their parents had the houses consecrated by learned Paṇḍits through *yajña* and recitation of prayers. It was only then that in the year 1934 the Guru and disciple moved into their new ashram. Life was now very intense and fulfilling. At five in the morning Gurudeva would call Sharika Devi from his window to come and study. She would carry the *Śivastotrāvalī* and come to him with great enthusiasm. After studying for one hour she would sit in meditation at the feet of the master. At 8 o'clock she would return to her cottage. Gurudeva would have his breakfast and walk in the garden. At that time his parents had also moved in with him. There were servants to attend to him, and our Gurudeva spent his time as an extraordinary saint who had all the trappings of a king. After 3 o'clock many people from the city used to come to be blessed by his presence. From seven to nine in the evening Swamiji would spend two hours in meditation. After taking his meal he would retire, and at 3 o'clock he would start his spiritual practice.

In this way the two great souls spent many years studying the scriptures and enjoying the bliss of meditation. Sharika Devi used to call her Guru Īśvara Svarūpa (embodiment of the Lord), and his house was called Īśvara Āśrama. Many reputed saints came and stayed at the ashram. With the presence of the parents the flow of visitors increased, and Gurudeva wanted solitude. So he retired by himself and only Sharika Devi could see him and that also to serve him his meals. In 1940 he moved to his house in the city and observed silence for four months. He studied the *Tantrāloka* and continued his meditation following the traditional way. Gurudeva himself related the following experience. The year was 1940. While Swamiji was absorbed in deep meditation at 2 o'clock at night, with God's grace he experienced enlightenment with the awakening of the six *cakra*s. The *cakra*s had a number of spokes. With the movement of the first *cakra*, the second, third, fourth, fifth and sixth started moving automatically. In the case of some *yogī*s the *cakra* in the forehead starts moving first and then the lower ones get activated. This state is described as the "demonical absorption" (*piśācāveśa*). Such a state is indicative of internal obstacles on the spiritual path. As a matter of fact, the opening of the six *cakra*s starting with the *mūlādhāra* (the lowest) leads to the attainment of the eight worldly and spiritual yogic powers. In a moment of supreme bliss Gurudeva narrated the above-mentioned experience to Deviji and myself.

Often, when Gurudeva started observing silence, some relation or close friend would die. In 1943, when Gurudeva started his practice of silence, a messenger arrived at 10 o'clock at night with the message that the revered master, Shri Mahtab Kak had taken his path towards the Supreme. When Deviji gave him the news, Gurudeva set out towards Rāmashram on foot.[2] When he saw his great master lying lifeless he wept bitterly. All his Guru-brothers consoled him and asked him to prepare for the rituals performed at the time of death. Together with many learned Paṇḍits Gurudeva carried his master's body to the cremation ground, while thousands of devotees sang songs in presence of the Almighty and showered flowers. A band played music to celebrate the merging of the soul of a great saint with the Lord, and thus the cremation ritual was performed. For eleven days there was the recitation of Śaiva scriptures and devotional songs under the guidance of learned Śaiva Paṇḍits. Following that, every year on the second day of the dark fortnight in the month of Phālgun (according to the Hindu calendar), or according to the calendar on the 19th of February he would perform a *yajña* in memory of his master. In this way he would show how one should have faith, love and devotion towards one's Guru.

In the year 1945 with the will of God I too had to move and stay with my introspective sister Sharika Devi. People who tread the spiritual path are often those who have suffered in life and they then shun the worldly life to take refuge at the feet of saints. Such a devotee would be termed as imperfect. The perfect seeker of salvation is one who has acquired the grace of the Lord through love and devotion towards the Supreme. Our Gurudeva and Sharika Devi were among those of the first category. I belong to the second class of devotees. My presence in the ashram brought a change in Gurudeva's daily life. Our compassionate Master taught me the *Gītā* in Kashmiri. I would study during the day and at night I would translate it into Hindi. Gurudeva would ask us to sit in meditation with him from four to six in the morning. Then, after taking bath he would have breakfast at 8 o'clock and spend the morning till noon in study. After lunch he would rest from two to four, then he would go on a walk from five to seven. Sometimes we would both accompany him. Before leaving he would give the following instructions: There should be no talking on the way. Watch the middle space as you take a step and then put the foot down. Concentrate on your incoming and outgoing breath.

2. The distance is about 14 km.

If someone speaks to you on the way, answer briefly. We always obeyed Gurudeva's orders. At 8 o'clock at night we would recite the evening prayer, then we would leave for our own cottage. In this way many happy years were spent.

In 1946 Gurudeva'a mother fell ill. She was bedridden for two years. During this time Gurudeva looked after his mother and served her in every way. In 1948 on the seventh day of the dark fortnight in the month of Jyeṣṭha she breathed her last in the ashram. Her body was taken to the city where she was cremated with all due rites. Being a worthy son he performed all the rituals pertaining to death in a devout manner. Exactly six months after his mother's death his father suddenly passed away. Gurudeva performed the *śrāddha* for his parents for a whole year. Even though he was an enlightened saint, Gurudeva paid his debt to his parents in an exemplary manner.

After the death of his parents Gurudeva started living like a *yogī*. He would make Sharika Devi and me sit in meditation in his presence and then teach us the Śaiva scriptures.

From 1948 Dr Lilian Silburn, a French scholar of Sanskrit, used to come to Srinagar to study the Śaiva texts with Gurudeva. She continued to come year after year and studied the main texts which she translated into French. Jaideva Singh from Varanasi, a musicologist and also a Sanskrit scholar studied the *Pratyabhijñāḥrdayam*, an important text by Kṣemarāja with Swamiji. He translated the text into Hindi and English. In this way Gurudeva would be absorbed in meditation and God-consciousness and at the same time read and teach the Śaiva scriptures. Thus the atmosphere of the ashram became so charged that many *siddha*s and *yogī*s would congregate there. Gurudeva's innate nature was introspective and Sharika Devi was also seeped in meditation. Therefore there was a constant stream of devotees who came for *darśana* and often stayed at the ashram which disturbed both the saints. As a result, in 1961 the entire property was sold. Gurudeva decided to make a small more accessible ashram near the road where all three of us could stay together along with Gopinath, our servant. Gurudeva's pure resolve had to be fulfilled. He spoke to his disciple Kamlaji who used to live near the main road. She and her parents were devotees of Swamiji. She gave one *kanāl* (500 square yards) of land to Swamiji for building a house. In a year's time a small and simple but attractive house was built with a beautiful garden. In 1962 Gurudeva celebrated the ritual of entering his new ashram in a festive way. Here it was decided that visitors would be allowed to stay only on Sundays when Swamiji would also be teaching the Śaiva texts.

Only Sharika Devi and myself were allowed to stay in his new house. At night no disciple or relation would be allowed to stay there. Provision was made for Gopinath who had served Gurudeva for thirty years. On Mondays Swamiji would observe silence in his room and no one was allowed in the ashram on that day. Gurudeva would be absorbed in *samādhi* from Sunday. Just as someone whose aim it is to accumulate wealth remains busy in finding the means to do so, as a scholar remains mindful only in his study, as a lover longs to see his beloved, in exactly the same way Gurudeva would become restless to have the vision of the Lord. On that day Gurudeva would not even shave. From 3 o'clock at night he would be seated on his *āsana* after washing his face. At eight in the morning Sharika Devi and I would place his breakfast on a low stool before him and would return downstairs. Seeing his glowing face, a faint residue of tears in his eyes, hearing his voice, calm but full of emotion would leave us feeling completely blessed. At one o'clock we would place his plate with lunch along with a *loṭā* of water and a vessel of curds in front of him and remove the breakfast dishes. While Gurudeva partook his lunch we waited in the staircase. After finishing his lunch Gurudeva would slightly tap on his plate and we would remove the utensils. Truly we would be so elated as if we just had a vision of the Lord. At 5 o'clock he would have *kahavā* (Kashmiri tea) and at night he would have either milk or rice. He hardly slept for three or four hours. On Tuesday he would emerge from his room at about 9 o'clock. Only looking at his saintly form gave one the feeling that he had surely realized the Almighty. I remember I would often childishly ask him about his spiritual experience. Compassionate and gracious as he was, he would sometimes reveal his ecstatic insight to us. But one day he said to me: "Are you my Guru that you ask me of my experiences?" I answered fearfully: "We are proud of the fact that we have the opportunity to serve our master, Lord Śiva, with whose grace we are endowed with the willpower to meditate wholeheartedly." He would be pleased with such an answer.

On Tuesday Gurudeva would teach his devotees the Śaiva scriptures. On Wednesday he would sometimes go and meet his disciples in the city. He returned at five regularly and would enjoy the peace and quiet of his room till 8 o'clock, when it would be time for dinner. But the extraordinary feature of Gurudeva was that he performed ordinary tasks while in a state of self-absorption and awareness. People with worldly ways would not dare to come near him.

India's former Prime Minister Indira Gandhi came to Gurudeva's ashram three times. Gurudeva was engaged in having the ashram cleaned when she came for the first time. As I looked down the lane outside the ashram there were a number of policemen. I went and reported to Gurudeva. He told me to continue my chores and that no one would enter without his permission. In the meantime a policeman came up and informed Gurudeva that Indira Gandhi wished to see him. Swamiji had two chairs placed in the garden. I said to Indiraji: "You have come without prior information." She replied: "Does one come to a temple after getting permission?" Her answer conveyed the essence of faith. When she came for the third time Gurudeva asked her: "Are your bodyguards trustworthy?" She answered him that she trusted them completely. Then Gurudeva asked her: "Is Rajiv Gandhi politically capable?" She replied: "I have made him competent, the rest is in the hands of fate." Then Swamiji asked her: "We have made a Satsang Hall and we wish to inaugurate it in the winter. Will you come for the inauguration?" Indiraji answered that she would certainly come if she was still alive. We will recall that it was in the year 1984. Sharika Devi said to me in an anguished voice: "The star of her fate has set." Both Gurudeva and Sharika Devi knew that she would die in a few days. And fate so conspired that three days after she left the ashram she was shot by her bodyguard. Gurudeva was quite upset by the news.

Once we had gone to Jammu with Gurudeva in the winter. Gopinath, our servant, had also accompanied us. Gurudeva expressed a desire to go to the shrine of Vaiṣṇavī Devī for two days. At that time the head of tourism Shri S.K. Raina who was Gurudeva's ardent devotee was posted there. He requested Gurudeva to come to Kaṭarā[3] by car where he would make all arrangements for his stay. He told Gurudeva that he would see that all provisions for his comfort would be made and that, after spending the night there, we would proceed to the shrine at 4 o'clock in the morning, and then return to Jammu on the same day. Gurudeva agreed. The next day we left for Kaṭarā reaching there at 4 o'clock in the afternoon. Gopinath had also accompanied us. Gurudeva saw the clean, decorated rooms in the State

3. Kaṭarā is a small town at the foot of the hill where the Vaiṣṇavī Devī shrine is located.

Guest House and decided to rest there for a while. We got busy having the evening meal prepared by Gopinath. We had tea at 6 o'clock and then we were asked to go to our room at seven and concentrate on our meditation. While Gurudeva was speaking to us in a matter-of-fact manner it seemed that in his heart of hearts he was merged with some past experience and was searching for something. His face was glowing with a divine lustre, his eyes were tearful and there was a serenity in his voice. It appeared that he was longing to see someone. However he soon retired to his room after speaking to us. There he spread his mat and sat in the lotus pose. After about half an hour Deviji quietly opened Gurudeva's door, beckoning me to come inside. We sat in a corner and started our meditation. After one hour Gurudeva was immersed in the internal joy of divinity. He was sobbing, and at the same time he was dancing with an aura of bliss. I was overwhelmed to see this spectacle, but Deviji who was experienced, realized that Gurudeva was in the midst of the wonder of *turīyānanda* (the second-last stage before merging into the Supreme).

After some time, when Gurudeva emerged somewhat in the external world he called out in a gentle voice: "Sharika, Sharika!" Even though his eyes were open he could not see her. Deviji called out softly: "Lord, I am here!" On hearing her he said in a sweet voice: "Did you see my divine state?" Deviji said: "I and Prabha both had the supreme *darśana*." Then he asked: "Did Gopinath also have *darśana*?" Deviji said, "He also came in once and had *darśana*." On hearing this Gurudeva was very pleased. Then, after a wash he had his meal. I asked: "Master, when will we leave for Devī's *darśana*?" He replied: "The Devī gave me her *darśana* right here. You three also had that vision. Now, what is the use of climbing up on the hill which will be a tiring effort. We will stay right here for the night and will return to Jammu in the morning." When we reached Jammu in the morning, Sri Raina saw us and he was surprised. Gurudeva let the matter pass without revealing the reason for not going up to the shrine.

We witnessed many extraordinary states of our Master. He always emphasized on awareness, and that one should be constantly immersed in the Divine. In the light of the *Vijñānabhairava* Swamiji stressed to watch the moment at the beginning and end of wakefulness and sleep. Great souls like Swamiji are sent in the world to uplift humanity. Our Gurudeva was indeed a rare realized being.

Our Master was by nature pure and childlike. But he was also known for his anger. Established in awareness he went about his daily chores. Through the senses of touch, speech and smell he extracted the honey of divine bliss of which his devotees had no knowledge. His vision was endless like the ocean. He could be hard like a stone and tender like the *śirīṣa* flower.[4] On the one hand he possessed the destructive powers of Lord Śiva, and on the other he was compassionate and the ultimate refuge like Lord Viṣṇu. He was calm and composed like the earth, but on the other hand he could get angry like Lord Rudra, the embodiment of the fire of death. But at the root of that anger was the desire to help his devotees. Verily, Gurudeva's nature was difficult like a tough mountain, and in order to understand him one had to traverse many thick forests and go through uneven valleys, confronting sometimes furious animals, at other times seeing the flow of a spring brimming with the unsullied comforting waters of compassion and purity. Truly, Gurudeva could be propitiated easily if one's heart was devout and pure. The famous scholar Paṇḍit Rameshvar Jha understood Gurudeva's true worth and his *Gurustuti* (Hymn in praise of the Master) revealed the divine nature of Gurudeva in poetic form. Respected late Professor Jiyalal Kaul has also described Gurudeva's attributes in his poem.

I can only say that living at his feet for almost a lifetime I found Gurudeva an embodiment of the following *śloka* of the *Bhagavad-Gītā*:

> *yasmānn 'odvijate loko lokānn 'odvijate ca yaḥ* ।
> *harṣāmarṣa-bhayodvegair mukto yaḥ sa ca me priyaḥ* ॥
> — *Bhagavad-Gītā* 12.15

> That man I love from whom the people do not shrink and who does not shrink from them, who is free from exaltation, fear, impatience, and excitement.[5]

I bow a million times to such a divine Master. Words fail to fully narrate Gurudeva's life. One could write a *Lakṣmaṇāyana*[6] — but it would be best to end this small account, hoping that it will give an idea of the immensity of his divine personality.*

4. The red *śirīṣa* flower has very soft petals and it is quoted in Sanskrit literature as the example of tenderness.
5. Translated by R.C. Zaehner.
6. In accordance with the *Rāmāyaṇa* describing the glory of Rāma.

* Translated from Hindi by Sarla Kumar.

5

Guru-Paramparā
Three Generations of Śaiva Saints

Ram Chandra Raina

FROM time to time Kashmir, known as *puṇya bhūmi* (holy land) and *ṛṣi war* (land of the *ṛṣis*), has given birth to a galaxy of Śaivite teachers, who were blessed with self-realization. Some of them were erudite scholars and brilliant philosophers. They lived, taught and blessed us and left their undying spirit behind to guide us for ever. Having had the good fortune of being introduced by my parents to them at an early age, I had an opportunity of sitting at the feet of two great spiritual giants, Mahāmaheśvara Shri Rāmapada and Mahāmaheśvara Shri Mahtab Kak whose very memory is blessed. I have also had the privilege of sitting sometimes physically and often mentally at the feet of Mahāmaheśvara Rājānaka Sri Lakshman Joo, the sole surviving teacher and exponent of Kashmir Śaivism. Nowadays such exalted souls are rarely to be found in the spiritual world, as revealed by the divine sage, Nārada, in the following aphorism, namely: *mahatsaṅgastu durlabho 'gamyo 'moghaśca.*[1] "Exalted souls are not so easy to find; they cannot be recognized as such, even if found; and once found, they are sure to benefit those who come in contact with them."

Mahāmaheśvara Shri Rāmapada, usually known as Swami Rāmaji, was born in CE 1853 as the son of Sri Sukhdev in Srinagar.[2] At the time of his birth the astrologers had predicted his emerging as a great saint. He learnt Śaivism under Sri Laljoo Kokroo, studied *Īśvara-Pratyabhijñā*, a standard and authoritative work on the

1. The philosophy of Love (*Bhakti-Sūtras* of Devarṣi Nārada), ed. Hanumanprasada Poddar, *sūtra* 39, p. 108.
2. According to Vikramī era, Swamiji was born in Saṁvat 1910. His father, Sri Sukhdev lived in Chinkral Mohalla in the city of Srinagar.

Trika philosophy of Recognition, under Sri Dayaram Ganz, and received initiation from Sri Mansaram Monga (*alias* Mana Kak), all the three of Srinagar.[3] Immediately after initiation, he immersed himself into penance and came to live in a hermitage (ashram)[4] dedicated by Rājānaka Sri Narayan Joo, the pioneer boat-builder and a renowned businessman of Srinagar. Highly learned and endowed with the faculty of reason, the Swamiji possessed deep insight into the philosophy and practice (*sādhanā*) of Śaiva lore and authoritatively resolved and interpreted difficult problems considered to be *rahasya* (mystic) or *gūḍhārtha* (secret). With remarkable progress in the spiritual realm, he had come to occupy that state in which he always lived and moved in the peace and bliss of consciousness. He felt great pleasure in teaching Śaiva Śāstras to his disciples and possessed great wit and humour. He breathed his last in CE 1914,[5] and left a number of spiritually advanced and learned disciples, most of them householders.

Mahāmaheśvara Mahtab Kak, usually known as Swami Mahtab Kak, was born in village Krandigam in the Tehsil and the District of Anantnag in CE 1862.[6] Renouncing his home, at a young age on the death of his parents, he learned Sanskrit and joined the hermitage of Swami Rāmaji, under whom he studied Śaivism and from whom he also received initiation. Upon Swami Rāmaji shedding his mortal frame, he was installed as the head of the ashram, where teaching in Śaivism continued to be imparted to the spiritually minded people and routine worship was performed daily. Sri Swamiji was temperamentally soft-spoken and sweet. Always cheerful, he loved to hear devotional songs, particularly those contained

---

3. Sri Laljoo Kokroo lived in Zaindar Mohalla and Shri Mansaram Monga lived in Shihiliteng Mohalla in the city of Srinagar. Sri Daya Ram Ganz lived in Sathu Bala, Srinagar. He was a very learned Śaiva philosopher. His son, Paṇḍit Rajakak Shastri was the first Principal of the Government Institute of Sanskrit (Pathsala) established in (Begh-i-Dilawarkhan) Srinagar.
4. This ashram (hermitage) known as "Śrī Rāma Śaiva Trika Āśrama" is situated on a lane branching from the central old city-road (running parallel to the Jhelum river) in Fateh Kadal (5th bridge from the Zero bridge) in the city of Srinagar.
5. According to the Vikramī era, the date of death is *caturdaśī* (14th) of the dark fortnight of the month of Māgha in Saṁvat 1971.
6. According to the Vikramī era, the date of birth falls on *caturthī* (4th) of the bright fortnight of the month of Kārttik, Saṁvat 1919.

in *Śivastotrāvalī* of Utpalācārya (a book in verse, studded with shining gems of thoughts and thrilling insight into truth; and composed in sonorous devotional songs in praise of Lord Śiva). My father (Sri Anand Joo Razdan of Safakadal), who was a devotee of Sri Swamiji as also of his revered Gurudeva, Sri Swami Rāmaji, used to carry me with himself, whenever he visited the hermitage. Young as I was, I received plenty of love and attention from the two divines, who also graciously used to offer me tea and morsels of food from their plates, or pieces of candy, which I gladly partook. On request from my father, Sri Swami Mahtab Kak would graciously condescend to come and live with us for a day or two on some occasions and bless us. What rudimentary knowledge of Śaivism I have picked up is, I believe, all due to the inspiration that I received from him and his emancipated Gurudeva. Alas, I suffered from lack of understanding and sufficient yearning and failed to attract the grace of the two god-men. I often recollect Sri Swami Mahtab Kak singing in a mood of ecstasy:

> *raṅgaḥ rasthiḥ zatsaiy kyahnaḥ rang hovum* ||
>
> What form did I not show in my formless nature?

He lived like a *jīvanmukta* in serene calm and bliss and always one with the Supreme. Lalleśvarī Yoginī identifies such a soul in the following prophetic saying:

> *cidānandam gyānprakāśam*
> *yimav cyunūya tim jīvanti mukti*
> *viśamis saṁsārins pāśas*
> *abodh gandoh śata śata ditiya* ||6 ||
>
> Those who achieve light–consciousness–bliss
> Are alone liberated while alive
> Tangled in the net of worldly existence
> Ignorant people tie hundreds of knots.*

Sri Swamiji left this world at the age of 86 years in 1943.[7] He left behind a number of disciples, endowed with divine wisdom, mostly householders.

---

* Translated by Jaishree Kak Odin, *To the Other Shore*: *Lalla's Life and Poetry*, New Delhi (Vitasta), 1999, p. 167 (No. 129 = No. 6 of Grierson's ed.)

7. According to the Vikramī era, the actual date of death is the *dvitīya* (second) of the bright fortnight of the month of Phālgun, Saṁvat 2000.

Mahāmaheśvara Rājānaka Sri Lakshman Joo, affectionately known by the name of "Īśvara Svarūpa," is[8] the sole-surviving exponent of the Kashmir School of Śaivism. Born as the son of Devi Srimati Aranimali and Rājānaka Sri Narayan Joo, the pioneer boat-builder and a renowned businessman of Kashmir, in 1907,[9] Īśvara Svarūpa was spiritually inclined from his very early age. He was a gentle and lovable child, who won the hearts of all. During his boyhood, as revealed by Sri Swami Mahtab Kak to my father, he used to lose his ordinary consciousness and fall into *samādhi*, which sometimes lasted for hours. Sri Swami Mahtab Kak had, however, predicted that that state of his would change, but will, in no case, impede his advancement in spiritual pursuit. The young aspirant for enlightenment and truth never found much to attract him in the ordinary dry-as-dust education imparted in school, which he attended for some time merely as a matter of form. But he passed his Matriculation examination in English and other subjects and with it turned away from bread-winning secular education to God-winning spiritual education. He passed many hours everyday in worship and intense meditation.

Not feeling himself quite at ease in the family environs of his parental house, Īśvara Svarūpa (at the age of 23), one fine morning, abandoned his home and retired to an old but celebrated ashram (hermitage), known as Sādhu-Gaṅgā (also called Sādhu Malyun) situated in the Kupwara tehsil of the Baramulla District in a dense forest away from the village habitation, which happened to be an abode of a succession of sages blessed with great yogic powers. After a short stay of about four months at this place, his parents, through the good offices of his venerable Gurudeva, succeeded in getting him back to Srinagar, where, however, he lived not in his old home but in an isolated hutment at Brari Nambal (a suburb of the city of Srinagar) on the shores of the Dal Lake.[10] Even this place did not suit him;

8. The date of writing was *c.* 1980s.

9. According to the Vikramī era, he was born in his parental house in Fateh Kadal, Srinagar city, on *dvādaśī* (12th) of the dark fortnight of Baiśākha, Saṁvat 1963.

10. Dal Lake is one of the most beautiful sheets of water in Kashmir. It is situated in the city of Srinagar measuring five miles from north to south and two miles from west to east. On three sides of the lake is a mountainous amphitheatre, whose summit is 3,000 to 4,000 ft above the sea level. Its dark green water reflects the lofty peaks of Mount Mahādeva.

he instead wanted to have a more secluded place outside the city of Srinagar. It was then that his parents, themselves spiritually inclined and already thrilled by the flashes of *samādhi* experienced by their son, built a separate house for him at a place in the vicinity of Nishat Bagh[11] on the shores of the Dal Lake. From the time he lived in this house, began his intense spiritual *sādhanā*. The quiet spot, where he used to meditate, lay on the slopes of Mount Mahādeva.[12] It was here that he, putting himself heart and soul in the practice of *prāṇika yoga*,[13] is said to have been blessed with self-realization. Later he moved to the present ashram in village Ishber[14] beyond Nishat Bagh. It was here that all the varieties of Śaiva *sādhanā*s (practices) and all the ideals of great religions were summoned up and perfected and even transcended by him. I have myself heard a talk on the Radio Kashmir, Srinagar, in which a question put to him during his interview at Īśvara Āśrama by the then Radio artist, Ghulam Rasool Nazki, a reputed scholar, writer and godly man of Kashmir, elicited a reply from Īśvara Svarūpa confirming that he had been blessed with *ātmasākṣātkāra* (self-realization).

11. Nishat Bagh meaning "garden of gladness" is one of the Mogul gardens, at a distance of about 11 km from Srinagar, on the shores of the Dal Lake.
12. Mount Mahādeva, about 12000 ft above the sea level, rises behind the Shalimar Garden, another Mogul Garden about 141/2 km distant from Srinagar. Hindus make a yearly pilgrimage to one of its lower peaks.
13. *Prāṇika yoga* is based on the control of *prāṇa*. *Prāṇa* is the vital *vāyu* that is exhaled and *apāna* is that *vāyu* which is inhaled and goes downwards towards the anus. *Suṣumnā* also called, *madhya-dhāma* is the middle *nāḍī*. These are two *nāḍī*s running parallel to each other on the *suṣumnā*. They are not physical but *prāṇika* and are known as *iḍā* and *piṅgalā*. *Prāṇa* passes through the *iḍā* and *apāna* through the *piṅgalā*. *Suṣumnā* too is a *prāṇika nāḍī* said to lie inside the spinal column. When through yogic practice, *prāṇa* and *apāna* get united and cause the *suṣumnā nāḍī* to open, *udāna śakti* comes into play bringing about the emergence of the fourth state of consciousness, viz. *turīya*. This state is followed by another state called *turīyātīta*, that which transcends *turīya*. It is the blissful state of pure consciousness in which the entire universe is felt as part of self.
14. Ishber village lies beyond the Nishat Bagh. From this village there is a path to the top of the ridge of the mountains above the Dal Lake. This was formerly the site of a shrine Sureśvarī as half way up is the sacred spring Śatadhārā. The summit called Barabal is 8,573 ft.

Īśvara Svarūpa learnt Sanskrit from competent teachers and the Śaiva literature from one of the renowned Śaiva scholars and grammarians of Kashmir, the late Rājānaka Śrī Maheśvara, a Paṇḍit of the old Archeological and Research Department of the Jammu and Kashmir State, who has several publications on Advaita system of thought to his credit. He received initiation at an early age from his Gurudeva Sri Swami Mahtab Kak, at whose feet he has had the unique good fortune of sitting and receiving guidance for more than forty years. He did not and does not spare himself from teaching Śaiva Śāstras to a large number of his disciples — men and women — and derives celestial happiness and bliss in celebrating, with perfect faith and devotion, the death anniversary of his great Gurudeva, when hundreds of people are fed after the *śrāddha* ceremony is performed with the help of learned brāhmaṇas. Apart from the poise, glow and vision which *ātmika* knowledge has brought to him, he is a living example of Maharshi Vasiṣṭha's grand ideal *antarayogī bahiḥ saṅgī* endorsed by the teaching of the *Bhagavad-Gītā*:

> *saktāḥ karmaṇyavidvāṁso yathā kurvanti bhārata* ।
> *kuryād vidvāṁstatha saktaścikīrṣur lokasaṁgraham* ॥3.25॥

> As the unwise act with attachment, O Bhārata, so should the wise, seeking maintenance of the world order, act without attachment.

Īśvara Svarūpa has a keen sense of humour. A spiritual man who cannot laugh, may only be a moral man. Īśvara Svarūpa can laugh without hurting one's feelings. I have seen him suffer fools with a deep sense of humour. And what fools most of us can be he alone knows. Though he sees one's inner nature, yet he never laughs at the disciple's weaknesses. He knows us better than we do; yet he treats us as we think we deserve. The slightest false step he corrects. He rescues his disciples even from grave errors without humiliating them. He is a *mahāpuruṣa*; in him one can perceive the largest magnitude of the Supreme, knowing as he does, his identity with the whole universe, as Self.

There are some souls who come to this world not drawn by their own *karma*, as is the normal case, but as if to work out the *karma* of others through their life. They take upon themselves the burden of humanity and suffer for the sake of the world. Their great concern is to solve the problems confronting suffering humanity, to relieve the misery and affliction which they see around them and to bring comfort and peace to the downtrodden and the helpless. They are liberated souls who have attained eternal peace. They take delight in the Self. They move in the world only for our good. Such a one is Īśvara Svarūpa, filled with compassion for all without any distinction of caste and creed. Śrī Sāmba (the son of Lord Kṛṣṇa), even though blessed with Supreme Consciousness and emancipated, thus supplicated for his reincarnation, with the sole purpose of helping the worldly people, to get liberated from the trammels of birth and death:

satyam bhūyo jananamaraṇe tvatprapanneṣu na sta-
statrapyekaṁ tava nutiphalaṁ janma yāce tadittham ।
trailokyeśaḥ śama iva paraḥ puṇyakāyo 'pyayoniḥ
saṁsārābdhau plava iva jagattāranāya sthiraḥ syām ॥

— *Sāmbapañcāśikā* v. 34

O Lord, it is true that those (your devotees), who have surrendered themselves to you, are for ever free from (the cycle of) birth and death. (Therefore, being your devotee, I am also free for ever from the cycle of birth and death.) Still, as a recompense for the prayers offered to you, I implore that yet another birth may be granted to me (I may be reborn), so that, in spite of being the master of three worlds (three states of wakefulness, dream and profound sleep),[15] being endowed with contentment, peacefulness and purity of body and being not born of a womb (having got embodied by sheer will),

---

15. The devotee has transcended these states and entered the fourth state called *turīya*. Rājānaka Sri Swami Lakshman Joo has defined the *turīya* state as the state of "Internal Individual Conscious Subjectivity," which according to him, can be realized within the first three by concentrating one's mind on subjectivity — (*i*) at the junction of the intake and outtake of respiration, or (*ii*) at the junction of the change of cognition from one object to another, or (*iii*) concentrating on objectlessness. According to him, these are the only three methods to realise Consciousness of this state. Beyond this is the fifth and the last state, known as *turīyātīta*, which Swamiji states to be a developed *turīya*, the 4th state, firmly held and universalized, and defines it as the state of "Internal Universal Conscious Subjectivity," in which the *sādhaka* experiences eternal peace, bliss and happiness and becomes one with Universal Consciousness.

> I remain as steady as a boat in carrying the living beings of the world across the ocean of this universe.

Great saints with strikingly impressive personality, both men and women, have lived in India. Their memory abides. Even among the poorest and the most depressed classes, great men have been born, who have won the respect of posterity by their wisdom, piety and devotion. Such men and women are still to be found today. In every part of India, the deeper things of the spirit of man, the problems of existence, the final mystery of God, the inner discipline of the soul have a place in the thoughts of living men and women today, perhaps here more than anywhere else in the world. There also is noticed a readiness to abandon everything that man holds dear in search of the inner truth, when the voice within the soul commands. As in the past, so today, there are saints and emancipated souls who suffer for others and make them free. It cannot, however, be denied that a large number of people are steeped in ignorance and amongst them many suffer from an inordinate pride in their ancient cultural glory. Unfortunately ignorance is passing for knowledge, cowardice for non-violence, and many evil actions as religious practices. We want energy, spirit of self-reliance, independence of thought and action, thirst for improvement and above all supreme endeavour for realization of the real purpose of life. All this can be achieved, if we get the sleeping soul roused to self-conscious activity by maintaining an abiding faith in its infinite potentiality, thus upholding the glory of the eternal and deathless *ātman*, the repository of all power and knowledge.

The modern scientist has come to look upon this universe as a play of the eternal infinite energy manifesting itself as all things. The philosopher thinks of the primary cause as a limitless power expressing itself in infinite ways both in the worlds of matter and thought. Kashmir Śaivism — the Trika — holds the Lord (Śiva), the ultimate reality and supreme consciousness as both the material and efficient cause of the universe, as everything and yet beyond everything. Among others, the distinctive feature of its metaphysics is that it does not recognize *māyā* as illusory reality, associated with *Brahman* and its Īśvara aspect though it is not *Brahman*, as in Vedānta. *Brahman* is never associated with anything but itself. Māyā to the Śaiva is *Śakti; Śakti* veiling herself as consciousness, but which, as being *Śakti*, is consciousness. And then Trika believes in *sādhanā* (practice), which is of the highest importance and more than anything else gives value to it. Humanity today needs a religion of Śakti — a power that accommodates a synthetic working of both the spiritual and physical forces in the achievement of a happy life, of which the realization of divinity in man is a very important and sacred objective. And what the intellectual world wants today is the sort of philosophy which not merely argues but experiments. My conviction is that the lofty, realistic and sound tenets of Trika will eminently meet the quest of the intellectual and the craving for happiness which all men seek. The great teacher Utpaladevācārya has, in his ecstatic mood, ordained a wider dispensation of divine grace in the following immortal couplet in his *Śivastotrāvalī*:

> *duḥkhānyapi sukhāyante viṣamapyamṛtāyate* ।
> *mokṣāyate ca saṁsāro yatra mārgaḥ sa śāṅkaraḥ* ॥20.22 ॥

> That path by which pain is converted into pleasure, poison is converted into ambrosia, and the world of becoming is made the seat of liberation, that is the path of Lord Śiva.

II.
The Ācārya of Kashmir Śaivism

अगाधसंशयाम्भोधिसमुत्तरणतारिणीम् ।
वन्दे विचित्रार्थपदां चित्रां तां गुरुभारतीम् ॥
— स्पन्दकारिका ४.१

agādha-saṁśayāmbhodhi-samuttaraṇa-tāriṇīm ।
vande vicitrārtha-padāṁ citrāṁ tāṁ guru-bhāratīm ॥
— *Spandakārikā* 4.1

I pay my homage
to that wonderful speech of my Guru
which is like a boat
for crossing the fathomless ocean of doubt
and is full of words which yield wonderful meaning.

18. Lilian Silburn with Swami Lakshman Joo, 1975.

19. Lilian Silburn studying with Swamiji, 1975.

20. Alexis Sanderson with Swami Lakshman Joo (c. 1975).

21. Tantra Sammelanam at Vārāṇaseya Saṁskṛta Viśvavidyālaya, 1965. Swami Lakshman Joo is sitting in the front row, fourth from left.

22. Thakur Jaideva Singh with his Master (*c*. 1980s).

23. Teaching in the Guptaganga Hall.

24. Pandit Jankinath Kaul 'Kamal' with his Master (*c.* 1985).

25. Teaching Tantrāloka under the Chinar Tree, 1985.

26. Teaching Tantrāloka under the Chinar Tree, 1985.

27-29. Teaching Tantrāloka under the Chinar Tree, 1985.

30-32. Teaching Tantrāloka under the Chinar Tree, 1985.

33 & 34. Ṭeaching Tantrāloka under the Chinar Tree, 1985.

6

Lilian Silburn and Swami Lakshman Joo
A Fertile Relationship

Jacqueline Chambron

Lilian Silburn was one of the pioneers who made the spiritual tradition and the texts of non-dualistic Śaivism of Kashmir known to the West by her studies and translations. This was possible thanks to her contact and study with Swami Lakshman Joo who taught her all the important texts. The times she spent in Kashmir, shortly after the Partition of India and in difficult circumstances, she had to undergo much hardship but her dedication was total. Besides being an excellent Sanskrit scholar she was immersed in spiritual practice and mystical experience which gave her access to the meaning of the texts and Swamiji's explanations. This spiritual understanding is reflected in her commentaries to the texts. The following is an extract from a biography under preparation by her chief disciple, Madame Jacqueline Chambron. (Editor)

WE find in the Preface of practically all the books of Lilian Silburn an expression of her profound gratitude for the help she received from Swami Lakshman Joo in her research and study of Śaivism. She describes him as a "very learned Paṇḍit and at the same time a true *yogī* and *jñānī*," who possesses the mystical knowledge described in the texts, of which he is one of the last masters who understands their profound meaning. During the years she was working with him — from 1949 till 1975 — she constantly referred the result of her research to the knowledge of the Swami. Their constant agreement and convergence of views was a source of happiness and sometimes also of consolation for both.

In 1952 she refers to her work with Swami Lakshman Joo as a source of joy:

> His constant joyfulness, our perfect understanding, his expression of gratitude after our time of working together, because he is so grateful for the task which I fulfil with regard to Trika.

In her Preface to the *Śivasūtras* Lilian describes her first trip to Kashmir in 1948, after passing her doctorate, and the months which she passed in solitude, in a ruin of a mud house, in the heart of the Kashmiri landscape.

She writes in a letter about fifteen years later:

> Since my arrival I was working with the Swami Lakshman Brahmacārin who possesses not only the knowledge of the Śaiva texts but who has an obvious mystical experience. I admired the greatness and simplicity of that great *yogī*. And yet, the monistic tradition of Kashmir Śaivism which was so much alive at the time of Abhinavagupta has partly disappeared, since the important technique of direct transmission (*anupāya*) has been forgotten, since the lineage of masters has been interrupted. It is now up to the disciple to discover the Self by his own effort, the master is there to give an example, to advise and to give explanations.

During the first weeks she started some exercises in order to arouse the *kuṇḍalinī*, as advised by the Swami. She climbed on the Śaṅkarācārya Hill which is crowned by the ancient Śiva temple early morning before sunrise and experienced, as she described later: "I succeeded in originating heat and bright lights which never disappeared since then . . . I tried hard to concentrate during six hours a day but never for three minutes could I stop the work of my mind. . . ."

Her sense of humour was infectious, and apart from the serious intellectual study she did with the Swami, during the long stays with him she was keen to distract him by all kinds of phantasies and surprises which were occasions to reveal a natural joyfulness.

Her last visit and study session with him was in 1975 when she came with some of her disciples.

Lilian Silburn

Preface to the Śivasūtras

After completing my thesis on "Instant et Cause" which I passed in Paris in 1948, I made a first journey to India and I met Swami Lakshman Joo in Kashmir. I received from him teaching about the *Śivasūtras* and their commentaries, as also about the *Spandakārikā* and the *Vijñānabhairava* which I translated (into French).

In that year I lived near him in a mud-hut which was abandoned, on the lonely slopes of the hills above the Dal Lake, towards which the terraces of the Nishat Garden descended. I lived several months in solitude, in the midst of that extraordinary landscape, where the nakedness of the rocky mountain, the subtle gentleness of the light and the immobility of the lake which was sometimes enveloped in mist combine and merge in a harmony and deep peace, which seems to be still pervaded by the presence of the great Śaivite masters who probably lived in this area. At least this is what makes us think, due to the presence of a spring which is still considered sacred, and a great *liṅga* of stone which has been discovered at this place under special circumstances by Swami Rāma who came from south India some years before.

When he returned to Kashmir after a long absence, he came to see the *liṅga* and the hut and he was surprised to find me there. He told me why he got this house built: Once when he was walking along the path above the Dal Lake he found this place fit for meditation and he was convinced that this is the site of a very ancient sanctuary. He got the earth dug up at that very place and discovered there a big *liṅga* in a lying position but intact. It was moved a few metres from there near to the spring.[1]

Afterwards it was closed in a small conical construction pompously called Śiva temple, and a few houses were built around it. The spring and the temple were locked and the place lost its great charm. However, at the occasion of certain festivals Swami Lakshman Joo and his disciples met there and it was a spectacle full of

1. The spring and the temple came to be called Gupta Gaṅgā. Later Swamiji got a *havanaśālā* (hall for sacrifice) constructed there and he used to perform *yajña* there. Another hall was built for his teaching and giving regular Sunday lectures, arranged by Dr Karan Singh and his "Dharmartha Trust." (Ed.)

beauty to see the devotees at the time of sunset spread out on the naked rocks and become immobilized in silent meditation on the mountain side, under the majestic guidance of the Swami.

In summer 1949 I was also fortunate to take part in the great expedition which the Swami undertook on foot to the large rock of the Mahādeva mountain where, according to Kṣemarāja, Vasugupta discovered the *Śivasūtras* engraved on the rock by Śiva.

We traversed the forest of the Mahārājā and had a picnic on the rock which, after having shown the *sūtras* for Vasugupta to read, again turned upside down under the water, taking its initial position and removing the divine text from sight. I tried in vain to swim under the rock, I could not decipher any inscription. But is it on the rock of Mahādeva or in the heart of Vasugupta that Śiva inscribed his wonderful Sūtras?

7

Swami Lakshman Joo and His Place in the Kashmirian Śaiva Tradition

Alexis Sanderson

In 1971 I completed a B.A. course in Sanskrit at Oxford. During the last year of that course I had strayed beyond the syllabus to read the *Dhvanyāloka* of the Kashmirian poetician Ānandavardhana and after studying the learned commentary on that classic by Abhinavagupta began to take an interest in that Śaiva author's theological and philosophical writings. Fascinated by what I found there I decided to devote myself to research in this area. Being conscious of the difficult and technical nature of the literature I saw the desirability of being trained by a Kashmirian scholar well-versed in this tradition and after discovering the existence of Swami Lakshman Joo from the publications of others who had studied with him I travelled to Kashmir in February 1972 at the age of 23 with the hope that he would accept me as a pupil. Provided with a letter of introduction I approached him with my request. He asked me what text I wished to study with him and when I replied that I wished to read all the extant literature, he asked me to return a week later for his answer. This postponement was repeated three times through an intermediary. After the fourth request to return I feared that I had asked for too much and was not to be accepted. But Swami Lakshman had merely been busy with other matters and when finally he was free to receive me again he did so without reservation, with the warmth and generosity towards all who sought his help that I was to see on many occasions as his pupil. He taught me for six years and for no reason other than the urge to propagate understanding that is the mark of the true teacher in any discipline. I cannot adequately express the gratitude that I feel towards him not only for the innumerable hours he devoted to my instruction but also for the perfect example that he gave me of dedicated teaching free of all thought of personal reward.

I had the funding from my college to pursue my studies in Kashmir for three years and I had the hope of more to come before I would have to look for a full-time teaching post. Nonetheless, it seemed to me to be inappropriate to ask Swami Lakshman Joo to work with me in the manner of a traditional Sanskrit teacher, reading through text after text, line by line. I therefore suggested that I would read on my own and bring my questions to him for discussion. He approved and thereafter we met for this purpose once or twice a week. In this way we covered the greater part of the literature that had been published in the Kashmir Series of Texts and Studies, devoting particular attention after my preliminary reading to the study of Abhinavagupta's *Tantrāloka*, his compendious analysis of the *Mālinīvijayottaratantra*. I brought to him all the problems that I encountered as I read and often had to go back to questions that we had already considered. Yet never once did he show even the slightest reluctance to continue to try to clarify his understanding of the texts for me, and this was so even when I had to address what I thought to be inconsistencies in his explanations. Again and again he patiently explained the differences of context that justified the differences of interpretation that he had proposed. When on occasion I remained unconvinced or perplexed he seemed only pleased by my refusal to rest with uncertainty. I never encountered in him the common evasion of the less committed teacher, who when confronted with a difficult question by a pupil is apt to escape his discomfiture by saying that it would take too long to explain or pretending that the matter would become clear later in the text.[1]

I was blocked only when my scepticism was applied to the metaphysical doctrine of his tradition's non-dualism. But it was inappropriate of me to venture into that territory since the purpose of my pupilage was to attempt to understand his understanding of the texts of Abhinavagupta and those texts themselves; and when I forgot this I was halted not by dogmatism but by the sincere expression of hope that I would come in time, perhaps in a future life, to assent to this position and so

1. I allude to the wit of the seventeenth-century south-Indian satirist Nīlakaṇṭhadīkṣita, Chief Minister in the court of Tirumal Nayak of Madurai, who mocks such second-rate teachers in his *Kaliviḍambana* with the words (v. 8): *vācyatāṁ samayo 'tītaḥ spaṣṭam agre bhaviṣyati* | *iti pāṭhayatāṁ granthe kāṭhinyaṁ kutra vartate* "Read on!," "Our time is up," "It will become clear later" — can there be difficulties anywhere in texts for those who teach them like this?"

open the way for myself through direct experience to what was for him no less than the ultimate goal of human existence. It is all the more remarkable in the light of this evident limitation of my approach to the study of his path that he was willing to devote so much time to my education.

The attentive reader will have noticed that I have distinguished here between the texts of Abhinavagupta and Swami Lakshman Joo's understanding of them, and will hope for my assessment of the accuracy and completeness of that understanding. For the two teachers are separated by approximately a thousand years. There was, of course, no doubt in the assertions of Swami Lakshman Joo's devotees that Abhinavagupta's Śaivism had reached them complete and unchanged; and when I asked Swami Lakshman Joo himself for his view of this matter he confirmed their faith. But systems of religious knowledge and practice such as this, which are rooted in the belief that they have been transmitted intact through an unbroken lineage of Gurus are more subject than most to the depredations of time. For if they fragment and contract, their teachers are barred from seeing this by their faith in the instruction received from their immediate predecessors and they will therefore be disinclined to reverse the process by recovering information from other sources, by searching, for example, for manuscripts of texts that were known to the authors whose works they consider valid but are no longer current among them. For such documents would be seen as mere texts divorced from living authority.

The Kashmirian Śaiva tradition has certainly not been immune in this regard. Around the turn of the tenth and eleventh centuries Abhinavagupta produced in the *Tantrāloka* his brilliant and compelling synthesis of the various Śaiva and Śākta traditions current among his contemporaries in Kashmir and beyond, conceiving them as a unified hierarchy encompassed by the "higher non-dualism" (*paramādvayavādaḥ*) propounded in the eighteenth chapter of the *Mālinīvijayottara*, and articulating as the upper terminus of this ascent of revelation a form of the Trika in which that system is fused with and coloured by core elements of the system of meditative worship of Kālī known as the Krama.[2] In doing so he drew

2. The *Tantrāloka* does not tell us the year of its composition. But we know that it was composed before Abhinavagupta's *Īśvarapratyabhijñāvivṛtivimarśinī*, which was completed, he tells us, in Kali 4115, Laukika [40]90 (= CE 1015). Two others of his works bear dates: the *Kramastotra*, completed in [40]66 (= CE 991), and the →

on a vast and diverse literature of Śaiva scriptures, commentaries, and *paddhatis*. His use of these sources commonly takes the form of paraphrases rather than direct citations and these often seemed to me excessively concise and consequently ambiguous. But these features that troubled me cannot be held against Abhinavagupta as defects. For if he had access to his sources, then so did the learned Śaiva audience for whom he was writing. The difficulties I encountered arise only if the source-text paraphrased is no longer accessible.

Now, in his thirteenth-century commentary on the *Tantrāloka* Jayaratha was inclined to cite these source-texts verbatim wherever he deemed this useful, so that in these instances the ambiguities can be resolved unless the source-text itself is obscure.[3] But he was writing some 250 years after the composition of the *Tantrāloka*[4] and already several of its scriptural sources seem not to have been available to him. We do not learn this from his telling us so. We strongly suspect it because in these cases he never cites the original when Abhinavagupta paraphrases it, and we establish it when on occasion he falls victim to a paraphrase's ambiguity by interpreting it incorrectly, which we can do if manuscripts of the texts in question have survived elsewhere.

→ *Bhairavastotra*, completed in [40]68 (= CE 993). For a detailed analysis of Abhinavagupta's hierarchy of Śaiva revelation within his Krama-influenced Trika and the doctrine of "higher non-dualism" that accommodates it, see Sanderson 2005, pp. 102-22.

3. This is so, for example, in the case of the Trika's *Triśirobhairavatantra*, the meaning of whose verses as transmitted in Jayaratha's commentary is often uncertain, in part because of their esoteric subject matter and in part because of the irregularity of their Sanskrit.

4. Jayaratha tells us in *Tantrālokaviveka* vol. 12, p. 432, concluding v. 28, that his father was a minister under Rājarāja. The historians of Kashmir have reliably reported the names of all their rulers and the durations of their reigns during the applicable period, and they make no mention of a Rājarāja. But it is evident that the name is a synonym of Rājadeva, who ruled Kashmir for 23 years from [Laukika] 4289, that is to say, from CE 1213 to 1236 (Jonarāja, *Rājataraṅgiṇī* vv. 75 and 87). The view of Rastogi (1979: 210), following the suggestion of Pandey (1963: 262), that this king is not Rājadeva but Jayasiṁha, who ruled Kashmir from 1128 to 1155, is unfounded, and excluded by other facts.

This is so, for example, in the case of the *Dīkṣottara*, a Śaiva Saiddhāntika work which has come down to us in manuscripts in the Tamil South.[5] Jayaratha never cites the original in his commentary on these passages and this lack is particularly striking in the case of the first of them, where citation is obviously necessary, since it lists without clarification six forms under which Śiva may be contemplated, namely world, embodiment, light, void, sound, and *mantra*.[6] The source here is *Dīkṣottara* 2.2-3b.[7] The rest of the chapter in which this passage occurs and the whole of the next are devoted to explaining the nature of each of the six. Jayaratha avoids drawing attention to this lacuna in his knowledge by citing instead passages without attribution from what are in fact other scriptural texts, namely the *Tantrasadbhāva*, the *Svāyambhuvasūtrasaṁgraha*, and the *Mālinīvijayottara*, poor substitutes for the *Dīkṣottara*, since they only partly clarify the matter in hand. That he had not read the *Dīkṣottara* itself can be inferred from the fact that he explains the void (*kham,=vyoma, śūnyam*) as referring to *śaktiḥ*, *vyāpinī*, and *samanā*, the three highest levels of the subtle resonance of *mantras*. This is a guess, and an inaccurate one. For the *Dīkṣottara* explains it in its second chapter as the void of Power (*śaktivyoma*) beyond the essence of sound (*śabdatattvam*),[8] and in the third chapter as referring to three voids that it terms *ayanaśūnyam*, *praśāntaśūnyam*, and *niṣkalaśūnyam*, the first located in the space from the uvula

---

5. This text, which is part of the *Niśvāsa* corpus, being presented as the last part of the *Niśvāsakārikā*, is cited or paraphrased in *Tantrāloka* 1.62c-63; 5.148-151; 5.148c-150, 8.9-10, 15.458c-459, 19.21-22, 24.4-5, 24.17c-21; and 28.65-71.

6. *Tantrāloka* 1.62c-63: *tato 'sya bahurūpatvam uktaṁ dīkṣottarādike* ǀ *bhuvanaṁ vigraho jyotiḥ khaṁ śabdo mantra eva ca* ǀ *bindunādādisaṁbhinnaḥ ṣaḍvidhaḥ śiva ucyate.*

7. *Dīkṣottara*, MS A, pp. 805, l. 9-806, l. 2; MS B, p. 37, ll. 4-6: 2.2 **ṣaḍvidhas* (A : *ṣaḍviṁśas* B) *tu śivo jñeyo yoginā sumahātmanā* ǀ **śabdo* (em. : *śabda* AB) **vyoma tathā* (corr. : *vyomatayā* A : *vyomas tathā* B) **jyotir* (corr. : *jyotiḥ* AB) *vigraho *bhuvanaṁ* (B : *bhuvanas* A) *tathā* ǀ 3 *mantramūrtis tu paramaḥ ṣaḍvidhas tu śivo 'vyayaḥ.*

8. *Dīkṣottara* MS A, p. 806, ll. 7-10; MS B, p. 37, ll. 11-14, covering the forms *śabdaḥ* and *vyoma*: *śabdatattve pare līnaḥ śabdāntargatamānasaḥ* ǁ 2.6 **paraṁ mokṣam avāpnoti* (B : *parame mokṣam āpnoti* A) *śabdāt sarvārthasiddhaye* ǀ *tasyātītaṁ paraṁ devi śaktivyoma prakīrtitam* ǀ 7 *tasya dhyānād bhavet siddhir *muktiś* (A : *mūrtiś* B) *caiva na saṁśayaḥ.*

to the mouth, the second at the top of the head, and the third beyond the body.[9]

Another example of an important scripture frequently drawn on by Abhinavagupta but apparently inaccessible to Jayaratha is the *Brahmayāmala* (/*Picumata*).[10] In *Tantrāloka* 27.29 Abhinavagupta paraphrases its listing of six types of skull-bowl that may be used as the substrate of worship known as a *tūraḥ*, ending with a five-member compound that is open to more than one interpretation.[11] Jayaratha takes the last of the six to be conveyed at the end of this compound by the words — *śaktikajākṛti*, taking them to mean "having the form of a Śakti lotus (*śaktikajam*)."[12] But comparison with the original, which survives in a Nepalese manuscript of CE 1052, shows that the words *śakti-* and *kaja-* should be understood to mean not "the Śakti lotus" but "the Śakti and the lotus" and therefore

---

9. *Dīkṣottara* MS A, pp. 812, l. 7-814, l. 4; MS B, p. 40, ll. 3-19: 3.2 **triśūnyam* (em. : *viśūnyaṁ* A : *viśūnye* B) *sarvatattveṣu gīyate surasundari* । *tasyāhaṁ saṁpravakṣyāmi lakṣaṇaṁ tu surārcite* ॥ 3 *vyāpakena samāyuktam ayanaṁ tat prakīrtitam* । *divārātryoś ca madhye tu veditavyaṁ prayatnataḥ* ॥ 4 *na rātrir na divā caiva *na ca* (em. : *nara* B : *nani* A) *bindu*kalās* (B : *kalakalā* A) *tathā* । *pañcadhā tu parityajya praśāntaṁ śūnyam ucyate* ॥ 5 *dehātītaṁ *tṛtīyaṁ tu* (A : *smṛtaṁsattu* B) *niṣkaleti vibhāvyate* । **nāsāyās* (conj. : *nāsāyān* AB) *tu yadātītaṁ tac chūnyaṁ ca tṛtīyakam* ॥ 6 **ghaṇṭikāntaparicchedaṁ* (conj. : *ghaṭikān tu paricchedaṁ* AB) **yāvat* (corr. : *yāvan* AB) *tanmukha*maṇḍalam* (A : *maṇṭapam* B) । *ayanaṁ śūnyam ity uktaṁ kathitaṁ jñānam uttamam* ॥ 7 **rasanāṁ* (conj. : *rasānāṁ* B : *nāsānāṁ* A) **śūnyataḥ* (corr. : *śūnyata* AB) *sthāpya vijñānam upajāyate* । **adhastāt tu parityajya* (A : *ayastas tu + + + jya* B) *pañcadhā *parameśvari* (A : *parameśvarī* B) ॥ 8 *praśāntaṁ śūnyam ity uktam ūrdhvaṁ kiṁcin na saṁspṛśet* । *etat *praśāntaśūnyaṁ* (A : *praśāntaṁ śūnyan* B) *tu jñātvā mucyeta bandhanāt* ॥ 9 **gamāgamaviyogena* (conj. : *gamāgamamayogena* A : *gamanāgamanayogena* B) *tṛtīyaṁ parikīrtitaṁ* । **viditaṁ* (A : *veditaṁ* B) *tad varārohe *dehamuktam* (A : *devi + ktam* B) *idaṁ smṛtam* ॥ 10 *tad evaṁ kathitaṁ devi śūnyam uktaṁ śivāgame.*

10. Abhinavagupta cites or paraphrases this text in *Tantrāloka* 4.60-65; 5.97c-100b; 13.145; 15.43c-44; 18.9; 23.43c-44b; 27.21c-23bb; 27.29; 28.384b; 28.409c-411a; 28.418c-419b; 28.422c-423b; and 29.11-12b.

11. *Tantrāloka* 27.29: *śrībrahmayāmale 'py uktaṁ pātraṁ gomukham uttamam* । *gajakūrmatalaṁ kumbhavṛttaśaktikajākṛti.*

12. *Tantrālokaviveka* on 27.29: *śaktikajaṁ guhyam.*

to be referring not to the sixth alone but to the fifth and the sixth.[13] Evidently Jayaratha had not seen the source and, forced to guess, has done so wrongly.[14]

That he had no access to the *Brahmayāmala*, or at least that he did not know it, is confirmed by his comments on *Tantrāloka* (4.60-65), in which Abhinavagupta paraphrases the *Brahmayāmala*'s teaching of a form of propitiation by means of which a person may raise himself to the status of each of the ascending ranks of initiate, the resulting status depending on the length of time for which he maintains the observance. The propitiation is that of the goddess Raktā, as is clearly stated in 4.63cd (*śrīmadraktārādhanakarmaṇi*) and 4.65b (*raktādevī*).[15] Now Raktā is one of the four goddesses that form the inner retinue of the principal deity in the system of the *Brahmayāmala*, the other three being Karālī, Caṇḍākṣī, and Mahocchuṣmā; and after this passage the *Brahmayāmala* goes on to teach propitiations of each of these remaining three followed by a fifth, collective propitiation. Jayaratha reveals that he is ignorant of the text, and hence of the deities worshipped on its authority,

13. *Brahmayāmala*, f. 33r3-4 (4.739c-741b): *mahāpātrasya vai devi lakṣaṇaṁ śr̥ṇu sāmpratam* || *gomukhaṁ gajapr̥ṣṭham vā gajakumbhas tathaiva ca* | *kūrmapr̥ṣṭhākr̥tiś caiva śaktipātraṁ tathaiva ca* || *ṣaṣṭha<ṁ> padmaṁ samākhyātaṁ kapālaṁ varavarṇṇini* "Hear now, O Goddess, the defining characteristics of human skull-bowls. [They are], O you of fine complexion, [that which has the shape of] a cow's face, an elephant's back, an elephant's frontal lobe, that which has the shape of a tortoise's back, the Śakti-bowl, and, sixth, the Lotus-bowl."

14. So *Tantrāloka* 27.29 means "And in the *Brahmayāmala* it is taught that the [skull-]bowl (*pātram*) [may be of the following six kinds:] (1) the excellent Cow-face (*gomukha*[*pātra*]*m*), (2) the Elephant-back (*gajatala*[*pātra*]*m*, i.e. *gajapr̥ṣṭhapātram*), (3) the Tortoise-back (*kūrmatala*[*pātra*]*m*, i.e. *kūrmapr̥ṣṭhapātram*), (4) that which is rounded like the frontal-lobe [of an elephant] (i.e. the *gajakumbhapātram* [the Elephant-lobe]), (5) that which has the [triangular] shape of Śakti (i.e. the *śaktipātram*), and (6) that which has the shape of a lotus (i.e. the *padmapātram*)."

15. *Tantrāloka* 4.63c-64: *tatraiva ca punaḥ śrīmadraktārādhanakarmaṇi* || *vidhiṁ proktaṁ sadā kurvan māsenācārya ucyate* | *pakṣeṇa sādhako 'rdhārdhāt putrakaḥ samayī tathā*. The source-text is *Brahmayāmala* 21.70b-71b (MS f. 101r4): *māsenācārya ucyate* | *pakṣeṇa sādhako hy eṣa bhūtale mantravigrahaḥ* | *prathaman tu vrataṁ hy etad raktāyāḥ parikīrtitam*, or rather a variant of this, since there is no reference here to the two lower grades of initiate.

because he takes *raktā-* in 4.63cd and 4.65b to be an epithetic name of the generic goddess Caṇḍikā.[16]

As a final example of the contraction in Kashmir of the available corpus of Śaiva scriptures by the time of Jayaratha I draw attention to the *Yogasaṁcāra*, a Kaula text of which Abhinavagupta made much use.[17] Here too it seems very likely that Jayaratha had no access to the text itself but knew it only through Abhinavagupta's paraphrases and citations. The content of some of the passages that draw on it is so obscure that direct citation would have been desirable, though in this case it may be that even if he had seen the original he would have been unable to take us much further.

The first use of this text in the *Tantrāloka* is a long direct citation of eighteen verses (4.127-144), an obscure passage for which Abhinavagupta offers no detailed explanation, excusing himself from doing so with the claim that the content is just too secret to be exposed.[18] Instead he offers in two verses before the passage and one after it what he takes to be its hidden gist, namely the process by which consciousness flows into each of the twelve faculties from a state of pure subjectivity through an intermediate conceptual state to a state of sensual apprehension of the object of cognition.[19] In my view Jayaratha has misunderstood how Abhinavagupta meant these verses to be interpreted. But this is not the appropriate place to demonstrate that. I wish only to show that the very obscurity of the cited passage, the absence of detailed analysis by Abhinavagupta, and lack of access to the source of the citation and therefore to its broader context, gave Jayaratha the freedom to add to the tradition an elaborate interpretation of his own, one that in the context of its production in thirteenth-century Kashmir could neither be verified nor refuted.

The passage begins with four verses which equate four parts of the human eye

16. *Tantrālokaviveka* on 4.63cd: *śrīmadraktāyāḥ śrīcaṇḍikāyā vidhāne.*

17. He draws on it in *Tantrāloka* 4.126c-144; 6.58cd; 12.23; 13.241c-242b; 15.65; 15.391c-396; 28.10c-14; 29.82c-91; 29.97-100b; and 32.10c-31c.

18. *Tantrāloka* 4.146ab: *na vyākhyātaṁ tu nirbhajya yato 'tisarahasyakam.*

19. *Tantrāloka* 4.125-126: *sā ca mātari vijñāne māne karaṇagocare | meye caturvidhaṁ bhāti rūpam aśritya sarvadā || śuddhasaṁvinmayī prācye jñāne śabdanarūpiṇī | karaṇe grahaṇākārā yataḥ śrīyogasaṁcare*; and 4.145: *atra tātparyataḥ proktam akṣe kramacatuṣṭayam | ekaikatra yatas tena dvādaśātmakatoditā.*

with four coloured circles of unnamed powers: the white of the eye with one of sixteen, the red margin with one of twelve, the grey iris with one of eight, and the black pupil with one of four. Given Abhinavagupta's statement of the gist of the passage and the fact that the field of the object and that of the faculties are regularly equated by Abhinavagupta with the moon and the sun and that these are considered by him to be sixteenfold and twelvefold, we can be sure that the sequence from sixteen to four was understood by him to represent the object, the external faculties, conceptual awareness, and the subject respectively. But Jayaratha's erroneous reading of Abhinavagupta's interpretation frees him to introduce a reading derived loosely from the Krama, even though not one of the passages of the *Yogasaṁcāra* quoted or paraphrased by Abhinavagupta reveals any connection with that system. He was no doubt encouraged by the fact that the citation was placed by Abhinavagupta in a Krama-based context, namely an exposition of the sequence of the Kālīs of the Cycle of the Nameless (*anākhyacakram*), reduced from thirteen to twelve to adapt them to his Trika-Krama synthesis.

Jayaratha connects the sixteen with the sixteen Kālīs which, he says, constitute the Cycle of the Nameless in the scripture *Kramasadbhāva*, taking these as representing the co-existence, within a higher fusion, of the object (*prameyam*), instruments of cognition (*pramāṇam*), subject (*pramātā*), and pure awareness (*pramā*), each of these four consisting of itself in predominance together with the other three subordinate within it, thus making the total of sixteen.[20] He equates

20. *Tantrālokaviveka*, vol. 3, p. 136, ll. 7-13, on 4.127: ***ye śvete cakṣurmaṇḍale dṛśyete*** *dṛśyamāne na raktamaṇḍalavad gupte* **tatra** *viśvakroḍīkārād* ***uttamaṁ*** *prameyapramāṇapramātṛpramāṇāṁ sarvasarvātmakatvāt* ***ṣoḍaśāraṁ cakraṁ*** *tiṣṭhati* [←-**stham**] *tadrūpatayā parisphuratīty arthaḥ. yadabhiprāyeṇaiva śrīkramasadbhāva-bhaṭṭārake anākhyacakre ṣoḍaśaiva devyaḥ pūjyatvenoktāḥ* "The circle with sixteen spokes is in the two white bands of the eye that are seen, that are visible, not hidden as the red circles are [by the eyelids]. That is to say, it is manifest in the form of these. It is [called] 'supreme' [here] because it encompasses everything. It is sixteen-spoked because the object of cognition, the means of cognition, the agent of cognition, and cognition each consist of all [four]. It is precisely to express this that sixteen is the number of goddesses prescribed for worship in the cycle of the Nameless in the venerable *Kramasadbhāva*."

In fact, there are seventeen Kālīs in this cycle in the *Kramasadbhāva*, as Jayaratha himself tells us in *Tantrālokaviveka*, vol. 3, p. 190, ll. 4-6: . . .

the twelve with the twelve Kālīs of the same cycle as it is taught by Abhinavagupta, saying that they are twelve because here the field of the object has been resorbed,

→ *śrīkramasadbhāvabhaṭṭārake anākhyacakre saptadaśa devyaḥ pūjyatvenoktāḥ*. Only an incomplete manuscript of this text has survived and the part it lacks includes that in which the cycle of the Nameless and its constituent goddesses are taught. Their number and names can, however, be established from another source with the help of an indication given by Jayaratha. For, after the words just cited he quotes the two verses of the beginning and the three-and-a-half verses of the end of the passage in the *Kramasadbhāva* in which these seventeen goddesses are detailed. In the beginning the first is identified as Sṛṣṭikālī and in the end the seventeenth is descibed as follows (ibid., ll. 16-18): *mahābhairavaghorasya caṇḍarūpasya sarvataḥ* | *grasate yā mahākālī *dvyaṣṭakaṁ* (conj.: *dvyaṣṭakā* Ed.) *kālanāśinī* || *saptādaśī tu sā kālī viddhi sarvārthakāriṇī*. Now, the *Kālīkulakramārcana*, a *paddhati* of the Krama composed by Vimalaprabodha, the Rājaguru of the Nepalese king Arimalla (r. CE 1200-1216), teaches a set of seventeen goddesses to be worshipped in the cycle of the Nameless, and their identity with those taught in the lost portion of the *Kramasadbhāva* is established both by circumstantial details given in the section of which this is a part — they match features distinctive of the *Kramasadbhāva* as we know it from the surviving portion — and by the fact that the seventeenth is named there Mahābhairavaghora-caṇḍagrasanakālī. This evidently is the name conveyed in the verses that Jayaratha quotes from the *Kramasadbhāva*. The seventeen are Sṛṣṭikālī, Sthitikālī, Saṁhārakālī, Raktakālī, Sukālī, Yamakālī, Mṛtyukālī, Bhadrakālī, Paramārkakālī, Mārtaṇḍakālī, Kālāgnirudrakālī, Mahākālakālī, Kṛṣakālī, Sarvāntakālī, Śivakālī, Krodhakālī, and Mahābhairavaghoracaṇḍagrasanakālī, these names being present in their *mantra*s given in f. 26r6-VI and (for the first twelve) ff. 13v6-14r5, which are formed by placing *āṁ phāṁ phīṁ mahā* before the vocative of the name with *kālī ambāpāda* after it. This is the series of thirteen taught in that order in the *Devīpañcaśataka* for the cycle of the Nameless with the addition of Kṛṣakālī, Sarvāntakālī, Śivakālī, and Krodhakālī between Mahākālakālī and the last, except that the last there has the slightly different name Mahābhairavacaṇḍograghorakālī (f. 21V [5.4ab]: *mahābhairavacaṇḍograghorā kālī parāvarā*). When Jayaratha says that the *Yogasaṁcāra*'s circle of sixteen is or is equivalent to the sixteen goddesses prescribed for worship in the *Kramasadbhāva*, he surely intends us to understand that the seventeenth is dropped as the goddess of the centre of the circle. But here we glimpse the artificiality of these manipulations. For the Kālīs that he equates with the *Yogasaṁcāra*'s circle of twelve are evidently those taught in the *Tantrāloka*, which →

leaving the fusion of the instruments of cognition (*pramāṇam*), the subject (*pramātā*), and pure awareness (*pramā*). The eight are then said to be these twelve reduced by the resorption of the four elements representing the instruments of cognition into the subject, leaving only the fusion of this subject and pure awareness. The four arise when the subject is resorbed in turn into pure awareness.

Having identified the sixteen and the twelve with sets of deities he goes on to do the same for the eight and the four. But here the Krama offers no obvious possibilities. He turns therefore to Abhinavagupta's Trika. He identifies the eight with the Trika's three goddesses (Parā, Parāparā, and Aparā), their three Bhairava consorts, and their ground divided similarly into male and female as Kuleśvara and Kuleśvarī, and the four with the three goddesses and their unitary ground Mātṛsadbhāva (which though masculine as the name of a *mantra* is identified in the Trika of Abhinavagupta with Parā in a higher form or with the goddess Kālasaṁkarṣiṇī).

All this is extremely unlikely to be what the author of the *Yogasaṁcāra* intended. Jayaratha cites no sources in support of his reading and it is improbable that any source would have supported it. For it combines in a transparently *ad hoc* fashion elements from two mutually exclusive forms of the Krama, the seventeen-Kālī system of the *Kramasadbhāva* and the thirteen-Kālī system of the *Devīpañcaśataka*, both reduced by one to suit the context following the lead given by Abhinavagupta in his adaptation of the second, and then equally arbitrarily combines these with sets of eight and four compiled from the Trika.

However, it would be wrong to accuse Jayaratha of personal intellectual dishonesty. He fails to disclose that he is guessing in such cases because he is participating in a culture of knowledge in which admission of ignorance or doubt is precluded for him by the obligation to pass on to his successors a corpus of interpretation that must mirror the original revelation on which it is based and therefore be free of the confessions of ignorance or uncertainty that are the very basis of enquiry in the very different world of modern historical scholarship.

→ are twelve there only as a result of Abhinavagupta's creative adjustment of the *Devīpañcaśataka*, in which (ff. 20r-21v [5.20-48.]) they are thirteen and in a somewhat different order from his (in the order also seen in the *Kramasadbhāva*); and there it is not the thirteenth (central) Kālī that is dropped but the fifth, Sukālī.

Wherever gaps appear in the edifice of knowledge they were to be filled by creative exegesis on the basis of available knowledge and the author's intuition; and we may say that this is one of the means by which traditions such as this, that are rooted in texts believed to be infallible, are kept alive and evolve in spite of the depredations of time.[21]

But the contraction of the textual base of the Kashmirian Śaiva tradition already evident in the thirteenth century in Jayaratha's commentary on the *Tantrāloka* is merely incipient. It is far more advanced in the centuries that followed. Since the time of Jayaratha the Kashmirian brahmin community has had to endure conditions that were certainly not favourable to the preservation of their traditions of learning and religion. For Kashmir passed under Muslim rule in 1320 and remained a Muslim state for five centuries, first under the independent Sultans of the Shāhmīrī dynasty, then under the Chaks (1555-86), the Mughals (1586-1753), and the Afghans of Kabul (1753-1819), before passing to the Sikhs of Lahore (1819-46) and the Hindu Dogras of Jammu (1846-1947). During the long period of Muslim rule all the non-brahmin population of the valley and many of the brahmins themselves had embraced Islam; those brahmins who remained were starved of the royal patronage that had sustained their Sanskrit scholarship and important aspects of their religion; and there were repeated outbreaks of persecution during which the brahmins, their temples, religious observances, and manuscripts suffered greatly.[22] Moreover,

21. Among other important Śaiva scriptural texts used by Abhinavagupta but apparently not accessible to Jayaratha are the *Kāmika*, *Bhairavakula*, *Gamaśāsana*, and *Ānandaśāstra*.

22. The historians of Kashmir report such persecutions under Sikandar (1389-1413), 'Alī Shāh (1413-20), Haidar Shāh (1470-72), Fath Shāh (1506-16), Muhammad Shāh (third reign: 1516-28), Shāh Jahān (1628-58), Muhammad Shāh (1719-48), Faqīr Ullāh Kanth (1767-68), Amīr Muhammad Khān Jawān Sher (1770-76), and Mīr Hazār Khan (1793). See Parmu 1969, pp. 97-98, 111-12, 130-31, 177, 198, 200-201, 360-61, 362, 369; Kilam 1955, pp. 40-47, 64-66, 81-86, 117-121, 165-67, 173-75, 203-05; Fortunately, there were periods of tolerance and good government during which the brahmin community was able to draw breath, notably the reigns of Zain-ul-'Ābidīn (1420-70), Hasan Shāh (1472-1484), the Mughals Akbar (1586-99) and Aurangzeb (1658-1707), and, during the Afghan period, Rājā Sukhajīvana (1753-62). But though those families that had survived persecution and had a tradition of Sanskrit →

during the time of Mughal and Sikh rule there was a dramatic reduction in the population of the valley that must have severely depleted the already greatly diminished brahmin community. Reliable population records do not exist for that period. But the *Tarīkh-ī-Hasan* of the Kashmirian historian Maulavi Hasan Shāh (1832-98) reports that a census carried out by the Mughal governor Saif Khan in 1670 showed that there were then 1,243,033 inhabitants in the valley, while Sir Walter Lawrence, who was Settlement Commissioner of Kashmir from 1889 to 1898, calculated that in 1835 there could have been no more than 200,000.[23] How many of these were brahmins is uncertain. But the census of 1891, by which time the population, benefitting from a return to stable government, had seen a phenomenal rise to 814,000, recorded that the followers of the brahmanical religion in the Kashmir valley constituted only 6.9 per cent of the total, about 56,000. If this, as is probable, was close to the proportion in 1835, then the brahmins at that time would have numbered no more than about 14,000. In 1877 the Sanskritist Georg Bühler reported (1877: 19) that according to a recent census there were no more than 40,000 to 50,000 brahmins in the valley, of whom about half, 24,000, lived in the capital. If this distribution was about the same in 1835, when the population was at its lowest ebb, then of the 14,000 brahmins that remained at that time only about 7,000 will have been in the capital, where such Sanskrit learning as survived was probably to be found; and of these only a small proportion will have belonged to the few families that had been able to maintain that learning. Bühler's informants told him in 1875-76 that these families were then no more than thirty or forty in number and that the Śaiva Gurus were drawn from among them.[24] Even if all these families

→ learning could return to their vocation what had been destroyed could not be recovered.

23. Sufi 1974, vol. 1, p. 276; Parmu 1969, pp. 392-93.

24. Bühler 1877, p. 20: "[The Kashmir brahmins] are divided into two halves, the aristocracy and the common herd. To the former belongs, firstly, a small number of particularly respected families — thirty or forty according to my informants — who have kept up, and still keep up, the study of Sanskrit, and live on *inām*s, allowances from the Mahārāja, and on fees which they receive for officiating as *ācārya*s, or superintendents of ceremonies before the domestic fire, and of *śrāddha*s, or sacrifices to the manes, and of the Śaiva worship. The other members of the aristocracy are the officials

maintained Śaiva learning, which is improbable, this is a perilously small base for the preservation of a complex religious culture under unfavourable conditions.

It is hardly surprising, then, to find evidence of a severe contraction in the number and range of the Śaiva scriptures preserved by the community since the advent of Muslim rule. Jayaratha was able to quote from the majority of those that had been utilized by Abhinavagupta. But of these numerous texts only the *Svacchanda*, *Netra*, *Vijñānabhairava*, *Mālinīvijayottara*, *Parātrīśikā*, *Mataṅga*, and part of the *Mr̥gendra* have survived in the manuscript tradition of the valley, largely, it would seem, because they were transmitted with running commentaries, or in the case of the fourth, with Vārttikas and the like, which having been composed in the golden age of Kashmirian Śaiva learning were the object of special veneration and much copied; and of these only the first two Tantras appear to have been supported throughout this period by a living tradition of ritual practice, since the worship of Svacchandabhairava and Amr̥teśabhairava that they teach was the basis of the *paddhati*s followed until recent times by the Śaiva Gurus of Kashmir for initiation (*dīkṣā*), fire-sacrifice (*agnikāryam*), and the post-mortuary rituals of cremation (*śivanirvāṇavidhiḥ*) and the offerings to the dead (*śivakriyā*, *śivaśrāddham*).

As for the Trika, we may infer with some confidence that it died out rather earlier as a system of ritual practice. For there is no trace in the surviving collections of Kashmirian manuscripts of any *paddhati* for Trika worship or initiation. The same conclusion is supported by the surviving manuscripts of those of Abhinavagupta's works, the *Tantrāloka* and the *Tantrasāra*, that cover this system in both its gnostic and practical aspects. For, the marginal annotations that these commonly contain are restricted to the chapters that deal with matters other than ritual. The demise of the Trika as a tradition sustained by ritual observance is also suggested by the character of the commentary on the Trika's *Parātrīśikā* composed

and the great traders, who have left the study of Sanskrit and taken to Persian. The plebs is composed of the so-called *Bāch-bhaṭṭas*, said to number 1,200 families, who gain their livelihood as performers of the manual work at the various ceremonies and as copyists, and by the priests at the *tīrtha*s or places of pilgrimage. The latter are, however, considered to rank a long way below the *Bāch-Bhaṭṭas*." On p. 24 (quoted above) he confirms that the Śaiva Gurus were among the first of these groups.

by Rājānaka Lakṣmīrāma (Lasa Kāka) at some time near the end of the eighteenth century or the beginning of the nineteenth.[25] For, that shows no knowledge of the Trika itself other than of its theoretical superstructure. It fails to recognize that the *Mantra* that is the basis of the course of worship and meditation taught in that text is *sauḥ*, the seed-syllable that embodies the Trika's Goddess Parābhaṭṭārikā. Instead it takes it to be the Aghoramantra, that is to say, the thirty-two-syllable *mantra* of Svacchandabhairava, thus substituting for the text's condensed form of Trika worship one constructed from the only system of Śaiva worship that had survived in Kashmir from early times down to the author's.[26] It is hard to believe that this substitution could have occurred if the Trika itself had still a living tradition of ritual at the time.[27]

---

25. This commentary does not give the date of its composition, but the same author tells us in the closing verse of his *Bhagavadgītātattvaprakāśikā* that he completed this work in Āśvina of the Śāka year 1732, that is to say, in CE 1811: *lakṣmīrāma iti dvijo 'tra nivasan kaśmīrabhūmaṇḍale meror mātur upāttadehajanano rājānagopālakāt* I *śrīśāke dviguṇādribhūparimite māse tathaivāśvine śuklāyāṁ pratipady ajāṅghrinirato gītāsu ṭīkāṁ vyadhāt.*

26. *Parātrīśikāvivṛti*, p. 14 on v. 26: *aghoramantreṇa ca saptaviṁśativāram aṣṭottaraśatākṣamālāpādena mantritām;* p. 15 on 28: *caturdaśavāram aghorābhijaptena puṣpena;* p. 16 on 30c-32b: *maheśvarīṁ parāṁ devīm aghoramantreṇa parayā bhaktyā atyādareṇa pūjayet*. He also imposes the *Svacchanda*'s system of worlds (*bhuvanāni*) (pp. 11-12 on v. 21). His engagement with the tradition of the *Svacchanda* and *Netra* is evidenced by a composite codex in Berlin which contains among a number of short Śaiva texts two attributed to this author that pertain to this field: (1) a **Niṣkalasvacchandadhyānavivaraṇa*, an analysis in 22 lines of the visualization-verse (*dhyānaślokaḥ*) of the *Svacchandodyota* (*madhyaprāṇaniviṣṭahaṁsa-* . . .) that is used in the worship of *Niṣkalasvacchanda* (colophon, f. 91v3v: *iti rājānakalasakākena vivaraṇaṁ viracitam*); and (2) a **Amṛteśvaradhyānavivṛti* in 17 lines on the visualization-verse of the *Netroddyota* (*dvāreśā* . . .) used in the worship of Amṛteśvarabhairava (colophon, f. 91vI17: *iti lasakākakṛtā vivṛtiḥ*).

27. How soon after Abhinavagupta it died out I cannot say. But I doubt that even Jayaratha was a Trika initiate. If we compare his commentary on the sections of the *Tantrāloka* that deal with these technical matters with his commentary on the *Vāmakeśvarīmata*, the root-Tantra of the Śākta cult of the goddess Tripurasundarī, we see a marked difference of approach. In the former I see nothing that could not be derived from his reading of the →

The same fate appears to have befallen the Krama. The existence of Kashmirian manuscripts of a few of its texts shows an enduring engagement with the gnostic aspects of this tradition;[28] and this engagement continued until relatively recent

relevant written sources, whereas the latter is highly technical, abounding in polemics against divergent views of the minutiae of ritual. It is probable, therefore, that Jayaratha's own ritual observance was in this later Śākta system rather than in that of the Trika. This does not mean that the Trika was not still alive among other practitioners: indeed he refers in his *Tantrālokaviveka* to the existence of Gurus in Kashmir whose ritual system combined those of the *Devyāyāmala* and the *Mādhavakula*, that is to say, a text of the Trika and a text of the Kālīkula (on 29.56: *atra hi keṣāṁ cana gurūṇāṁ śrīdevyāyāmalaśrīmādhavakulārthasammelanayā sampradāyaḥ samasti*). However, it alerts us to the danger of assuming that if an author comments on the sections of a text that deal with ritual he must himself have been a practitioner of those rituals. By Jayaratha's time the *Tantrāloka* had achieved an eminence by virtue of its theoretical sophistication that made it an authority for a wider range of Śaivas than those who were followers of the Trika. We see this from the fact that it is much cited in Jayaratha's commentary on the *Vāmakeśvarīmata* and in South Indian commentaries on other non-Trika Śākta works, such as the *Mahārthamañjarīparimala* (Krama), and the *Yoginīhṛdayadīpikā* (Śrīvidyā).

28. We have Kashmirian manuscripts of the following Krama texts: the *Kālikāstotra* of Jñānanetra *alias* Śivānanda, the Old Kashmiri *Mahānayaprakāśa* of Śitikaṇṭha with a Sanskrit commentary, the Prakrit *Mahārthamañjarī* of the South Indian Maheśvarānanda with a short redaction of his Sanskrit auto-commentary (*-parimala*), the *Chummāsaṁketaprakāśa* of Niṣkriyānandanātha, which is a Sanskrit commentary on 105 Old Kashmiri Krama aphorisms known as *chummāḥ* and also incorporates a series of 30 Old Kashmiri verses on the oral instructions (*kathāḥ, carcāḥ*) of the Krama, and the related Sanskrit *Vātūlanāthasūtra* with its commentary by Anantaśakti. The *Mahārthamañjarī* was particularly widely read. It appears commonly in composite Kashmirian codices of the kind that bring together for pious study (*adhyayanam*) a number of gnostic works, often both Śaiva and Vedāntic, such as this, the *Vijñānabhairava*, the *Paramārthasāra* and *Bodhapañcadaśikā* of Abhinavagupta, the *Śivastotrāvalī* of Utpaladeva, the *Spandakārikā*, the *Ātmabodha* of Śaṅkarācārya, the *Kaivalyopaniṣad*, the *Atharvaśiropaniṣad*, the *Mahopaniṣad*, and the *Bhagavadgītā*; see, for example, manuscripts 5389, 5407, 5615, 5705 and 5737 in Ehlers 2006. The catalogue of the Sanskrit manuscripts in the Research and Publication Department in Srinagar lists 25 of this text (Raina 1989, ser. nos. 2240-65), of which 21 are in composite codices.

times. We see it around the middle of the eighteenth century in the *Vijñānabhairavavivr̥ti* of the Śiva[svāmin] Upādhyāya (Śivopādhyāya)[29] who wrote during the rule of Rājā Sukhajīvana (1753-63),[30] and in the early nineteenth century in the *Śivarātrirahasya*, whose author, also called Śiva[svāmin] Upādhyāya, is said, in a note at the end of a manuscript of this work, to have been alive in Kashmir during the reign of Ranjit Singh (1819-39).[31] For that work draws on the pentads of the Krama to provide an inner meaning for the five faces of the cone-shaped *liṅga* of baked clay (*pañcaputtalaliṅgam*), known as the *sañĕ pŏṭul*ᵘ in Kashmiri, which is prescribed in this text for worship during the annual Śivarātri festival.[32] We also

29. See pp. 66-69 of that work.

30. *Vijñānabhairavavivr̥ti* p. 144, v. 5.

31. Stein 1894, No. 3669 *ḍha: granthakartā kaśmīreṣu mahārājaraṇajitsiṁhasya samaye jīvann āsīt*. It is very likely that our author is the Śivasvāmin/Śivarāma/Śivopādhyāya who, as Stein reports (1892, p. xiii), is praised in a versified colophon at the end of the *editio princeps* of the *Rājataraṅgiṇī* of Kalhaṇa for having preserved in his home the only copy of that work in Kashmir. Stein tells us (ibid.) that Troyer, the editor, reports that his edition was based on a copy of that manuscript, which Mr. Moorcroft had obtained on loan from Śivasvāmin through the intercession of the Trikeśvara in the course of an official visit to the Valley in CE 1822/23. When Georg Bühler visited Kashmir in 1877 he found the same manuscript with Keśavarāma, Śivarāma's grandson in the male line, and adds that Śivarāma and his descendants to the present day have been the hereditary Gurus of the Trika family. The Trika family is that known in the vernacular as Tikku/Tikkoo, so that the term Trikeśvara used in the colophon of the *editio princeps* evidently denotes the patriarch of that clan. The vernacular name of the Upādhyāya clan (*jātiḥ*, Kshm. *zāt*) is Padey.

32. *Śivarātrirahasya*, vv. 83c-84b, equating the five-faced image with the body and the five senses: *mr̥ṇmaye deha evāsau pañcendriyamukhaḥ smr̥taḥ* || *puttalatvaṁ vimr̥śyāsya na kuryān mamatāṁ budhaḥ* | *pañcaputtalaliṅgasya pūjanārtho 'yam īritaḥ*; 89c-96b, equating the five faces of the image with (1) the five recipients of the Krama's worship of the *pīṭhacakram* (Pīṭha, Śmaśāna, Kṣetrapāla, Melāpa, and Yāga), (2) the five gross elements from ether to earth, (3) the five sense-objects from sound to odour, (4) the five Cause-deities from Sadāśiva to Brahmā, (5) the goddesses of the five flows (Vāmeśvarī, Khecarī, Dikcarī, Saṁhārabhakṣiṇī/Gocarī, and Raudraraudreśvarī/Bhūcarī), (6) and the five →

see knowledge of the Krama in the *Gāyatrīmantravivr̥ti* of Śivasvāmin/Śivarāma

phases of cognition (*udyamaḥ, avabhāsanam, carvaṇam, kālagrāsaḥ,* and *viśrāntiḥ*): *vimr̥śyaṁ pañcadhā rūpaṁ caitanyakulapañcake* ‖ 90 *mr̥nmaye puttale dehe pañcadhātvaṁ smr̥taṁ budhaiḥ* | *prathamaṁ praṇavaḥ pīṭhaṁ vyoma vāmeśvarī tathā* ‖ 91 **sadāśivodyamau* (corr. : *sadāśivodyamau* Cod.) *caiva pīṭhadehaḥ prakīrtitaḥ* | *tataḥ śrīkhecarīdevī vāyuḥ sparśo 'vabhāsanam* ‖ 92 *īśvaraḥ kāladāhātmā śmaśānaṁ cintayed budhaḥ* | *prakāśānandarūpasya kṣetrasya parirakṣaṇāt* ‖ 93 *melāpayāgayugmena kṣetrapālo 'bhidhīyate* | *rūpaṁ śrīdikcarī tejo mahārudro 'pi *carvaṇam* (em. : *darśanam* Cod.) ‖ 94 *vyāptaṁ *saṁhārabhakṣiṇyā* (em. : *saṁsārabhakṣiṇyā* Cod.) *sāmarasyātmakaṁ jalam* | *ukto melāpaśabdena pañcavāhopadeśakaiḥ* ‖ 95 *raso jalaṁ *gocarī* (em. : *khecarī* Cod.) *ca kālagrāsaś ca keśavaḥ* | **alaṅgrāsātmako* (em. : *alaṅgārāstmake* Ed.) *yāgo *raudraraudreśvarīśritaḥ* (corr. : *raudraraudrīśvarīśritaḥ* Cod.) ‖ 96 *pr̥thivī gandho bhūcarī ca viśrāntir ātmabhūs tathā*. This draws without acknowledgement on the *Mahānayaprakāśa* published in the Trivandrum Sanskrit Series, three verses of which are also cited without attribution in the *Vijñānabhairavavivr̥ti*, p. 67, ll. 10-13, ll. 18-19 (=Trivandrum *Mahānayaprakāśa* 7.126-127 and 143). This text, then, can be added to works of the Krama that were studied in Kashmir into the late eighteenth or early nineteenth century. It is unfortunate that in spite of this to my knowledge no Kashmirian manuscript of the text has come to light.

The term *puttalaḥ* here renders Kashmiri *pŏtul*ᵘ / *putul*ᵘ "an idol, image" (Grierson 1915, s.v.). For *sañĕ pŏtul*ᵘ see Grierson 1915, s.v. meaning "an image on which one sprinkles water," from *sañ* "the sprinkling of water [on a deity]" (cf. Grierson 1915, s.v). For the presence of the *sañĕ pŏtul*ᵘ in the ritual of Hērath (*śivarātriḥ*) see the drawing of the *pūjā*-layout in Handu 1978, where it is called *sanyā putalū*. The name is appropriate because, as that layout shows, it is placed on a *bhadrapīṭhaḥ* with a channel for the run-off of the liquids that must be poured over it. Cf. *Śivarātripūjāpaddhati* folio side 26, l. 3: *snānārthaṁ bhadrapīṭhe*; and 62, ll. 1-4: *śivarātryādiviśeṣadivaseṣv atiśuddhāmbunā sahitaiḥ pañcadaśadravyaiś ceti ṣoḍaśa mahāsnānāni devāya dadyāt*. For its being made of baked clay and representing the *liṅga* (84c and 90a) see Madan 1961, p. 130. The Śivarātri worship overcoded by Śivopādhyāya is the Kashmirian Smārta form (with Devī, Vaṭuka, and Rāma [v. 87ab: *devīvaṭukarāmādipūjakaḥ*]; cf. Madan 1961, p. 130), not that of the strictly Śaiva cult of Svacchandabhairava/Amrteśvarabhairava (taught in the fragmentary *Śivarātripūjāpaddhati* MS); and this fact underlines the theoretical, non-ritual character of the Krama here.

Upādhyāya, probably the same,[33] who is said, in a similar note at the end of a manuscript of the text, to have been living at the beginning of the same reign.[34] But no Kashmirian manuscript of any *paddhati* of this system has come to light to prove the survival of its rites, nor any manuscript of any of its scriptures, which were still available to Jayaratha.

The tradition of ritual based on the *Svacchanda* and *Netra*, which from at least the tenth century seems to have been the predominant form of Śaivism in the valley, clung on somewhat longer. When Georg Bühler observed the traditions of Kashmir in 1875-76, he reported that it was customary among the Śaiva brahmins of the valley to undergo an elaborate ceremony of Śaiva initiation following the *Kalādīkṣā*[*paddhati*]. He acquired manuscripts of this text, which are now preserved in the collection of the Bhandarkar Oriental Research Institute in Pune. These contain redactions of the work of that name originally composed by the Kashmirian Guru Manodadatta in CE 1335/36 but subsequently expanded and containing in one redaction a series of hymns of which the latest is the *Śambhukr̥pāmanoharastava* composed by Rājānaka Ratnakaṇṭha in the seventeenth century.[35] The procedure laid out for initiation in this text is based on the *Svacchanda*, with some ancillary matter from the *Netra*. We can be sure, then, that though the Trika had died out in all but its doctrinal superstructure, and the Krama too, this other ritual tradition at least had survived into the late nineteenth century.

However, it did so in a manner that presaged its demise. For Bühler tells us

33. *Gāyatrīmantravivr̥ti*, final colophon: *samāpteyaṁ gāyatrīmantravivr̥tiḥ. kr̥tiḥ śrīśivasvāminaḥ. upādhyāyaklotpannaśivarāmaprakāśitā* | *śrīvidyātuṣṭaye bhūyād gāyatrīvivr̥tiḥ parā*. In this work Śivarāma quotes the *Chummāsaṁketaprakāśa* (f. 17V3-6): *vannavihīnaniruttaru khassaru* (em.: *khasmaruṇa* Cod.) *jagasa mūlapakiti gāyatra* **repha* (em. : *ka* A) | *takārahakāravikassaru vannacitra ciñceya* **vicitra* (em. : *vicitta* Cod.) *iti chummāsaṅketaprakāśe*.

34. Stein 1894, No. 2668 *ka*: *kr̥tir iyaṁ paṇḍitaśivarāmasya kāśmīrikopādhyāyavaṁśaprasūtasya yaḥ śrīmahārājaraṇajitsiṁhasya kāśmīrarājyārambhe jīvitavān*.

35. The hymn appears in *Kalādīkṣāpaddhati*, BORI MS 157 of 1886-92, 220r6-201vI5. Ratnakaṇṭha's works and copies of manuscripts prepared by him bear dates that extend from 1648/49 to 1685/86. For a list of these compositions and manuscripts and their dates see Stein 1979, vol. 1, pp. 46-47. The Stein collection of manuscripts from Kashmir in the Bodleian library in Oxford contains several of the latter not mentioned in that listing.

that his Śaiva brahmin acquaintances informed him that they attributed no special value to their Śaiva ceremonies but underwent them simply as a matter of family tradition. In this respect they showed themselves ignorant of one of the cardinal Śaiva doctrines, found throughout the scriptures and in all exegetical traditions, namely that Śaiva initiation effects a transformation of the self (*ātmasaṁskāraḥ*) that guarantees liberation at death.[36] It is possible that Bühler could have found a more learned Śaiva informant among the brahmins of Kashmir, one who would have given him this doctrinally correct view of the purpose and value of initiation. But it is surely a further indication of the decline of Śaivism by this time that those to whom he did speak showed no knowledge of the very belief that had articulated and justified the Śaivas' conviction of the superiority of their path to all others. It is unlikely that his informants were merely feigning ignorance in this matter, a

36. Bühler 1877, pp. 23-24: "Kashmirian Śaivism did, and does not, content itself simply with the worship of Śiva emblems, as is the case among the Smārta Brāhmans in Mahārāṣṭra and Gujarāt. It is a real separate religion, with peculiar ceremonies and sacrifices and transcendental doctrines. There exists, for those who are willing to enter it, a regular order for which a special initiation, both by a *mantra* and a *dīkṣā* consisting of complicated ceremonies, is required. The *mantra* is frequently given first, and the *dīkṣā* years afterwards. The rites to be performed at the latter are very numerous, and are described in the *Kalādīkṣās* of the Government collection. They are Tantric imitations of the Vedic rites. The *gurus* are those Sanskrit-speaking Paṇḍits who have been initiated. Śaivas appear to modify their Vedic daily and occasional rites by adding new Tantric ones, for which the *Kriyākāṇḍa* of Somaśambhu is the guiding authority. My acquaintances were either unable or unwilling to tell me the purpose of their Śaiva mysteries. They said that they did not consider them to be a special road to heaven or to final liberation, nor particularly to add to their sanctity. But they thought that it was better to be initiated, as it had been the custom of the country from time immemorial." The distinction drawn here between the giving of the *mantra* (*mantropadeśaḥ*) and *dīkṣā* proper is that between the preliminary *samayadīkṣā* that makes one a *samayī* and the full initiation known as the *nirvāṇadīkṣā* which makes one a [*nirvāṇa*]*dīkṣitaḥ* (/ *putrakaḥ*). The ceremony of the former is set out in the short Kashmirian *Śiṣyasaṁskāra*[*paddhati*] (c. 140 *granthas*). The only inaccurate statement in this passage is the author's judgement that the initiation consists of Tantric imitations of the Vedic rites. This is true of the postmortuary rites (Sanderson 1995: 31-36) but not of initiation.

possibility of which Bühler himself was aware, since the doctrine that Śaiva initiation liberates was not an esoteric teaching to be concealed from the uninitiated. On the contrary it had been an essential element of how the Śaivas presented themselves to others, their justification for their transcendence of what they saw as the mundane religion (*laukiko dharmaḥ*) of the brahmanical tradition. It was openly declared in inscriptions and well known to their opponents.[37] Only if Śaivism were the religion of an embattled minority in the midst of an orthodox brahmanical community could we easily imagine that Śaivas might choose to play down the significance that they attached to their ceremonies. But there can have been no need for this in Kashmir, where Śaivism was the faith of the majority.[38]

The end of this last surviving tradition of Śaiva ritual was indeed approaching. When I was in Kashmir a century later in the 1970s I was told that the practice of Śaiva initiation had been abandoned some fifty years earlier, and I heard the same concerning the Śaiva post-mortuary rituals, though a printed text of the *paddhatis* for these, published in 1936, could still be purchased.[39] It appears, then, that the last remnants of the proper Śaiva ritual practice current in the time of

37. The Śaiva doctrine that initiation liberates the soul was attacked early in the seventh century by the Buddhist Dharmakīrti in his *Pramāṇavārttikakārikā, Pramāṇasiddhipariccheda*, vv: 259c-69c. His criticisms have been addressed by Abhinavagupta's pupil Kṣemarāja in his examination of initiation (*dīkṣāvicāraḥ*) at the end of his commentary on the fifth Paṭala of the *Svacchanda* (*Svacchandoddyota* vol. 3, pp. 73, l. 10-84, l. 9). Within the fold of orthodox Brahmanism we find the doctrine attacked by Aparārka, who ruled Koṅkaṇ from 1110 to 1140, in his commentary on *Yājñavalkyasmṛti* 1.7 in the context of a lengthy diatribe against the view that the Śaiva scriptures should be counted among the means of valid knowledge of religious duty.

38. Bühler 1877, p. 23: "As regards their *bhakti*, or worship, nearly all Kashmirians are Śaivas. A few families only are Śāktas . . . . There are also a small number of Vaiṣṇavas, ..."

39. These *paddhatis* are in *Karmakāṇḍa, Caturthapustakam*, compiled by Paṇḍit Keshav Bhaṭṭ Jyotishī (1873-1946), pp. 205-456. They are (1) the *śivanirvāṇapaddhatiḥ* for cremation (pp. 205-292), (2) the *vaidikadaśāhnikapretakriyā* followed by the Śaiva version, *śivakriyāvidhiḥ*, for the offerings to the departed during the ten days after death (pp. 293-312); (3) the *annapūripūjāvidhiḥ* for the worship of an image made of boiled rice (Kashmiri *anapūr*[u]) placed on a wooden

Abhinavagupta, as opposed to that of non-initiated devotees of Śiva following Smārta models, had ceased in the valley close to the time of Swami Lakshman Joo's birth in 1907, and, more crucially, that the Trika and Krama rituals had died out considerably earlier and perhaps had not been performed for several centuries.

It is evident, then, that when I studied the Trika under Swami Lakshman Joo's guidance his expertise, great though it was, could not be expected to extend to those parts of the surviving literature that are devoted to the Trika's rituals, which in the case of the *Tantrāloka* amount to about half of the whole.[40] This was certainly a disadvantage for one who was seeking to understand Abhinavagupta's Trika and the related systems in their totality. For ritual, as the attention given to it in the *Tantrāloka* attests, had been a fundamental constituent of those traditions. Indeed, one might say in accordance with mainstream Śaiva thinking in India that it was the base sustaining all other aspects of the religion.

→ platform (the *śivapīṭhaḥ*) in the *śrāddha* (pp. 313-38); (4) the *śivāṣṭakāvidhiḥ* for the fire-sacrifice between the *annapūripūjāvidhiḥ* and the presentation of the *Śrāddha* offerings (pp. 338-53); (5) the Śākta *māsānumāsikaśrāddhavidhau śivānvaṣṭakāvidhiḥ* for the preparation of the rice ball (*piṇḍaḥ*) in the seventeen *Śrāddha*s offered to the deceased during the course of the first year after death (pp. 354-57); (6) the *sāṁvatsarikaśivaśrāddhavidhiḥ* for the annual *Śrāddha* (pp. 358-77); (7) the *ekoddiṣṭaśivaśrāddhavidhiḥ* for the *Śrāddha* offered after the *annapūripūjāvidhiḥ* and *śivāṣṭakāvidhiḥ* and before the *śivānvaṣṭakāvidhiḥ* to the deceased (father or mother) in the year after death (pp. 377-91); (8) the *śivasapiṇḍīkaraṇavidhiḥ* for the *Śrāddha* in which after the first year after death has passed the deceased is raised to the status of an ancestor (pp. 391-409); (9) the Śākta *śivadīpaśrāddhavidhiḥ* for an additional *Śrāddha* for the deceased during the first year after death involving the lighting of nine lamps into the central of which Caṇḍā Kāpālinī (the primary goddess of the *Brahmayāmala*) is invoked as the destroyer of Death (pp. 410-52); and (10) the *śivavaiśvadevādinityakarmavidhiḥ* for the daily rites of food preparation, etc. (pp. 452-56). The preceding part (pp. 1-205) covers the Brahmanical Viṣṇuśrāddha. The volume has been photographically reproduced in Chandra 1984.

40. The chapters in the *Tantrāloka* that are devoted to ritual, namely Āhnikas 15-33, comprise 2,637 verses out of the total of 5859. They cover initiation, consecration to Office, cremation, *Śrāddha,* worship, both daily and periodic, and the installation of images and other substrates of worship.

However, one should not conclude from this that Swami Lakshman Joo's Śaivism was not a living tradition carrying forward the heritage of the past. Firstly, in the years that he taught me I came to appreciate not only the depth and thoroughness of his understanding of the non-ritualistic aspects of his tradition and the literature that expounds them but also his personal faith in these as the means of self-realization, a faith manifest both in his own unswerving commitment to a life of Śaiva meditation and study and in the deep devotion of the many disciples whose religious life he inspired and guided. His interpretation of the texts was rooted not only in his pupilage with his teacher Rājānaka Maheśvara,[41]

41. Swami Lakshman Joo acknowledges Rājānaka Maheśvara (Maheshvarnāth Rāzdān) as his teacher in the Śaivaśāstras in two Sanskrit verses at the end of his editions of the *Bhagavadgītārthasaṁgraha* and *Śivastotrāvalī*, praising his learning in Sanskrit Grammar, Sāṁkhya, Yoga, and other Śāstras, and his deep devotion to Śiva (*sāṁkhyayogādiśāstrajñaḥ pāṇinīye patañjaliḥ* । *śivārkaraśmisaṁpātavyākośa-hṛdayāmbujaḥ* । *mahāmāheśvaraḥ śrīmān rājānakamaheśvaraḥ* । *śaivaśāstraguruḥ sa me vākpuṣpair astu pūjitaḥ*). See also the *Śrīpādukāstuti* of Swami Lakshman Joo's disciple Jiya Lal Kaul (1902-1967), in which he reports that his Kashmirian Guru studied all the works of Kashmirian Śaiva learning under the guidance of this scholar: *mukundarājānakavaryasūnur maheśvarākhyo hi gurur garīyān* ॥ *babhūva vidyāgurur asya dhīmān mahātmanaḥ puṇyavratasya tatra* । *satpātranyastāṁ hi tathā svavidyāṁ saṁśobhayām āsa guruḥ sa nūnam* ॥ *tasmāt sutīrthād vidhivat tadānīṁ śaivāgamācāryakṛtāni tāni* । *sarvāṇi śāstrāṇi pariśrameṇa papāṭha śīghraṁ gurur asmadīyaḥ* (vv. 19c-21). It is said that his pupilage lasted seven years, ending in or not long before 1934, when he moved from the city to a secluded house constructed for him by his father on the hillside above Ishabar village in the ancient Sureśvarīkṣetra.

Son of Rājānaka Mukunda and the representative of "an ancient family of scholars" (*Śivasūtravimarśinī*, KSTS ed., p. iii), Rājānaka Maheśvara worked in Srinagar as one of the Sanskrit Paṇḍits of the Research Department of the Jammu and Kashmir State. His scholarly assistance and the loan of his manuscripts are acknowledged in the prefaces of many of the editions of Śaiva texts in the Kashmir Series of Texts and Studies between 1911 and 1930. But I have heard it said, and I have long suspected this, that his contribution to the preparation of these and other editions went far beyond the mere assistance or satisfactory discharge of undefined duties for which he was cursorily acknowledged by the Superintendent identified as the sole editor on their title pages.

but also in his own lived experience, and if I came on occasion to the opinion that it departed to some degree from the intention of the texts themselves these departures were evidence that the tradition had not declined into a mere repetition of the formulations of the past but was indeed still a living force with the capacity for creative exegesis that enables such traditions to evolve.

Secondly, the fact that Swami Lakshman Joo's Trika lacked the rituals taught in the *Tantrāloka* is perfectly defensible within the terms of the Trika of Abhinavagupta himself and may well have been inherited from an established tradition that had long co-existed with the ritualistic Śaivism that survived in Kashmir into the early twentieth century. It is true that according to major Śaiva scriptures and the school of Saiddhāntika Śaiva exegesis that flourished in Kashmir in the tenth century alongside the traditions of the *Svacchanda*, *Netra*, the Trika, and the Krama there can be no valid Śaivism without ritual, since it was held that no person has the authority to adopt Śaiva observances and study the scriptures unless he has gone through that ceremony, and that no person may be a Guru of the system with the right and duty to initiate others, teach the scriptures, and consecrate images unless he has been first initiated and then ritually consecrated to that office by his predecessor. Moreover, the ritual of initiation was considered not merely an unavoidable rite of passage into the practice in the religion but also as essential to the attainment of the liberation that is the religion's goal. For it was held that the "impurity" (*malaḥ*) that prevents the soul's liberation, though imperceptible, is a substance (*dravyam*), that therefore what is needed to remove it is not gnosis (*jñānam*) but action (*kriyā*, *vyāpāraḥ*), and that the only action capable of bringing about this effect is the ceremony of initiation performed by Śiva himself through the person of the officiating Guru. But Abhinavagupta developed his Trika on the foundation of opposition to this mainstream view. For him "impurity" is nothing but ignorance of one's identity with Śiva and it is therefore knowledge of that identity rather than the action of ritual that has the power to remove it. The rituals of the Trika, both initiation and post-initiatory worship, are efficacious in his view only inasmuch as they embody, enact, and inculcate this liberating knowledge. Furthermore, while knowledge may work through ritual, thereby rendering the latter efficacious, it need not do so. It may also proceed to its effect with the help of more subtle means, namely meditational practices, the gradual cultivation of liberating insight, or direct intuition, these being seen as an ascending hierarchy in which consciousness throws off the contraction that is its impurity through immersion in action (*kriyā*), conceptual knowledge (*jñānam*), or its own preconceptual dynamism (*icchā*), all culminating in the same enlightenment but by a progressively more direct path of access. These three modes of immersion in Śivahood (*samāveśaḥ*) are, he explains, the *āṇavaḥ samāveśaḥ*, *śāktaḥ samāveśaḥ*, and *śāmbhavaḥ samāveśaḥ* taught in the *Mālinīvijayottara*, also known as the three methods or paths of access (*upāyaḥ*), that is to say, immersion that starts from (1) the contracted state of the psycho-physical individual (*aṇuḥ*), (2) the pure knowledge that is the power (*śaktiḥ*) of Śiva in the form of the conceptual cognition of ultimate reality, and (3) the intuition of [one's identity with] Śiva (*śambhuḥ*) in the preconceptual vitality of consciousness. Ritual is accommodated in this scheme merely as a lower extension of the first and lowest of these methods, there being higher action of a purely meditational kind that involves the cultivation of non-conceptual self-realization through such means as imaginative visualizations, meditation on the vital energies, and the repetition of *mantra*s in harmony with the flow of the breath.[42]

Ritual, then, is not indispensable in Abhinavagupta's view; and he applies this position, as we might expect, to all aspects of the Trika. Thus for him it was not necessary that all should pass through the ceremonies of initiation and consecration in order to qualify as Gurus in this tradition. Some could become empowered to occupy this role by a purely internal process of self-realization, through a figurative initiation and consecration performed by the goddesses that are their own cognitive powers.[43]

---

42. For a presentation of the ritualistic and gnostic positions of the two Kashmirian schools, with references to the relevant textual sources see Sanderson 1992, pp. 282-91; 1995, pp. 36-47.

43. See *Tantrāloka* 4.42c-43bb: *yasya svato 'yaṁ sattarkaḥ sarvatraivādhikāravān* ǁ 43 *abhiṣiktaḥ svasaṁvittidevībhir dīkṣitaś ca saḥ* | *sa eva sarvācāryāṇāṁ madhye mukhyaḥ prakīrtitaḥ* ǁ 44 *tatsaṁnidhāne nānyeṣu kalpiteṣv adhikāritā* | *sa samastaṁ ca śāstrārthaṁ sattarkād eva manyate* ǁ 45 *śuddhavidyā hi tan nāsti satyaṁ yad yan na bhāsayet*. See also *Parātrīśikā* 18 (cited in this context in *Tantrāloka* 4.49): *adṛṣṭamaṇḍalo 'py evaṁ yaḥ kaścid vetti tattvataḥ* | *sa siddhibhāg bhaven nityaṁ sa yogī sa ca dīkṣitaḥ*. Abhinavagupta terms such a Guru "natural" (*akalpitaḥ*, *sāṁsiddhikaḥ*) as opposed to the "made" (*kalpitaḥ*) Guru, one who acquires his office by passing through the usual external ceremonies (*Tantrāloka* 4.70c-71): *yena kenāpy upāyena gurum ārādhya bhaktitaḥ* ǁ *taddīkṣākrama-yogena śāstrārthaṁ vetty asau tataḥ* | *abhiṣekaṁ samāsādya yo bhavet sa tu kalpitaḥ*.

It is evident that Abhinavagupta did not venture to propose this ritual-free Trika as the norm. The *Mālinīvijayottara*, the scripture on which he chose to base his Trika, devotes too much attention to the rituals of initiation and consecration for this to have been a plausible strategy; and it is in any case probable that in his time the Trika maintained a broad base of adherents for whom these externals were predominant in practice. The Trika of meditation and gnosis alone is thus propounded as the path of an élite. Moreover, the mere fact that he sanctioned this alternative is not of itself conclusive evidence that it developed with the support of his authority as a distinct tradition over and above one that maintained its rituals, a tradition that in course of time, after the demise of those rituals, was inherited and passed on by Swami Lakshman Joo. To make that conclusion plausible we need evidence that the Trika of the kind advocated for the élite by Abhinavagupta in the tenth century and propounded by Swami Lakshman Joo in the twentieth already existed well before the latter's time within the Kashmirian brahmin community as a tradition of meditation and gnosis followed by persons who had not received Śaiva initiation in the formal, ritualistic sense, but whose ritual life was or had been restricted, as Swami Lakshman Joo's appeared to be, to the common brahmanical inheritance of Smārta observance.

Now, evidence of just this kind exists. It is found in the *Mṛtitattvānusmaraṇa*, an unpublished Kashmirian Sanskrit verse treatise in Purāṇic style attributed in its chapter colophons to the *Bhṛṅgīśasaṁhitā*, which sets out the beliefs and rituals associated with death and the destiny of the soul thereafter, the rituals being of the common Smārta variety rather than the Śaiva but with an admixture of subordinate Śaiva elements. It tells us that it is to be recited by the family priest (*guruḥ*) in the home after the death of the father, mother, or teacher for the benefit of the deceased, the recitation beginning on the first day and ending on the twelfth.[44] Its survival in numerous manuscripts and the fact that these reveal a work that like the *Kalādīkṣāpaddhati* has evolved distinct versions suggest that this was indeed a text in widespread use and one, therefore, that is likely to provide an accurate picture of common practice in the Kashmirian brahmin community of its time.[45] When

44. *Mṛtitattvānusmaraṇa*, f. IV8-10 (1.15-16b): *śrotavyaṁ parayā bhaktyā hy etad gurumukhāt priye | mṛtitattvānusmaraṇaṁ pitṛmātṛgurukṣaye | prathamaṁ dinam ārabhya dvādaśāntaṁ samāpayet.*

45. I have examined closely only two of these manuscripts, one in the SuUB in →

that time was is uncertain; but it was definitely well before that of Swami Lakshman Joo, since one of two manuscripts of the text deposited in the Bhandarkar Oriental Research Institute in Pune was acquired in the years 1884-86 and is probably considerably older than that, being on very old paper.[46] As for how much earlier it was composed I can say at present only that it was not in existence before the fifteenth century, since it includes in a list of those who should not be invited to eat the *Śrāddha* meal any brahmin who has learned to read the Perso-Arabic script (*yavanākṣarapāṭhakaḥ*).[47] For it was only during the reign of Sultan Zain-ul-'Ābidīn

Göttingen, from which the citations given here are drawn, and the other in the Bibliothèque Nationale in Paris. They show slightly different redactions and their divergences no doubt reflect adjustments made over time as the text was passed on from generation to generation in independent lines of family priests. I have not made a systematic search for other manuscripts of this text, but I noted the presence of six in the collection of 1884 Kashmirian manuscripts acquired by Klaus-Ludwig Janert, perhaps the uncatalogued manuscript library of General Rājā Sir Rām Singh (1861-99), second son of Mahārāja Raṇbīr Singh, said in 1927 to have been transferred to the Raghunāth Temple Library in Jammu (Ehlers 2006-07), when I examined it in September 1997 shortly after its arrival in the SBB-PK. Among other manuscripts that I have noted are six in the collection of the Research and Publication Department of the Jammu and Kashmir Government (Raina 1989, ser. nos. 2425-30). The *Bhṛṅgīśasaṁhitā* of which it claims to be part exists only as the fictional locus of attribution for this and a number of other independent works on aspects of brahmanical observance in Kashmir. Apart from the *Mṛtitattvānusmaraṇa* there are various texts attributed to this source, the great majority of which promote the sacred sites of the valley, glorifying the former deeds of Śiva and other gods as the source of the sanctity of these places, and specifying the rites and ascetic restraints to be undertaken there for various purposes. But only one, the *Vitastāmāhātmya*, is comparable in size to the *Mṛtitattvānusmaraṇa* (which is of about 1,000 verses), the others being much shorter tracts.

46. Sharma 1976, p. 366.

47. *Mṛtitattvānusmaraṇa*, ff. 47V10-48r1 (10.6c-10): *śrāddhe vivarjayet paṅguṁ kāṇaṁ kubjam apīśvari* ‖ 7 *mūkam andhaṁ mahādevi kuṣṭinaṁ śvitriṇaṁ tathā* । *yakṣmiṇaṁ patitaṁ cāpi dyūtastrīpaṇyasevinam* ‖ 8 *madhupānaratam cāpi vedabhraṣṭam athāpi vā* । *ācārabhraṣṭaṁ deveśi varjayeta pramehiṇam* ‖ 9 *grahaṇīrogagrastaṁ ca* (48r) *yavanākṣarapāṭhakam* । *kṛṣikarmaratam cāpi sandhyāsnānavivarjitam* ‖ 10 *rasavikrayiṇaṁ cāpi varjayec-chrāddhabhojane* । *ete proktā mahādevi brāhmaṇāḥ paṅktidūṣakāḥ.*

(1419-1470) that a significant number of Kashmirian brahmins began to learn Persian, doing so in order to qualify to hold positions in the administration.[48]

Now, the ninth chapter of the text outlines the means by which men can ensure that when they die they will be spared the sufferings of the dead described at length earlier in the work. It explains that there are three paths to this end and that these are for three distinct classes of aspirants: ritual (*karma*) for ritualists (*karmī*), meditation (*yogaḥ*) for *yogins*, and gnosis (*jñānam*) for gnostics (*jñānī*), the last for those who have accomplished the first.[49] The path of ritual (*karmamārgaḥ*)

48. See Bühler 1877, p. 20, quoted above (n. 24). The members of his class of "the officials and the great traders, who have left off the study of Sanskrit and taken to Persian" are those that came to be known in Kashmir by the Persian term *kār-kun* "manager, officer" (Kashmiri *kôrkun* "a Persian-knowing Brahmin employed by Government" [Grierson 1915, s.v.]). On the emergence of the Kārkuns in the reign of Zain-ul-'Ābidīn and the founding by that king of schools for the teaching of Persian see Parmu 1969, p. 144. The language of official communication in Kashmir continued to be Persian throughout the Sikh rule and into that of the Dogras. When Mahārāja Pratāp Singh (b. 1850, r. 1885-1925) changed it to Urdu, the Kārkun brahmins protested (Sufi 1974, p. 487). The rest of brahmin society comprised, as we have seen, (1) those families of high status that had kept to the study of Sanskrit, with whom the Kārkuns intermarried, and (2) families of lower status whose men did not take to Persian but served as priests (*bāca-baṭh*), with whom the other brahmins, therefore, would not marry or, until after 1948, eat. The *Mr̥titattvānusmaraṇa* is probably a product of this sub-caste, since it was its members that performed the rituals taught in it for their client families. The same is surely true of the other compositions attributed to the *Bhr̥ṅgīśasaṁhitā*. The term *bāca-baṭh* has been said to render Sanskrit *bhāṣābhaṭṭaḥ* in the meaning "a brahmin of the language," i.e. "a Sanskrit-knowing brahmin" (Grierson 1915, s.v; Madan 1989, pp. 19-20). That *bāca-* renders *bhāṣā* is implausible. I propose that the true meaning was somewhat derogatory or condescending, in keeping with their status, namely "gift-taking brahmin," since there is Kashmiri *bôc*ᵘ "a man who lives upon what he can get in the way of gifts, and is ignorant of any trade or business" (Grierson 1915, s.v.).

49. *Mr̥titattvānusmaraṇa*, f. 39r5-7 (9.3c-5b): *trividhā kathitā *vede* (conj. : *veda* Cod.) *tantre ca sura sundari* ॥ 4 *adhikāraprabhedena yātanāyā viniḥsr̥tiḥ* । *yogināṁ yogajālena karmiṇāṁ karmaṇā tathā* ॥ 5 *tathaiva kr̥takarmāṇāṁ sāṅkhyānāṁ jñānayogataḥ*. The term →

consists of the common observances, ceremonial and charitable, of the brahmanical tradition, with daily worship in the form of the Smārta *pañcāyatanapūjā* offered to the five deities Śiva, Viṣṇu, Sūrya, Gaṇeśa and Devī;[50] the path of meditation (*yogamārgaḥ*) is that of attaining identity with Śiva by withdrawing the vital energy into the central channel (*suṣumnā*) by regulating the breath (*prāṇāyāmaḥ*) while mentally repeating the syllable *oṁ* (*praṇavoccāram*), so that *kuṇḍalinī* ascends through that channel, penetrating the six centres (*ṣaḍ ādhārāḥ*) and reaching the cranial aperture (*brahmarandhram*);[51] and the path of gnosis (*jñānamārgaḥ*) is the cultivation of awareness of one's identity with Śiva through one or other of the three paths of access (*upāyatrayam*) taught in the Trika of Abhinavagupta. That it is the Trika that is intended is apparent in the fact that the verses defining these three paths (9.74c-77b) are lifted from the *Mālinīvijayottara* (2.23, 22, 21). That it is Abhinavagupta's Trika is apparent in the fact that it was there that the three paths were brought to the fore to provide through the creative exegesis of their scriptural

→ *sāṅkhyaḥ* here denotes a person who adopts the path of gnosis (*jñānī*), not a follower of the Sāṁkhya school.

50. *Mr̥titattvānusmaraṇa*, f. 39vII-13 (9.17c-18) *nirmālyam apanīyātha pañcāyatanam arcayet* | 18 *śivaṁ viṣṇum ca sūryaṁ ca gaṇapaṁ pārvatīṁ tathā* | *śaṅkhaṁ dūtīm apīśāni pūjayeta vidhānataḥ*. The *dūtī* here is the bell, an element imported from Kashmirian Tantric worship. Cf. *Śivanirvāṇapaddhati*, p. 216; *Svacchandoddyota*, vol. 2, p. 293. The conch (*śaṅkhaḥ*) and the bell are first worshipped and then blown and rung. For a *paddhati* of the Kashmirian Smārta *pañcāyatanapūjā*, but with Viṣṇu as the principal, see the *Viṣṇupañcāyatanapūjāvidhi* on pp. 27-54 of the *Nityakarmavidhi* of Paṇḍit Keshav Bhaṭṭ Jyotiṣī. In the case of the *Mr̥titattvānusmaraṇa* Śiva is the principal among the five deities. The daily worship that it prescribes is, then, a *Śivapañcāyatanapūjā*.

51. *Mr̥titattvānusmaraṇa*, f. 42rII-vi (9.60-62b): *niyataṁ saṁyamet prāṇaṁ yuktiyuktaṁ maheśvari* | *ūrdhvarecakato vāyuṁ malinaṁ ca tyajed bahiḥ* | 61 *piṅgalānāḍito devi tataḥ śuddhaṁ prapūrayet* | *iḍayā. kumbhayet paścāt suṣumṇāyāṁ yathārthataḥ* || 62 *sarvatra praṇavoccāraṁ vidadhyād devy atandritaḥ*; and f. 42v3-7 (9.64-67b): *yogaṁ yuñjyāt priye tāvat pūrakumbhakarecakaiḥ* | *yāvat kuṇḍalinībodho jāyate surasundari* || 65 *mūlādhārādiṣaṭcakrāṇy ākramya kramaśaḥ priye* | *bhūmyādisthānabhūtāni tattatsiddhim avāpnuyāt* || 66 *tataḥ karandhre saṁprāpya śivenaikyaṁ yathāvidhi* | *tatsaṁparkasamudbhūtaṁ pibed amr̥tam adbhutam* || 67 *pītvāmr̥taṁ ca paramaṁ bhavet sākṣāc chivo 'ciram*.

definitions a comprehensive account of all the Trika's practice.[52] Since the Trika practice taught here lacks the rituals that Abhinavagupta accommodates as a lower level within the lowest of these three paths of access, and since the ritual life that is said to be transcended by it is not that of the Trika or any other Tantric Śaiva system but simply that of the common brahmanical tradition of the uninitiated devotee, it is evident that the *Mṛtitattvānusmaraṇa* already shows us the Trika in the form and context that it had in the Śaivism of Swami Lakshman Joo, that is to say, as a system of meditation and gnosis co-existing with Smārta rather than properly Śaiva ritual observance.

---

52. *Mṛtitattvānusmaraṇa*, f. 42v10-43v12 (9.69-88 and Paṭala colophon): *adhunā jñāninām mārgaṁ śṛṇuṣvāvahitānaghe* | *kṛtvā karmāṇy anekāni kāraṇaṁ jñānasantateḥ* || 70 *praśamaṁ paramaṁ prāpto bhavet svasthāśayah pumān* | *indriyārthavirāmeṇa ṣaḍvargavijayena ca* || 71 *manaḥsaṅkalpavirato caitanyaṁ bhāvayet sudhīḥ* | *ṣaṭtriṁśattattvavijñānaṁ svīkṛtya gurutaḥ priye* || 72 (43r) *śivo 'ham iti sarvatra bhāvayed avikalpataḥ* | *aikyaṁ kṛtvā prakāśasya vimarśasya ca sundari* || 73 *paramaḥ sa samāveśaḥ śivajñane prakīrtitaḥ* | *upāyatritayaṁ cātropadiṣṭaṁ paramaṁ mayā* || 74 *teṣv ekatra naras tiṣṭhañ śivaṁ sākṣātkaroty alam* | *akiñciccintakasyaiva guruṇā pratibodhataḥ* || 75 *utpadyate ya āveśaḥ śāmbhavo 'sāv udāhṛtaḥ* | *uccārarahitaṁ vastu cetasaiva vikalpayan* || 76 *yaṁ samāveśam āpnoti śāktaḥ so 'trābhidhīyate* | *uccārakaraṇadhyānavarṇasthānaprakalpanaiḥ* || 77 *yo bhavet sa samāveśaḥ samyag āṇava ucyate* | *upāyatrayam ālambya gurūddiṣṭena vartmanā* || 78 *prayāti śivasāyujyaṁ yatra gatvā na śocate* | *bhrāntibhājām idaṁ devi jagat sarvaṁ pravartate* || 79 *nāmādirahiraṁ yadvat kanakam kuṇḍalādiṣu* | *eka eva śivo devi sarvatattvasamāśrayaḥ* || 80 *tadanugrahapātrāṇāṁ pratibhāty avikalpataḥ* | *jagacchivādvayaṁ vyaktaṁ bhedas tatra *vikalpataḥ* (conj. : *vikalpitaḥ* Cod.) || 81 *mohapātram idaṁ viśvaṁ chāyājalapiśācavat* | (43v) *śivo 'ham iti yaḥ śaśvad dṛḍhaṁ bhāvayate budhaḥ* || 82 *jīvanmuktaḥ sa eveśi na śocati kṛtākṛte* | *śivādvayapadasthasya puṁso devi viśeṣataḥ* || 83 *siddhyaṣṭakadharasyeha dāsāḥ sarve surādayaḥ* | *mahāpralayavātānāṁ koṭayo vāntu yāntu vā* || 84 *mahāpralayasūryāṇāṁ koṭayaḥ pratapantu vā* | *kalpāntasāgarāṇāṁ ca koṭayaḥ pravahantu vā* || 85 *sarveṣāṁ bhayahetūnāṁ sannidhāne 'py upasthite* | *manaścāñcalyamuktasya na bhayaṁ vidyate kvacit* || 86 *itthaṁ hi vartamānasya sādhor asya mahātmanaḥ* | *śāntasya śāntacittasya ko yamaḥ kā ca yātanā* || 87 *iti te jagadīśāni yātanāyā vinissṛtiḥ* | *niṣkāmakarmaniṣṭhānāṁ yogināṁ jñānināṁ tathā* | *trividhā kathitā samyag anurodhāt taveśvari* || 88 *śrotavyaṁ paṭhitavyaṁ ca śāstram etad rahasyakam* | *sarvapāpaharaṁ devi jantūnāṁ kalināśanam* || *iti śrībhṛṅgīśasaṁhitāyāṁ bhairavībhairavasaṁvāde karmayogajñānamārgaprakāśanaṁ nāma navamaḥ paṭalaḥ*. The verses in this passage (74c-77b) that have been lifted from the *Mālinīvijayottara* (2.21-23) deviate only in 75d, which has *vikalpayan* where the manuscripts and testimonia of *Mālinīvijayottara* (2.22b, ed. Vasudeva 2004, p. 22) have *vicintayan*.

Swami Lakshman Joo left no comprehensive commentary or systematic clarification of his understanding of the Trika, but he devoted countless hours to expounding its literature; and his oral interpretations of a number of its texts survive indirectly in the translations published by Jaideva Singh Thakur (1893-1986), who, as I was able to witness during my years in Kashmir, went through every sentence of these texts with Swami Lakshman Joo and did his best to make his renderings conform to his teacher's explanations. Those who have mastered the works of Abhinavagupta and wish to see how the tradition of the Trika had continued to evolve thereafter will find much evidence in these materials, though it will, of course, frequently be difficult to determine what has been inherited and what is Swami Lakshman Joo's own contribution. As further testimony of the quality of his Śaiva scholarship we have his critical editions of the *Bhagavadgītārthasaṁgraha* of Abhinavagupta and the *Śivastotrāvalī* of Utpaladeva; and we can appreciate the vitality and originality of his exegesis in two short independent treatises: (1) his Hindi *Kramanayapradīpikā*, which builds upon and in some respects modifies Jayaratha's interpretation of Abhinavagupta's presentation of the Krama in the *Tantrāloka*, including his interpretation of the problematic passage of the *Yogasaṁcāra* discussed above, and (2) his Sanskrit *Kuṇḍalinīvijñānarahasya*, the text of a lecture given in Benares in 1965, which offers an original synthetic vision of the *Tantrāloka*'s scattered statements on the nature and manifestations of *kuṇḍalinī*.[53]

The instruction that I received from Swami Lakshman Joo was of inestimable benefit to me. I was able in later years to explore for myself, and am still exploring, various matters that were not of concern to him, such as the independent histories of the various traditions out of which Abhinavagupta had fashioned his brilliant synthesis, the ritual systems that animated them, the nature of their co-existence and interaction, and the relation between these and broader currents in the religion and society of the early medieval period in Kashmir and beyond, drawing for this

53. In 1978 I began an English translation of this treatise of six pages for Swami Lakshman Joo and left it with him when I had to leave Kashmir having reached only the fourth line of the fifth page. This draft, which, I presume, was found among his papers, was published as it stands, incomplete, unrevised, and, since it was unsigned, without indication of its translator, in Bhatt 1995, pp. 27-29.

purpose on the abundant literature then unknown to scholarship that has survived in manuscripts in other parts of the Indian world, on epigraphical records, and on a tradition of academic analysis very different from that which drove the creators and preservers of this splendid Kashmirian heritage. But it is my years with Swami Lakshman Joo that I value above all. For these subsequent explorations grew out of and were inspired by the breadth and depth of his vision of the Trika. Though I was a scholar committed to historical analysis rather than a Śaiva seeking enlightenment, I was able, I hope, through his instruction to develop a sense of how he saw and experienced his tradition from the inside; and this confirmed in me the conviction that an essential part of my task was to develop an understanding grounded in an awareness of how the various Śaiva traditions perceived themselves. I do not believe that I could have made significant progress in the intellectual and aesthetic appreciation of the world-view of Abhinavagupta and his contemporaries if Swami Lakshman Joo had not taken such pains to initiate me into his grasp of it; and without that my subsequent attempts to broaden my understanding of the history of Śaivism would have lacked a vital foundation. I feel myself immensely fortunate to have been brought by Swami Lakshman Joo into close contact with Śaivism as a living tradition, one that preserved the ability not only to read its literature accurately but also to expound it with comprehensive vision and inspiring conviction. I remember him with profound gratitude and unreserved admiration.

Abbreviations

BORI	:	Bhandarkar Oriental Research Institute, Pune
Cod.	:	The reading of the manuscript
conj.	:	My conjectural emendation
corr.	:	My correction
em.	:	My emendation
IFI	:	Institut français d'Indologie, Pondicherry
KSTS	:	Kashmir Series of Texts and Studies
MS/Hs	:	Manuscript/Handschrift
NAK	:	National Archives of Nepal, Kathmandu
NGMPP	:	Nepal-German Manuscript Preservation Project
SBB-PK	:	Staatsbibliothek zu Berlin — Preussischer Kulturbesitz

SuUBG : Staats- und Universitätsbibliothek, Göttingen

T : Transcript

References

***Amṛteśvaradhyānavivṛti* of Lasa Kāka [Rājānaka Lakṣmīrāma], SBB-PK, Hs or 11664, ff. [91]vI-17 (top line on left of page, bottom on right).

Karmakāṇḍa, vol. 4: *Karmakāṇḍam, Caturthapustakam*, ed. Paṇḍita Keśavabhaṭṭa Jyotirvid, Bombay: Nirnaya-Sagara Press, 1936.

Kalādīkṣāpaddhati, BORI MS 157 of 1886-92. Paper; Śāradā script; no date.

Kaliviḍambana of Nīlakaṇṭhadīkṣita = Vasudeva 2005, pp. 320-76.

Kālīkulakramārcana of Vimalaprabodha, NAK MS 5-5188, NGMPP Reel No. A148/10. Paper; Newari script; no date, but probably seventeenth century.

Kuṇḍalinīvijñānarahasya of Rājānaka Lakṣmaṇa [Lakshman Raina, Swami Lakshman Joo]. *Sarasvatī Suṣamā* (Vāraṇaseyasaṁskṛtaviśvavidyālaya patrikā) 20/1, Saṁvat 2022 (1965), pp. 57-62.

Kramanayapradīpikā [Hindi] of Rājānaka Lakṣmaṇa [Lakshman Raina, Swami Lakshman Joo], Jammu: R.C. Printing Press, 1958.

Kramasadbhāva: *Kālīkulakramasadbhāva*, NAK MS 1-76, NGMPP Reel No. A 203/23. Paper; Newari script; up to 7.2 (incomplete); no date, but probably seventeenth century.

Gāyatrīmantravivṛti of Śivarāmasvāmin/Śivasvāmin Upādhyāya, SuUBG, MS Mu I 30, ff. 16r[23a]8-24v[31b]12. Paper; Śāradā script; no date.

Chummāsaṁketaprakāśa of Niṣkriyānandanātha, SBB-PK, Hs or 11387 (*Triṁśaccarcārahasya*). Paper; Śāradā script; no date; incomplete.

Tantrāloka of Abhinavagupta with the commentary (*-viveka*) of Rājānaka Jayaratha, ed. Mukund Rām Śāstrī, KSTS 23, 28, 30, 35, 29, 41, 47, 59, 52, 57, 58, Bombay and Srinagar, 1918-38.

Dīkṣottara, MS IFI T. 17 (**A**); MS IFI T, 150 (**B**). Modern Devanāgarī paper transcripts of Grantha manuscripts (IFI MS No. 4 *Niśvāsakārikā*; no date; and Madras Government Oriental Manuscripts Library, MS No. R14403 *Niśvāsakārikā*; no date).

Devīpañcaśataka: *Kālīkulapañcaśataka*, Kathmandu, Kaisar Library, MS No. 524 (*Kālikākuśe*), NGMPP Reel No. C 49/3. Palm-leaf; Maithila script; [Lakṣmaṇa] Saṁvat 122 (= a year between CE 1230 and 1242).

Nityakarmavidhi, ed. Paṇḍita Keśavabhaṭṭa Jyotirvid, Srinagar: Krishna Printing Press, no date.

Niṣkalasvacchandadhyānavivaraṇa of Lasa Kāka [Rājānaka Lakṣmīrāma], SBB-PK, Hs or 11664, ff. [91]r1-[91]v3.

Parātrīśikāvivṛti of Lasa Kāka [Rājānaka Lakṣmīrāma], ed. Jagaddhara Zadu Shastri, KSTS 69, Srinagar, 1947.

Pramāṇavārttikakārikā of Dharmakīrti, ed. Miyasaka Yūshō, *Acta Indologica* 2, 1971/72.

Brahmayāmala, NAK MS 3-370, NGMPP Reel No. A 42/6. Palm-leaf; early Newari script; AD 1052.

Bhagavadgītātattvaprakāśikā of Lasa Kāka [Rājānaka Lakṣmīrāma], SuUBG, MS Mu 1 22. Paper; Śāradā script; no date.

Bhagavadgītārthasaṁgraha: *Srimad Bhagavad Gita With Commentary by Mahāmāheśvara Rājānaka Abhinavagupta*, ed. Pandit Lakshman Raina Brahmachārī [Swami Lakshman Joo], Srinagar: Kashmir Pratap Steam Press, 1933.

Mahānayaprakāśa (anonymous), ed. K. Sāmbaśiva Śastrī, Trivandrum Sanskrit Series 130, Citrodayamañjarī 19, Trivandrum, 1937.

Mālinīvijayottara: *Mālinīvijayottaratantra*, ed. Madhusudan Kaul Shastri, KSTS 37, Srinagar, 1922.

Mṛtitattvānusmaraṇa, SuUBG, MS Mu I 108. Paper; Śāradā script; no date.

Yājñavalkyasmṛtiṭīkā of Aparārka, ed. the Paṇḍits of the Ānandāśrama, Pune, 1903-4, 2 vols., Ānandāśramasaṁskṛtagranthāvalī, 46.

Rājataraṅgiṇī of Jonarāja, ed. Śrīkaṇṭh Kaul, Hoshiarpur: V.V.R.I. Press, 1967.

Rājataraṅgiṇī of Kalhaṇa: *Kalhaṇa's Rājataraṅgiṇī or Chroncile of the Kings of Kashmir*, ed. M.A. Stein, Bombay: Educational Society's Press, 1892.

Vijñānabhairavavivṛti of Śivopādhyāya, ed. Mukunda Rama Shastri, KSTS 8, Bombay, 1918.

Śivanirvāṇapaddhati = *Karmakāṇḍa*, vol. 4, pp. 202-92.

Śivarātripūjāpaddhati, SBB-PK, Hs or 11279. Birch-bark; Śāradā; disordered folios, each incomplete through damage; no folio numbers. Abbreviated title in margin of folio sides 6, 51, 59: *Śivarāpū*.

Śivarātrirahasya of Śivopādhyāya [Nityasvatantrakavi], Oxford, Bodleian Library, MS Stein Or. e. 24, ff. 1-4r. Paper; Śāradā script; no date.

Śivasūtravimarśinī of Kṣemarāja, ed. J.C. Chatterji, KSTS I, Srinagar, 1911.

Śivastotrāvalī of Utpaladeva with the commentary (*-vivṛti*) of Kṣemarāja, ed. Rājānaka Lakṣmaṇa [Lakshman Raina, Swami Lakshman Joo], Chowkhamba Sanskrit Series 15, Varanasi, 1964.

Śiṣyasaṁskāra[paddhati], Paris, Bibliothèque Nationale, MS Sanscrit 505 C. Paper; Śāradā script; no date; acquired in 1898.

Śrīpādukāstuti of Jiya Lal Kaul. In *Śrīrāmeśvarācāryaviracita Śrīgurustutiḥ Prabhādevīracita-bhāṣāṭikopetā* (Srinagara: Īśvara Āśrama, Vikrama 2033), Part 2.

Svacchandoddyota: Svacchandatantra with the commentary (*-uddyota*) of Kṣemarāja, ed. Madhusūdan Kaul Śāstrī, KSTS 31, 38, 44, 48, 51, 53, 56, Bombay, 1921-35.

Secondary Sources

Bhatt, S. (ed.), 1995, *Kashmiri Paṇḍits — A Cultural Heritage*, New Delhi: Lancer Books.

Bühler, Georg, 1877, *Detailed Report of a Tour in Search of Sanskrit Manuscripts Made in Kaśmīr, Rajputana, and Central India*, London: Trübner. Extra Number of the Journal of the Bombay Branch of the Royal Asiatic Society.

Chandra, Lokesh, 1984, *Sanskrit Texts from Kashmir*, vol. 7, Śatapiṭaka Series, Indo-Asian Literature, no. 333, New Delhi: Sharada Rani.

Ehlers, Gerhard, 2006, *Die Śāradā-Handschriften der Sammlung Janert der Staatsbibliothek zu Berlin — Preussischer Kulturbesitz*, Stuttgart: Franz Steiner Verlag, Verzeichnis der orientalischen Handschriften in Deutschland, Band II, 16,òIndische Handschriften Teil 16.

Grierson, Sir George, assisted by Mukundarāma Śāstrī of Srinagar, 1915, *A Dictionary of the Kāshmīrī Language compiled partly from materials left by the late Paṇḍit Īśvara Kaula*, Hertford: Asiatic Society of Bengal, Bibliotheca Indica, New Series, No. 1405.

Handu, Premanatha, 1978, *Śrīvaṭukapūjāvidhiḥ*, Srinagar.

Kilam, Jia Lal [1955], *A History of Kashmiri Pandits*, Srinagar: S.N. Dar.

Madan, T.N., 1961, "*Herath*, A Religious Ritual and its Secular Aspect," in *Aspects of Religion in Indian Society*, ed. Lalita Prasad Vidyarthi, Meerut: Kedar Nath Ram Nath, pp. 129-39.

———, 1989, *Family and Kinship — A Study of the Pandits of Rural Kashmir*, 2nd enlarged edn., Delhi: Oxford University Press.

Pandey, K.C., 1963, *Abhinavagupta — An Historical and Philosophical Study*, 2nd edn., revised and enlarged, Varanasi: Chowkhamba Sanskrit Series Office, Chowkhamba Sanskrit Series, Vol. 1.

Parmu, R.K., 1969, *A History of Muslim Rule in Kashmir*, 1320-1819, Delhi: People's Publishing House.

[Raina, A.K.] 1989, *A Catalogue of Sanskrit Manuscripts*, Srinagar: The Research and

Publication Department, Jammu and Kashmir Government. Based on a draft prepared by Śrīkaṇṭh Kaul and Dīnānātha Yach.

Rastogi, Navjivan, 1979, *Krama Tantricism of Kashmir*, vol. 1, Delhi: Motilal Banarsidass.

Sanderson, Alexis, 1992, "The Doctrine of the Mālinīvijayottaratantra," in *Ritual and Speculation in Early Tantrism: Studies in Honour of André Padoux*, ed. T. Goudriaan, pp. 281-312, Albany: State University of New York Press.

———, 1995, "Meaning in Tantric Ritual," in *Essais sur le Rituel III: Colloque du Centenaire de la Section des Sciences religieuses de l' òcole Pratique des Hautes òtudes*, ed. A.M. Blondeau and K. Schipper, pp. 15-95, Louvain and Paris: Peeters.

———, 2005, "A Commentary on the Opening Verses of the *Tantrasāra* of Abhinavagupta," in *Sāmarasya: Studies in Indian Arts, Philosophy, and Interreligious Dialogue*, ed. Sadananda Das and Ernst Fürlinger, pp. 89-148, New Delhi: D.K. Printworld.

Sharma, Har Datta, 1976, *Descriptive Catalogue of the Government Collections of Manuscripts Deposited at the Bhandarkar Oriental Research Institute*, vol. XVI, Part II, Poona: BORI.

Stein, M.A., 1892. See *Rājataraṅgiṇī* of Kalhaṇa.

———, 1894, Catalogue of Sanskrit Manuscripts in the Raghunatha Temple Library of His Highness the Maharaja of Jammu and Kashmir, Bombay: Nirnaya-Sagara Press.

———, 1979, *Kalhaṇa's Rājataraṅgiṇī — A Chronicle of the Kings of Kaśmīr*, tr. with an Introduction, Commentary and Notes, 2 vols. Delhi: Motilal Banarsidass. Reprinted from the edition of 1900.

Sufi, G.M.D, 1974, *Kashīr, A History of Kashmir*, 2 vols. New Delhi: Light and Life Publishers.

Vasudeva, Somadeva, 2004, *The Yoga of the Mālinīvijayottaratantra Chapters 1-4, 7, 11-17*, Critical Edition, Translation & Notes, Pondicherry: Institut français d'Indologie/òcole française d'Extrême-Orient, Collection Indologie - 97.

———, 2005 (ed., tr.), *Three Satires, Nīlakaṇṭha, Kṣemendra & Bhallaṭa*, New York: New York University Press/JJC Foundation.

8

Tribute to the Sage of Kashmir

Kapila Vatsyayan

It is indeed a privilege to write a few lines as tribute to the sage of Kashmir, Swami Lakshman Joo. I was neither a pupil, nor devotee, nor fortunate enough to sit at his feet for the many discourses he gave or participate in *yajñas*. Nevertheless, I knew of him and his teachings through many in Srinagar, and of his teachings through Thakur Jaideva Singh, whom I knew both as a musicologist and an ardent admirer and devout *śiṣya* of Swami Lakshman Joo.

Nishat was no strange place for me. My grandmother had lived there far away from the family city house in Srinagar to recoup from her illness. My mother[1] knew the garden and the upper terraces of Nishat like the palm of her hand. Each tree, each flower, blossom and fruit had been her long-time companions. She spoke to each with the intimacy of filial love and affection.

Long after, when visits to Kashmir were less frequent, although regular, a visit to Nishat, specially the area beyond the formal garden and its vicinity was a must, almost a pilgrimage. It was on one such visit,[2] when she herself (mother) was no longer physically active to stride across hills and mountains, that she and I hesitatingly without notice or prior appointment arrived at the doorstep of Swamiji's ashram and while she sat in the car, I went in, to be greeted warmly by Swamiji's disciple, Prabha Devi. I introduced not so much myself but told her about my

1. Satyavathi Malik, eminent Hindi writer, born and brought up in Srinagar, Kashmir, deeply devoted to the culture of Kashmir, also founder of many institutions of literature, music and dance in Kashmir, as also in Calcutta and Delhi.
2. It must have been in the 1970s.

mother and my long-term desire to have *darśana* of Swamiji. Not only was the rapport instant, but more she eagerly accompanied me to bring mother in. We walked steadily and in silence to sit in the porch waiting for his arrival.

Yes, he arrived, clad in white — with the clear luminosity of one who had experienced. His slight frame radiated *tejas* and *ojas.* No words were necessary and none exchanged for nearly twenty minutes. This was communication perfect at another level and dimension.

With trepidation I broke the silence and spoke of Thakur Jaideva Singh. He responded warmly and affectionately. However, it was evident that my mother and he were speaking to each other without words and any external signs.

I was all too conscious of my ignorance about Kashmir Śaivism, dared ask no questions, but I had filled myself with the essence of Kashmir Śaivism, in the human embodiment in whose presence I found myself. No more was desired or asked for.

Over decades I have known Swami Lakshman Joo through his writings and the writings of others, particularly Thakur Jaideva Singh, Janakinath Kamal and of course Bettinaji who has imbibed so deeply and sensitively his teachings.

This is neither occasion nor am I competent to speak about the profundity of his experience and the depths of his comprehension about Kashmir Śaivism. Each time I have picked up his short, simply-written book containing his lectures on Kashmir Śaivism I have been struck by the fact that his depth of experience and vastness of knowledge is matched by a direct simple articulation in words: Who else could communicate through simple similies and analogues the complexity of the Theory of the Alphabet (*Mātṛkācakra*) and the Theory of Reflection (*Pratibiṁbavādaḥ*). Only two excerpts from his writing in his words give a glimpse of this ability to communicate complexity through simplicity and depth.

The first in the context of the Theory of the Alphabet, where he employs the motif of the cup-shaped mirror, and the second in the context of the Theory of Reflection. In the first case, he says:

> The reflection of the universe, which has been explained earlier as being in the form of a cup-shaped mirror, is represented by the sixteenth letter of the Sanskrit alphabet, *visarga*, the letter *ḥ*. In Devanāgarī script the letter *ḥ* takes the form of the two points of the

colon ":". And these two points of the *visarga* (:), represent the two cups in which the reflection of the universe takes place. These two points are known as *Śiva Bindu* and *Śakti Bindu*.

In the second, explaining *svātantrya:*

In the ordinary worldly course sound is reflected outwardly in ether and inwardly in the ear. Touch is reflected outwardly in air and inwardly in the skin. Form is reflected outwardly in fire and in a mirror and inwardly in the eye. Taste is reflected outwardly in water and inwardly in the tougue. Smell is reflected outwardly in the earth and inwardly in the nose. These reflections, however, are just like the reflection in a mirror. They only take place individually. All five reflections are not available at once, only one thing is reflected in each. In a mirror form is reflected. Touch cannot be reflected in a mirror nor can taste, smell, or sound. A mirror will only reflect form. It is only in Supreme God Consciousness that you find all five reflected at once. In fact, although these reflections are experienced individually in all of the organs, sight in the eye, sound in the ear, etc. these reflections could not even be observed if consciousness were not there. Awareness is needed and this is found in consciousness and not in the organs.

The universe, therefore, is reflected in the mirror of consciousness, not in the organs nor in the five gross elements. These are merely *tattvas* and cannot reflect anything. The real reflector is consciousness. In consciousness, however, you see only the reflected thing and not anything that is reflected. That which is reflected (*bimba*) is in fact *svātantrya*. This whole universe is the reflection in God Consciousness of *svātantrya*. There is no additional class of similar objects existing outside of this world that He reflects in His nature. The outside element, that which is reflected, is only *svātantrya*. The infinite variety which is created is only the expansion of *svātantrya*.

You can understand this by taking the example of cause and effect. When a potter makes a pot he takes clay and gives form to that clay with his potter's instruments such as a stick, string, and potter's wheel. Within the potter's creative activity two kinds of causes can be distinguished. There is the material cause which in Sanskrit is

> called *upādāna kāraṇa*. This is that cause that travels with the effect. It cannot and does not become separated from the effect. Secondly, there is the formal cause which in Sanskrit is called *nimitta kāraṇa*. The formal cause does not travel with the effect. The material cause is the potter's clay and the formal cause is the potter himself and his stick, string, and wheel. In the ordinary worldly course the reflected object (*bimba*) seems to be the cause of the reflection (*pratibiṁba*) because the reflected object cannot exist without that which is reflected. We have seen, however, that all reflection is really a reflection in God Consciousness. If the reflected object is really the cause of the reflection then what kind of cause is it? Is it the material cause, which travels with the effect, or is it the formal cause, which does not travel with the effect? It cannot be the material cause because that would mean that there is something outside of God Consciousness which travels to become part of the effect which is the reflection. Yet, it is our theory in Śaivism that nothing can exist outside of God Consciousness.
>
> This universe, therefore, is found in the reflector of God Consciousness, not through the agency of anything of which it is a reflection (*bimba*) but through His *svātantrya* where the universe is contained in a seed form. *Svātantrya* is the seed of everything. Everything exists in the mirror of God Consciousness with *svātantrya* as its cause.*

What else can one add as tribute? The master's words are the most precious as they emerge from deep experience and reflection.

Swami Lakshman Joo was indeed the carrier of the long and profoundly important stream of Kashmir Śaivism. Here was a contemporary embodiment of the sage tradition of an Abhinavagupta, Utpaladeva, Kṣemarāja, and others.

It is gratifying to note that his legacy of both experience and scholarship is being fostered by another generation of Indian and foreign scholars.

---

* Swami Lakshman Joo, *Kashmir Shaivism. The Secret Supreme*, Delhi, 1991, pp. 29-32.

9

The Power of Pure Awareness

Bettina Bäumer

yadhībalena viśvaṁ bhaktānaṁ śivapathaṁ bhāti ।
tamahamavadhānarūpaṁ sadgurumamalaṁ sadā vande ॥

I worship that pure *sadguru*
whose nature is Awareness
by whose spiritual power
the universe shines as the path of Śiva
for the devotees.

— Abhinavagupta, *Dehasthadevatācakrastotra* v. 4

MYSTERIOUS are the ways of the Divine, beyond our thinking, planning and even desiring. As the *Kaṭha Upaniṣad* says, unless one is chosen by Him, one cannot reach the goal and realize one's essential nature (cp. *Kaṭha* 2.23). All my intellectual as well as spiritual search for about 20 years in India could not have found the Real, had I not met my Master in Swami Lakshman Joo, and had he not accepted me as his disciple.

It was the attraction of Indian spirituality, of the Upaniṣads and of Sri Ramaṇa Maharshi, which made me study Sanskrit and then come to India in 1967. I had not only searched through the texts, I was also guided by competent teachers (above all Swami Abhishiktananda and R. Panikkar). And yet, after practising meditation and studying the texts for so many years, I could only reach a certain point in my spiritual life and I still felt something lacking. However, I had started reading some of the texts of Kashmir Śaivism along with French translations and introductions by Lilian Silburn, a disciple of Swami Lakshman Joo. These texts exerted a powerful attraction on me. But it was still in the books and I lacked practical experience.

I was also fortunate to know personally and even closely both, Lilian Silburn and Thakur Jaideva Singh, Swamiji's scholar-disciples in Paris and Varanasi respectively. Each in her or his own way, through their books and through their personalities, conveyed something of the mystical spirit of Kashmir Śaivism. It is through them that I felt more and more attracted by Swami Lakshman Joo and by this great spiritual tradition.

I was basically shy, and when two letters sent to Īśvara Āśrama, seeking Swamiji's permission to come, remained unanswered, I did not dare simply to go to Kashmir and try my luck. It was only when Thakur Jaideva Singh passed away in May 1986, and since he had entrusted me with the completion of his book *Parātrīśikā Vivaraṇa* (by Abhinavagupta) which he had studied with his master, that I had a concrete reason for going to Kashmir. My prayer in these years preceding my meeting with him was very simple but intense: may it be granted to me to meet him at least once in his lifetime. This prayer was more than fulfilled.

Externally there were two circumstances which made the meeting possible: the publication of *Parātrīśikā Vivaraṇa* for which I wanted to seek his blessing and guidance, and the fact that I was invited to Srinagar by the Indian Council for Philosophical Research for a Seminar on Kashmir Śaivism in September 1986, which would bring together the most important Indian scholars on the subject. But much more important than the external reason for going to Kashmir was my internal situation. For, after the death of two of my great spiritual friends (Jaideva Singh and P.Y. Deshpande), and after the separation from my first teacher, I was in a kind of vacuum. This was perhaps a better condition for meeting my master than any other reason. And yet, I could not know what was in store for me.

Coming to Srinagar for the first time, and that too with a group of scholars of Kashmir Śaivism, was not only exciting, but I could feel the elevation and at the same time apprehension which remained so characteristic whenever I came to the master.

It was known that Swamiji generally received people only on Sunday. That first Sunday afternoon the whole group of scholars had arranged a meeting where they could have his *darśana* and ask questions. But I was sure that I wanted to meet him personally before all these intellectuals, because my search was more than intellectual. So I quietly arranged a taxi to take me one Sunday morning at seven, possibly before anybody else would reach the ashram.

It was one of those indescribably transparent, beautiful autumn mornings, when the mountains reflected clearly in the Dal Lake, where only a few *śikhara*s were moving calmly. Apples, hanging red on the trees, were being harvested. I stopped on the way and bought a basket full, not to go with empty hands. The air was pure and fresh, more so after a hot monsoon in Varanasi. The mountains were pointing sharply towards the sky. After searching at Guptagaṅgā Temple, my Paṇḍit and I finally reached the door of the ashram. A simple wooden door painted in white, with no name on it. By that time it was about 8 a.m. I knocked at the door which would become so symbolic for me for "entering within" (*samāveśa*). I was still full of apprehension: Was I worthy to have his *darśana*? A boy opened the door and said that this was not the time to meet Swamiji, and that we should come in the afternoon. By then I had gained courage and I insisted to see Prabha Devi, about whom Jaideva Singh had spoken to me, and to whom I could explain my case. She was kind enough to meet us and I gave the reference of Jaideva Singh. She understood. She went upstairs to ask Swamiji whether he would meet us at this hour. Again I passed some anxious moments. As a Christian I had never really understood what "the fear of God" means, it was only in the proximity of Swami Lakshman Joo that this expression was filled with meaning.

I cannot recall how many minutes passed, but Swamiji was gracious. He came down the steep stairs from his upper room — a tall upright figure wrapped in deep silence, moving slowly, as if emerging directly from *samādhi*. From his entire body emanated an atmosphere of an extremely subtle, transparent, peaceful and transcendent state which immediately elevated and purified whoever met him and was open to the divine influence. And in spite of the fear and apprehension one would feel in his presence, this transcendent state was paired with great compassion, with a love that was beyond the personal. Within seconds of this first *darśana* all these feelings came to my mind, and the only and spontaneous reaction was to fall at his feet. He only slowed down his movement, he remained in his natural, silent and transcendent state. He sat down on his usual *āsana* in the open verandah. I was allowed to sit in front of him, and before uttering any word I could only be merged in this atmosphere of peace, of power and concentration which radiated from him. All the words I wanted to utter seemed so shallow in his presence. Yet, I had to speak about Jaideva Singh, about my responsibility to edit and publish his translation of *Parātrīśikā Vivaraṇa*, and I was seeking Swamiji's blessing for this work. He took keen interest and promised to look through the manuscript before it was published. But all this was only the external connection. At a much deeper level I knew that I had "arrived," that my search was fulfilled. I craved nothing but to be accepted, to be guided and initiated by him. I only dared to ask this question: "Is initiation necessary for understanding Kashmir Śaivism?" which he answered in the affirmative. I had expressed my deepest desire, hoping that one day it would be fulfilled.

In fact, as expected, the afternoon meeting with the scholars of the seminar was of a quite different nature, and Swamiji became impatient with the purely intellectual questions. I did not care what was said, I remained there, in front of the master, absorbed in his presence. Even in his anger and apparent irritation, the same divine power was there in its purity. After this first day I had a very powerful dream — in fact, more than a dream: We were in the same hall at Guptagaṅgā, when the crowd dispersed I found myself alone with Swamiji. I fell at his feet in *sāṣṭāṅga praṇāma*, but was incapable of getting up. I was like glued to the ground in total surrender. Swamiji himself pulled me up. When I recounted this dream to him he was happy. It was sign of confirmation.

I would take about seven months after this first meeting until I could come to him again and receive what he had promised me. In between it was a time of testing, of physical and mental suffering, until I was found worthy to come in his presence.

The next occasion was his birthday, for which he had invited me explicitly. It was an occasion to learn his ways and the ways of his devotees. Within me the certainty was growing that he was my Guru and there was none else in this world who could carry me to my final destination — which we call God. As he went on testing my sincerity and firmness by rejecting me many times, the inner certainty became still stronger. There was no other way — as the Upaniṣad says: *nānyaḥ panthā vidyate 'yanāya.** Waiting for initiation became unbearable, the only alternative would have been suicide. . . . The words of Utpaladeva are so true.

> In whatever state of being —
> Life, death or anything else —
> May I worship you constantly

* *Śvetāśvatara Upaniṣad* 3.8.

In your imperishable body
That embraces the whole world
And consists of the bliss of eternal consciousness.

— *Śivastotrāvalī* 13.3

Finally came the appointed day — and only later did I realize how fortunate I was to be accepted in such a short time. Other devotees were waiting for years to receive initiation. On the day of my initiation there were only few people in the ashram. Swamiji sent them all away and finally I was alone with my master in the *maṇḍapa* in the garden. At that blessed moment he gave all his attention to me, and the indescribable happened. It was pure recognition — *pratyabhijñā*. No complicated ritual, no more testing, but the direct transmission in its total purity. Tears of joy and purification were flowing, as if the burden of so many lives was lifted, and I felt light, like a feather. He opened the door and removed all the obstacles so that I could enter within — *samāveśa*.

I can also never forget the graciousness of Sharika Deviji who was a powerful mediator and a discrete helper, as her sister Prabhaji.

I was more and more led to see the divinity in the master, to watch all his actions, words, moods, and above all his powerful silence as an expression of his divine state. His piercing look could destroy the ego which was interfering all the time. It was like a laser ray in modern medicine, which can pierce and touch the point of the disease — but in order to liberate and to heal.

And with all that, with his incredible power, there was the perfect naturalness, the utter simplicity, the overwhelming sense of joy and humour, and the love and care for his devotees, his generosity. In his perfection he incarnated all the high ideas of Kashmir Śaivism.

Some powerful experiences which he granted me were like signposts on the inner path. Only afterwards did I realize what they meant.

One beautiful afternoon, it was a day off from the ashram, I walked to Harwan with Rajan, my *gurubhāī*, along the clear stream lined with willows, overlooking the Dal Lake. I only knew Harwan as an ancient Buddhist site, but I did not know what it meant in the life of Swamiji and of his master Mahtab Kak. When we climbed up to the ruins of the Buddhist monastery and sat down, the hills behind us and the vast valley before us, I was suddenly drawn within by an irresistible force. Everything outside vanished and there was an unending depth, a beauty without fear. I was lost for a long time. When I opened my eyes, I found the same beauty, the same deep reality, the same radiance in every atom of the universe. I could not decide which beauty was greater, inner or outer, and again and again closed my eyes. But the bliss within and the bliss outside were not different, and the alternation itself was bliss. While the experience was going on, there was not a thought, no interpretation — only a sea of bliss. Nothing else mattered, no past, no future.

It was only afterwards when I came across an explanation of *krama-mudrā* that I understood what it was. The day after this experience I went to Swamiji and felt like telling him about it — but the moment I saw him he smiled. He knew not only what had happened to me — in fact, it was He who had done it! How foolish could I be to tell him something which was entirely his grace.

His guidance was so subtle, and as in the above case, mostly it happened without words. Often a gesture, a look, a smile would confirm the experience. There was an incredible clarity in his presence.

One Sunday afternoon there were not many devotees in the ashram. Swamiji was sitting in his easy chair towards the wall right of the *maṇḍapa*. I was facing him, at a distance of three or four metres, and I was sitting cross-legged against a tree. Other devotees were grouped around. It was quiet, Swamiji was in a radiant mood, but relaxed. As I was leaning against the tree, I suddenly lost consciousness of the outer world. I felt as if streams of light were pouring over my body from above my head, enwrapping the body in a triangle of light. The light was flowing down and also flowing out from inside. It was a dynamic radiance, indescribably blissful. When, after a considerable time, I opened my eyes with difficulty, I saw that Gurudeva's eyes were on me with an incredible grace. I could hardly bear his look, although it was nothing but grace. Afterwards even my *gurubhāī* commented: "you were full of radiance."

Such was the grace of the master who could do anything, in his presence or absence, if only one was open to it. When, after several visits, I came again to the ashram after two years, I saw that Swamiji was busy building an octagonal wooden shrine around the very tree where I had had the experience. Then only I was told that this tree was very special, that he used to sit under it in *samādhi* at his earlier birthdays. Now he called it Parabhairava Dhāma and made an enclosure around it to preserve its sanctity. He used to remove his chappals and said that this is holy ground. No wonder I could feel the vibration, even without knowing.

Whenever Swamiji was teaching a Sanskrit text or some stray verses from *Tantrāloka, Netra Tantra* or other texts, it would give me such vibrations of that total unity of word and meaning, which Kālidāsa compares with the union of Śiva and Pārvatī (*Raghuvaṁśa* invocation). When he used to sit under the huge Chinar tree, teaching his disciples, it was as if he was Abhinavagupta himself. Once he taught *Gurunāthaparāmarśa* to Paṇḍit Kokiloo and the Devīs, and I was fortunate to be present. He was in such a state of consciousness that there was a total identity between him, Abhinavagupta (who is described in the poem) and Śiva — the state of *ahantā*. He was overflowing with the inner states described in the texts.

No less powerful was — and is — his guidance through dreams. The clarity of consciousness which one could feel in his presence is here transmitted at another level. In some dreams even Swamiji was teaching me Sanskrit texts!

Whenever I stayed in the house of Swamiji's brother Sri Nīlkaṇṭha Raina and his wife Arunditi, I was happy to combine work on the texts — mainly *Parātrīśikā Vivaraṇa* and Abhinavagupta's *stotras* and *Tantrasāra* (for my German book) — because every moment in Gurudeva's presence would illumine the meaning of the texts. I often thought, if I could spend my whole life in this way, I would need nothing else.

Apart from Swamiji's birthday celebrations which were blissful for everyone, my special attraction was the annual (or bi-annual) *yajña* which Swamiji used to celebrate for his master Mahtab Kak. At the first *yajña* I attended after my initiation I did not know what was in store for me. All the more powerful was this first experience. I could observe the preparations going on for days on end, and it was a privilege when Swamiji allowed me to help in cleaning the offerings: rice, sesamum, *bilva* leaves, etc. Whatever was to be offered in the sacred fire had to be spotless, pure, another lesson how the outer and the inner were to correspond. Swamiji would not tolerate any imperfection, even in minute details.

It may be more authentic to translate here the entry in my diary after the first *yajña* with Gurudeva:

Havanśālā, Guptagaṅgā 10 September 1987

Yesterday's *yajña* was overwhelming. It was so intense that today I am feeling like emptied — but in the best sense. Ritual as an intensification, concentration of *sat:* every action is done in the fullness of consciousness. Swamiji was divine, he illustrated the Tantric dictum: *śivībhūtvā śivaṁ yajet* ("becoming Śiva one should worship Śiva"). The *jīvanmukta* as *yajamāna*. Nine hours of most intense contemplation. How can I describe it? The entire ritual lasted from 9 a.m. till 11 p.m., the *yajña* from 9 to 5, followed by *śrāddha* for his Guru until 6 p.m., and then followed by *prasāda* in which a few hundred people participated. First *pūjā* with the *kalaśa* under the photo of Swami Mahtab Kak. On the big *vedi* (*sthaṇḍila*) firewood is arranged. After consecration of the *vedi* and exchange of *ṭīkā* and *mantras* with the Paṇḍits, Swamiji sits down on his *āsana* facing east. The fire is kindled and the *havana* begins. The first recitation is a long *Gaṇeśastotra*. I am fortunate to sit in the opposite corner near the Devīs (Sharikaji and Prabhaji), in full view of Swamiji, through the fire. His gestures are so perfect, his concentration the whole day is total, he radiates an inner fullness which is transmitted to the smallest things. The fire becomes mightier, the mountain of offerings becomes like a fiery, huge *Śivaliṅga*: flowers, leaves, nuts, sesamum, rice, *guṛ*, ghee, coconuts. The symbolism is so overwhelming: the Fire of Consciousness (*cidāgni*) in which everything is offered, purified. The recitations were powerful — from *Ṛgveda* Puruṣasūkta and Nāsadīyasūkta, to *Śivastotrāvalī*, to *Sāmbapañcāśikā*, *Pañcastavī*, etc. to *Bhagavad-Gītā* and lastly *Bhairavastava* of Abhinavagupta. When the *Saṁgrahastotra* of Utpaladeva was recited, it was too strong to bear — every word sank too deep. Tears were flowing. Their tune of recitation is so enchanting. It started with *Sāmbapañcāśikā* that the meaning of the text, the tone of the recitation and the offerings in the fire became such a dense unity that it became almost unbearable: ritual and mysticism all in one.

The fire was *Agni, Sūrya, Śiva, cit, prāṇa, vāk, kuṇḍalinī* rising.

I understood that the spiritual transformation which Swamiji wants to operate in me can happen completely in and through this sacred

> action: here he is totally mediator to the Divine. Therefore he told me explicitly to take part in the *yajña*, therefore he allowed me to participate fully, from the preparations to the *pūrṇāhuti* and to the *prasāda*. Everything is a spiritual process made visible. In me *cakra*s are opening, the Śakti is rising forcefully, it is a total purification.
>
> At the time of the *śrāddha* for Swamiji Mahtab Kak, Swamiji burst in tears, as if he saw his Guru. It was so moving to see him like this, he was literally shaken.
>
> Today only ashes remain.

Every one of the *yajña*s I was fortunate to attend was a unique experience. That last one which he could celebrate in the Guptagaṅgā Temple, before terrorism engulfed Kashmir, and before Sharika Devi's and his own *samādhi*, was particularly memorable (September 1990). He was in a tremendous state of Bhairava. At the end of the *yajña*, when he sprinkled us with the holy water from the *kalaśa*, his look was piercing, a mixture of divine power, fierceness, joy. I was completely intoxicated, which he noticed. When only a few devotees were left around him, about 11 in the night, he suddenly looked at me and called me. I went to do *praṇāma*, and the indescribable happened. He blessed me by placing his right foot on my head. He knew it would be the last time (the last time of the full *yajña*, not the last meeting). But nobody understood when, on the next day, he ordered all the branches of the apple trees in the garden of Guptagaṅgā to be cut though the apples were still green. He foresaw the *pralaya* that was to follow, and this was a sign.

In January 1991, when terrorism already dominated Kashmir, I felt an irresistible call to meet my master and Deviji. There was no outer communication. The obstacles seemed insurmountable: snow on the airfield of Srinagar made my plane return twice to Delhi. A bomb explosion at Lal Chauk, at the heart of Srinagar, made everybody advise me not to go. But the third attempt was successful. By grace of the master I met Deviji's nephew in the plane and could go with him to the ashram. Swamiji was surprised to see me at such an unexpected time, and he was graceful. But I was shocked to find Deviji in a semi-conscious state. I had never seen her sick or weak, she was always an image of grace, of radiance, of quiet and self-effacing presence near her master. Seeing her in this condition tears came to my eyes. I sat before her in silence, when she suddenly got up, as if pulled by some unknown force. She not only opened her eyes, but she blessed me with her hand and gave me such a piercing look which contained and expressed everything: the experience of her life in the proximity of the divine master, an inner strength in spite of physical weakness, and a total grace pouring out. It was her last blessing. Three days later she would give up her body, as if saying "now it is enough." I have never seen a more beautiful death — or rather *samādhi.*

To be a witness of the last two days of Deviji in the ashram and of Swamiji's divine state in this situation was an extraordinary privilege, and beyond words to be described. The night after Deviji was brought to Jammu on her "last journey," Swamiji called us to his upper room where he was in a God-intoxicated state. All the time, since Deviji's departure, we were reciting *mantras*, especially the Amṛteśvara Bhairava Mantra.

It was clear why the call to come was so strong and made me overcome all obstacles.

In different ways the master had prepared me for his physical disappearance, even though I was not ready for it. One afternoon in the ashram, when he was sitting in the verandah, he suddenly said in a serious tone: "I am now going to where I have come from." There was an uneasy silence among the few devotees present. I could not withhold my tears. I dared to ask: "Who will be there to guide us then?" After a few minutes of total silence, Swamiji said: "I shall send somebody."

In fact, the only real preparation for continuing to live without the grace, the power, the clarity and the joy of his physical presence was to learn more and more to enter into that state of pure awareness, of God-consciousness, as he loved to say, that was his. His consciousness was the measure of Reality — *pramāṇa.* He was like the Himalaya in Kālidāsa's verse where he describes it as "the measuring rod of the earth" (*pṛthivyāḥ iva mānadaṇḍaḥ* — *Kumārasambhava* 1.1). Our usual standards are so shallow and so far from Reality.

In our age of spiritual exhibitionism and commercialization, Swamiji remained hidden in his greatness. But his hidden power continues to inspire and to elevate, not only his immediate disciples, but even those who have never met him in the body.

Mudrā

Divine seal imprinted on the world:
mudrā
the age-old gesture springing from the soil —
this tree: *mudrā* of the cosmos,
each tree, each blade of grass:
a *mudrā*
of the Divine Dancer.

Man the living tree —
hands manifest his mood
his joy, his pain —
outward.

The tree grows, bearing fruit;
gestures become slow,
im-pressive.

Mudrā turns within,
becomes the soul's attitude
mirror of a divine image
imprinted in the depth.

The flow goes inwards, outwards,
Śakti's vibration
In silent stillness of the Centre
or
breaking forth in ecstatic dance.
No difference.

The tree growing, the child dancing,
the Man of God lost within —
all are His *mudrā,*
flowing from the Void
in cosmic joy: *jagadānanda*

III.
The Enlightening Master

गुरुरुपायः ॥ ६ ॥

gururupāyaḥ ॥6॥

गृणाति उपदिशति तात्त्विकार्थमिति गुरुः, सोऽत्र व्याप्तिप्रदर्शकत्वेन उपायः ।
गुरुर्वा पारमेश्वरी अनुग्राहिका शक्तिः ।
— शिवसूत्र विमर्शिनी २.६

gṛṇāti upadiśati tāttvika-arthamiti guruḥ so'tra vyāpti-pradarśakatvena upāyaḥ ।
gururvā pārameśvarī anugrāhikā śaktiḥ ।
—*Śivasūtra Vimarśinī* 2.6

The Guru is the means (to liberation). (Sūtra)

Guru is one who teaches the essential truth.
He is the means because he shows (the way of) pervasion.
Or Guru is the power of Divine grace. (*Vimarśinī*)

35. Swamiji in *samādhi* on his Birthday. (*c.* early 1980s).

36. Swamiji with Devis Sharika and Prabha in Iśvara Āśrama.

37. Swamiji with Sharika Devi in the verandah on their usual *āsana*.

38. Swamiji with devotees in Nishat Bagh.

39. Deep concentration.

40. In his natural *āsana*.

41. Teaching under the Chinar tree, 1989.

42. In a relaxed mood, 1989.

43. Sharika Devi, 1989.

44. Devi Sharika at the feet of her Master in the upper ashram (*c*. 1930s).

45. Sharika Devi with Swamiji.

46. The Yoginī.

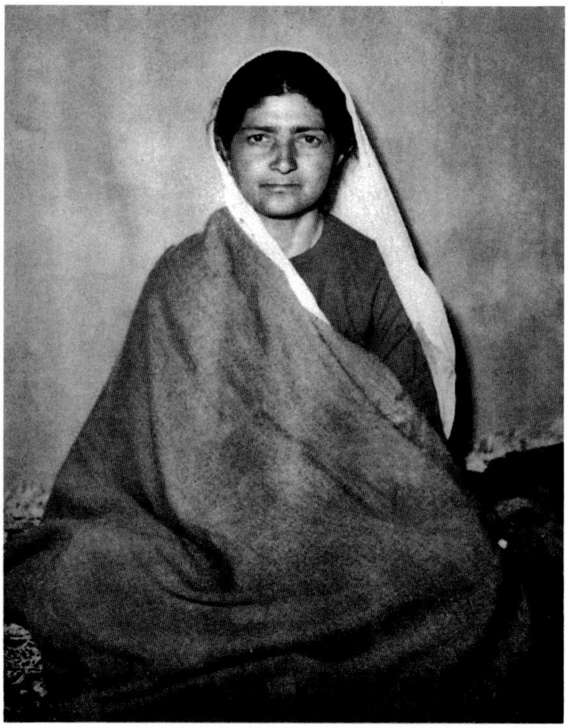

10

The Making of a Yoginī

Mohan Lal Sopory

I REALLY consider myself very fortunate, that I remained associated with Śrī 108 Swami Īśvara Svarūpa, Swami Lakshman Joo. Swamiji's elder sister Gunawati was married to my respected elder brother, Jawaharlalji. Therefore there was a great deal of amity between the two families. Once Swamiji remarked, "When I entered this house for the first time with my sister, I perceived the presence of a particular person with whom I had been closely associated in my last life. But I did not reveal this knowledge to anybody. Suddenly, one day a young girl appeared before me and the old remembrance returned as if a certain recognition occurred." This young girl was my elder sister Sushri Sharika Devi who had a saintly disposition from childhood. Often when we played together, she would mould a *Śivaliṅga* out of mud. She would enjoy worshipping it or she would write *rāma rāma* on paper for the whole day and then consign it to a river. This was for her play as a child, which continued for many years. After some years it was destined that a *Haṭha-Yoga* ascetic came to our house. Our father welcomed him and gave him the facility of staying with us. Sharika Devi learnt the technique of *prāṇayāma* from him. In a short while she started experiencing absorption in the Self. One day Swamiji Maharaj came to our house and discerned her state of inner contemplation. He gave me the following command: "Bring her to me. I will resolve many of the knots in the path of *yoga*. She will thus gain mastery in the practice of *yoga*." I was still a child and replied simply, "Maharaj, our parents will be unhappy." Swamiji said that through his blessing I would not experience any impediment. Even if I came at night I would not be beset by dogs or thieves, nor would my parents raise any objection. I accepted his order and thus Sharika and I started going to Swamiji.

This was Sharika Devi's first attempt to go to Swamiji. At this time Sharika would accompany me to Swamiji and would learn Sanskrit grammar, meditation, etc. from him from 4 a.m. to 9 a.m. and I would proceed to school and later to college in pursuit of my education. One day Swamiji said to me, "You and I will camp at the beautiful spot called Gopītīrtha, near Nishat for a few days." Swamiji had taught me the technique of meditation while I was still a child. I felt very happy with the prospect. Through Gurudeva's inspiration Sharika Devi, my younger sister Prabha and my nephew Motilalji also came there after some time. They were accompanied by Swami Muktananda.[1] After a few days Sharika Devi said to Swamiji, "Grant me the state whereby I can attain my true divine nature." It was six o'clock in the evening. Swamiji was seated on a deck chair. He said, "The vision of the Supreme within the self comes only with intense meditation and relinquishment of worldly desires. I am an ordinary person. How can I grant your wish?" Deviji was adamant. She said, "You are the embodiment of Lord Śiva. I am certain that you have the power to do so. My unflinching devotion will finally make you relent." After uttering these words a flood of tears started to flow and continued till 12 o'clock at night. Muktanandaji was watching this scene. Both the children (Prabha and Motilal) were sleeping, Swamiji instructed me to take them and lay them under the chinar tree outside. Seeing the unabated torrent of tears of Sharikaji Muktananda said to Swamiji, "Are you intent of killing this girl?" There is a law governing the relationship between the devotee and the Lord. This spectacle appeared to be one where a child was insisting on getting the moon. Muktanandaji went out of the tent. I was watching the awesome divine play with folded hands. After 12 o'clock Swamiji appeared as Lord Śiva Himself. He said to Deviji, "Come before me and recite the *Śivastotrāvalī* worshipping me as Lord Śiva." Deviji did so for one hour weeping continuously. It was 4 o'clock when Swamiji placed his right hand on her head. With the touch of Swamiji's hand, Devi's tears dried up and she was lost in herself for twenty minutes. After this she said to Swamiji, "I am now experiencing the fullsome state of *samādhi*, replete with divine fragrance." Swamiji understood her state of complete spiritual fulfilment. He said: "Now you can ask for all the boons you want and I will grant them." She begged that she should remain celibate and always immersed in meditation. These two wishes she asked for happily but she hesitated to ask for the third, but Swamiji pleaded with

1. Not to be confused with Swami Muktananda of Ganeshpuri who came much later to Swamiji.

her to ask for that also. Thus she had no option but to ask for her third boon wherein she wished that she and the master would stay together for ever. Then Swamiji said, *tathā-astu* ("let it be so") and her three prayers were granted.

By this time dawn was about to break. Gurudeva took Deviji to a nearby stream which was full of water. He unrobed her and bathed her there with his own hands. Then he washed her face and put on her clothes. We were strolling near the stream. Deviji, while chewing a toothstick, gazed at Swamiji and said: "I am truly manifest in every atom. Your power is pervading everywhere. I can give salvation to Mohan Lal." Swamiji was listening to every word silently. By this time they had reached the tent. He said: "The time is not yet ripe for you to remain in this state. There are still many tasks for you in this world. When the time comes I will restore your original state." After ages, it is only the very fortunate who experience such spiritual states. Those who witness these are indeed blessed.

Swamiji was now silent and Deviji who began experiencing the objective world again was in tears. She implored her Master to restore her divine state. It seemed as if the moon had lost its power to cool or a snake had been deprived of its gem.[2] When Deviji found that her state of complete fullness and bliss would not be recovered she became almost mad. She could not see with one eye and developed low fever. Seeing her in this condition Swamiji considered it best to send her home. We quickly breakfasted and packed, asking Muktanandaji and the two children to return home separately. The three of us hired a *toṅgā* (horse-cart). Swamiji sat in front while Sharika Devi and I sat at the back. By the time the *toṅgā* reached opposite Nehru Park Deviji abused Swamiji. He turned to look upon Sharika and I felt as if I had the *darśana* of Lord Śiva, I presume that Deviji saw the manifestation of Lord Śiva in all His glory in Swamiji. She now begged for forgiveness in all humility. After some time we reached the city and dropped Swamiji at his residence in Fateh Kadal. Then Sharika and I proceeded to our residence in Saraf Kadal.

Our parents were upset when they saw Deviji who was sick. They laid her on a bed and after a couple of days her condition worsened. They called the famous doctor Dinanath Ganju. He saw her and said that the girl would not survive beyond a few days. After this he left. In the meantime my mother sent me to Swamiji. Deviji was experiencing the last states of life.

2. In Hindu mythology the cobra has a gem in its hood.

When I arrived at Swamiji's residence he said, "When you return from college bring a quarter kilo of grapes." When I returned at 4 o'clock I gave the grapes to Swamiji who picked just three grapes and said: "Put these in Sharikaji's mouth, one by one." An absolute miracle occurred when she ate the grapes. Whereas previously she could not even drink water she now opened her eyes, stretched herself and started looking all around.

This was the glory of Swami Lakshman Joo who was no ordinary *yogī* but a *yogīrāja* who had achieved yogic powers even as a child. He had a unique technique of meditation whereby he could interact in the objective world while he remained absorbed in the Self. He was in contact with people yet he was aloof. Swamiji was truly an exceptional scholar who knew all the subtleties of Śaiva Śāstras and above all he was a phenomenal Gurudeva who transcended all conceptions of a renunciate.

In the days to come two beautiful houses were built on the Īśvara hill near Nishat by the respective parents of these two great souls. I had started going to college. Gurudeva was very fond of me and wanted me to stay with him but my mother pleaded with him and said: "O Lord how can I see both my children renounce the world?" Then Swamiji answered: "Very well! You can get Mohan Lal married. He will remain devoted to me even while he is a family man."

One day I went to Swamiji and he took me for a boat ride in the Dal Lake. When the boat reached the middle of the lake, suddenly a cyclonic wind arose. The boat became unsteady and people on the shore feared that it would capsize. Swamiji asked me and the boatman to close our eyes for five minutes. He forbade the boatman to ply the oars. Thus the three of us sat motionless. Suddenly the rain and storm abated and after some time we came ashore. Such was the supernatural divine power of Swami Lakshman Joo.[3]

I was studying in college. One day Swamiji said, "You have a few holidays, so let us go to Draphan, which is beyond Harwan and the hunting ground of kings." I gladly accepted Swamiji's command and reached Swamiji's residence on the following day. We had taken a bag of rice, a mud pot and some salt from Harwan. We walked for several hours and reached a spot called "Darvanya." Swamiji said:

3. Compare the stilling of the storm by Jesus. (Ed.)

"We will rest here and then make arrangements for meal." I collected some small dry twigs and made a cooking oven with stones, Swamiji lit the fire and he placed the earthenware pot with some water and rice on the fire. We used a stick instead of a ladle. He added a little salt and soon the rice was ready. He covered the rice and placed it on coals. Then he went to the stream with pure bubbling water. The forest was very dense. We had no plates for serving the rice. I was watching this *līlā* (divine play) with amazement. Swamiji got two stones from the water and served the rice on them asking me to start eating. We were hungry and enjoyed the meal. We had some cold water and then sat on a mat under a tree. We could hear the roar of wild animals and the chirping birds all around us. I felt very frightened. Swamiji lit a fire.

"Now no wild animal will attack you. You can meditate without any anxiety." I sat in front of the fire till twelve at night. Swamiji was immersed in *samādhi*. At dawn we bathed and returned home. Every action of our Gurudeva was replete with divinity.

Once, when I was still a child I visited Swamiji's house with Deviji. He said: "I will take Sharikaji to Hariparvat at night." I did not accompany them. Swamiji tied a turban on Sharika's head and took her to Hariparvat disguised as a boy. When they returned home in the morning Sharika Devi said to me: "I had a vision of all the gods, and even the seven sages appeared to me. All the rocks at Hariparvat are manifestations of various gods. It is for this reason that it is considered a sacred place where all one's wishes are granted." Thereafter I too visited Hariparvat off and on.

When the old memories ring in the mind I am carried to a splendid world of beatitude. Thus I experienced many wonderful events. Whenever I met my Master he looked upon me with the same compassionate loving manner that I had known as a child. In 1991 when he returned from America he had become physically very weak. My heart sank. Understanding my state he reassured me that he was in a divine blissful state of mind and that it was only natural that the body lost its vitality at the end of life.

Words cannot describe the glory of our Gurudeva. My entire life was filled with his grace. I make this offering of adoration at his holy feet.

11

The Ascent to the Lord

Sarla Kumar

IT was the day Man landed on the moon — it was the day my Lord and Master Swami Lakshman Joo catapulted me into the realm of the Divine, a sphere of which I was hitherto oblivious. Maybe I had a vague distant premonition that there was another dimension to life but suddenly I shed my old self and became a new being. Such was the impact, the revelation, the grace, the bliss, that it defies articulation.

My sister, Mrs Rajni Rai was a close devotee of our Gurudeva. I marvelled at the equanimity of mind with which she faced the vicissitudes of life. She was blessed with our Master's grace and had reached a state of deep concentration and understanding. She often became immersed in the void of consciousness. During the last years of her life she suffered from Parkinson's disease which reduced her to a state of helplessness. Many years earlier Gurudeva had predicted: "Some terrible physical disability will befall you. May the Lord protect you." His blessing sustained her and she never lost heart. Her God-consciousness and awareness remained with her in spite of extreme physical pain. Such was the power of Swamiji's grace.

Even from childhood, I was in search of a spiritual guide but I could not surrender to anyone. And then, as if the time was ripe, I came face to face with our living God. Inexperienced and naïve as I was, I wrote to Swamiji seeking a *mantra*. My sister was my emissary. Swamiji said that he would give it to me when he met me but I had pleaded so fervently that he relented and sent me the *mantra* by post. I sat down with my *mālā* but nothing happened.

Then our Master came to Delhi and I sought an appointment. When I went to the place of his residence, he was not there. I tried again and still could not get his *darśana*. I was sure that he was testing me. Was my resolve firm enough? The third time he kept the appointment — for me it was my tryst with the Divine.

Uninitiated and unacquainted as I was with the norms that should be observed when one seeks the divine path, I did not take any offering of flowers, fruit or sweets. How foolish I was! I was at the threshold of the temple of Lord Bhairava and did not have the sense of carrying a token thanksgiving. I only carried a heart that was sincere, and was searching and He knew it.

He sat with a smile playing on his face — the picture of purity, the essence of the Supreme, the very Lord manifested on earth. I do not know what happened — he only looked at me and gave me the same *mantra* that he had sent by post. But some miracle had occurred! The floodgates of joy suddenly opened within me. I was carried to another divine realm. I was wonderstruck! Suddenly I heard him say, "Sing a *bhajana* as Guru-*dakṣiṇā*!" Imagine, he lifted the opprobrium of my shameful conduct with such supreme graciousness.

I returned home as if in a daze. Fortunately, I was alone. For three days and three nights I could not sleep. Yet I was as fresh as a daisy. I was floating on ether. I could not hold my tears. The only refrain which came back again and again was:

> *tumāro chāḍ dūsrī gati nāhīn*
> *sovata jāgata śaraṇa tihārī*
>
> Leaving you there is no other way
> Whether sleeping or waking, I surrender to you.

After some weeks I went to Lucknow, where my husband was posted. There too, I was bathed with this effulgence, this indescribable lightness of being, the presence of "anotherness" within me. Yet to the outside world I was the same old Sarla.

More than thirty-nine years have elapsed since the first *śaktipāta*. He gave me *nirākāra dhyāna* (formless meditation) two years after he had first blessed me, thus leading me to find and experience the Supreme within myself. How fortunate I am that the embodiment of Lord Śiva accepted me, a worthless worm, as His disciple, and sanctified not only this life but all future births. His compassion and grace are immeasurable, His presence overflowing with bliss and divinity, His gaze is like that of a thousand suns burning all impurity. He showered his blessings on me without my even being aware that his grace was flowing like the Gaṅgā. He wrote the following letter to me:

om

Guptaganga
20th December

Dear Sarla ja.

I do not know why I did not write to you so far. Truly telling you that you are always in my mind and I do send you my blessings though not in words but in my thought.

I hope you are doing your abyas. regularly and with great devotion. In fact Abyas done with devotion & love towards Lord Carrys one nearer to Him.

Our shastras teaches us Kundalini yoga and that yoga Comes nearer as soon as you have reached the higher limit of your Abyas.

I wish you become one of our ancient Devi's just like Meera & Lalleshwari. Convey my best wishes to your husband and also to your Sister Rajni jee Rai.

yours as ever,
Lakshman Joo

Swamiji performed the *yajña* for His Master, Swami Mahtab Kak with great love and devotion. On these occasions and on His birthday he manifested his *Śiva svarūpa*. The hall at Guptagaṅgā near his residence "Īśvara Āśrama" on the outskirts of Srinagar would be full of devotees. Swamiji performed the *homa* reciting *mantra*s and would be merged in the spirit of Śiva. At a particular moment all the devotees formed a chain placing the hand on the shoulder of the devotee who sat in front. The chain of enchanted *bhakta*s was connected to Swamiji. Suddenly a current of ecstasy passed through all the devotees as the Supreme Being transmitted His divinity. This miracle occurred at every *yajña* that Swamiji performed.

The Guru scolds not only to bless but also to wash away the impurities of the disciple. At one *yajña* I sat among the devotees and was praying not so much for grace as for the well-being of my family.

Swamiji being omniscient and omnipresent knew my thoughts even though I was sitting at quite a distance from Him. Later in the day a Mahātmā came there and Swamiji rose from His seat to welcome him. Everyone rushed to him to seek his blessing and *prasāda*. I followed Deviji (Swamiji's disciple who had experienced the highest state of divinity), while Swamiji was seated close by. I asked for *prasāda* for myself and also for my son Sanjeev. Swamiji heard me and reprimanded me angrily, "Sanjeev! Sanjeev! Sanjeev! If you keep thinking of your family, you will never rise spiritually. Sanjeev will get whatever he is destined to get. You must never forget your goal. You have come alone in this world and you will go alone!" By scolding me in the presence of many disciples He freed me from the web of attachment. Thus he once again put me on the supreme path. O how can I ever forget that moment! Glory be to my divine Master!

In the 118th verse of the *Vijñānabhairava* it is stated:

> *kṣutādyante bhaye śoke gahvare vā raṇāddrute* |
> *kutūhale kṣudhādyante brahmasattā samīpagā* ||

> At the beginning and end of sneezing, in a state of fear or sorrow, (standing) on top of an abyss or while fleeing from a battlefield, at the moment of intense curiosity, at the beginning and end of hunger; such a state comes close to the experience of *Brahman*.

Once I was facing a moment of extreme crisis and was terror-stricken. I stood looking out of the window at the impending danger. Suddenly I had a vision. I lost all consciousness of my surroundings and stood engulfed by manifold shafts of light with Swamiji descending on each of them. I was dazed and spellbound. After some time when I regained normal consciousness, the danger had passed and I stood wonderstruck and unable to speak. When I went to Srinagar again and met Swamiji in person, I related my experience to Him. He smiled and said ever so gently, "The Guru takes the form of Devī sometimes. You had the vision of the Devī," such was the power of our Master, who had all the *siddhi*s but concealed them, and to the uninitiated He might have appeared as an ordinary human being.

Four days before he shed his mortal frame, he was aware of the devotees around him. I knelt by His bedside along with my sister and my dear Guru *bahin* Bettina. I was not thinking of His pain as he was beyond it. Selfish as all humans are, knowing that I would not see Him again in His human form, I was begging for His grace. He gave me such a piercing look that whenever I recall it, His presence becomes alive again. O how can I ever forget it!

Finally, when he gave up his physical form and took *mahāsamādhi*, I felt bereft, lost, rudderless, and desolate. But gradually he came and held my hand. He beckoned me and said, "I am here with you always, you only have to think of me." How true He has been to His promise. He devises means whereby I can take one more step towards Him. The path is long, the terrain is wild and difficult but I do not despair as He is with me.;

12

The Scientist and the Saint

Sudhir K. Sopory

It is a privilege to write on Swami Lakshman Joo whom we used to call with reverence Īśvara Svarūpa.

My mother's sister, Shobha Sivananda, told me once that to write about one's Gurudeva is like pointing the sun at midday and telling others that he is the source of light. Īśvara Svarūpa was indeed an incarnation of the supreme spirit, Lord Śiva. His presence is to be felt and therefore it is difficult to record his attributes within the boundary of our limited power of description through language. If we know Him, then we cannot describe Him. What I am attempting to reflect in this chapter is my association with him and also to glance at him as a teacher and a philosopher, and finally as a Guru who always cared and showed concern for his devotees. In this context I will illustrate this more specifically with regard to two of his prime disciples, Sharika Devi and Prabha Devi, about whom I have some personal knowledge. These attributes will only reflect a drop of his ocean-wide God personification. It is beyond me to record his perfection mainly due to my own limitations and also due to the fact that saints of Īśvara Svarūpa's stature do not reveal themselves. They act and intermingle like common persons, which more often than not sends deceiving signals.

A Brief Account of My Association

In the excitement of writing about Īśvara Svarūpa, most of us try to narrate our association with him. It becomes our intention to put across to the reader the fact of our closeness with him. I am also not above this temptation.[1] I would therefore write only briefly about my experience in his presence.

Our family association with Īśvara Svarūpa relates to his being the younger brother of my father's first wife, and also through his most accomplished disciples, Sharika Devi and Prabha Devi, who are my father's younger sisters. Īśvara Svarūpa, whom I will from now onwards call Swamiji, used to come to our house on a very regular basis. I remember having gone out also on many occasions with him to different places for what used to be for us wonderful picnics. Swamiji used to tell my uncle, Shri Mohan Lal, to arrange such outdoor gatherings since he had his own buses.

From my childhood I have seen him on every occasion in our house. One such function that he used to attend was *pāna*, a day that is celebrated by Kashmiri Paṇḍits for Goddess Lakṣmī. On this day everybody used to get up very early to participate in the preparations for the *pūjā*. Swamiji used to come in the evening and would sit in an anteroom to the kitchen. Prabhaji would recite the story of how a king who had lost all his kingdom got it back after he joined in *pāna pūjā* that was performed by his wife whom the king had exiled from his kingdom. Following the *pūjā*, Swamiji would have his dinner. We used to wait all the year for this day since Swamiji used to spend maximum time in our house on this day. His presence was always soothing to all.

One occasion when I saw the power of His presence was at the time of my elder brother's marriage. It started raining heavily on the previous day. My mother was worried and approached Swamiji. He assured all of us that the rain would stop and within a few hours, it stopped pouring. He cured my brother who could not get up because of a major problem in his leg. For us he was all-in-one, saint, scholar and healer. Everyone would go to Him for all kinds of problems, and people found so much solace in his assurance. His blessing was sufficient on many occasions to carry one's life forward.

I once travelled with him alone in a train from Hardwar to Dehradun. I had gone to see him at Hardwar. He had come to Hardwar with Sharika Devi and Prabha Devi. After spending the day in his presence, I enquired if he would come to Dehradun. He immediately accepted to come along and see my mother who had come from Srinagar to Dehradun to stay with her brother. It has been one of the few occasions that I was with him alone in the train.

The Dar family at Dehradun were also devotees of Swamiji. My mother's sister, Daya Tankha, who had been given the name Shobha Sivananda by Swami

Sivananda, has written a number of books and poems on her Guru. In later years she used to stay with us for a few months in a year when I was a Professor at Jawaharlal Nehru University. Once she showed me a postcard written by Swamiji to her. She had written to him about the deteriorating health of her husband and wanted him to bless her and assure her that her husband would get well. This was a repeat letter despite an earlier assurance that had come from Swamiji. This time, probably to show that his assurance should be taken seriously and no more communications to follow, Swamiji replied on the same postcard which was sent by my aunt to Him. Strangely this postcard on one side has Swamiji's writing and on the other side my aunt's request. The same postcard returned with his message and with changed address. I was surprised to see this postcard when she showed it to me. It is preserved as his blessing by my cousin sister. I have also preserved a postcard written to me by Swamiji. This was in response to my telegram I had sent on his birthday. I was then doing my Ph.D. I remember how elated I was to get his response. He also once sent me his recorded blessings, at the insistence of my mother, when I was in Germany. In fact, before I was proceeding for my higher studies abroad, my mother-in-law requested him to keep his hand of grace on me. He told her that she need not worry about his going abroad and added "he is just moving out into another garden and he will be going out so often that you may not feel that he is out of India."

Lakshman Joo: Saint, Teacher and Philosopher

What I have described above has been the experience of many who have come in contact with Him. Our perception may, however, vary. And our presentation will also vary with different shades and colours. This is probably due to our limited power and knowledge of perceiving him. He is the same, yet we describe him differently. It is difficult to perceive without the limitations of the perceiver. It may be possible only if one has reached a similar state of God-consciousness. The basic cause of our limitation in understanding Swamiji is our memory and of course ignorance. I can only say that Swamiji was apparently not a "miracle Swami," yet each one of us must have had some experience which communicated to us his divine power. His presence was empowering and not overpowering. In his presence one would feel the kindling of the fire of Śiva. This fire had the power to burn away all the impurities and limitations of the mind stuff. This fiery power could also be used to bake and ignite the mind and energies of his devotees. Anything and everything that one desired to know was reflected in his speech, silence and smile.

One aspect of Swamiji, besides possessing godly power, was his extensive knowledge and command on Kashmir Śaivism and its teaching through his own experience. Though we were in close association with Swamiji during our childhood, yet at the age, being engrossed in one's own study and the pressure from parents and teachers, I did not find any time to devote to the study of Kashmir Śaivism. On our visits on Sunday to the ashram sometimes I have sat through his discourses, but little did I realize that the subject matter being taught had such deep meaning and philosophy. We used to watch which of his students were attentive and were absorbing the subject. Not that we understood, but based on many conversations that some were engrossed in while the class was on, I could gather that not many were interested to get to know what was being taught. My own ignorance on the subject followed me most of my life. I did read some books but did not get the real meaning and essence of these texts. It is only now that through Prabha Devi, who has showered her grace by staying with us during the winter season, that I have slowly started appreciating the doctrine of Kashmir Śaivism. I am still not able to devote as much time as I should. Nevertheless, listening to his commentaries and reading his books, some of which have been printed only lately, I now feel that one should have spent time to listen to Prabhaji who in the style of her Master, makes things very easy and comprehensible for persons like me to understand. It is clear that Śaivism is not concerned with only speculative and pure thought but is a synthesis of religion, philosophy and ethics. At times this philosophy looks very complicated, but by listening to his remarks and interpretation, which I sometimes do through the tapes that have been recorded of his discourses, the jigsaw just disappears and all the pieces that were not fitting would find their own places. The questions would slowly disappear and the answers would unfold automatically. In fact, if one concentrates on his teachings over a period of time, one finds that you do not even need answers. The silence and the quietness overpowers the noise of reading and communicating.

Knowledge-seeking can also boost one's ego. Swamiji's teachings can shift the balance from the ego of individual I to the Universal I. In order to get the best out of a Master like Swamiji, one has to put aside one's ego and knowledge. The *jñāna-*

yoga has to help one to reach thoughtlessness, a state of pure consciousness. Prabhaji once told us the following incident, at a function held at Īśvara Āśrama at DLF, Gurgaon, in honour of her being bestowed an award in the memory of Thakur Jaideva Singh. This award was given by Trika Interreligious Trust, Varanasi. Prabhaji narrated that when Thakur Jaideva Singh approached Swamiji to learn certain texts and understand Śaivism, Swamiji asked him if he wanted to learn as a scholar that he was, or as an ignorant person. The prompt reply came, "as an ignorant person." Swamiji then told him that now he could teach him, and now he would not only be able to grasp the subject but also develop a feel for it. Through Swamiji's teachings, for the first time, the cosmic nature and edifice of Kashmir Śaivism moved outside the Himalayan state into the whole of India, and to many parts of the world.

Swamiji would teach his disciples and help them at the same time to elevate themselves. However, one question that always arises in the mind of many is why is it that not many of his devotees, except a few, could grasp the subject and learn from his teachings. It is difficult to find an answer! I feel the problem has been with the learners rather than the Master. While reading *Yogasūtras* of Patañjali its first verse as commented by Swami Satchidananda reads:

> Now when a sincere seeker approaches an enlightened teacher, with the right attitude of discipline (viz. free from preconceived notions and prejudices) and full of intelligent faith and receptivity, and with right spirit of enquiry at the right time and right place, communication of *yoga* takes place.

Another *śloka* composed by Acharya Rameshvar Jha, when translated, reads as:

> When the sun shines all living beings get into action and positive energy flows. However some organisms, like the owl, get away form the shining bright light. The fault is in the nature of the owl and not in the Sun.

This question I also once asked Prabha Devi. She told me that Swamiji knew that only few are able to grasp his teachings and many of those who attended his discourses came only for *darśana* and not really for learning. In fact, one day he told her that the reason he asks her to leave the main door open for a long time after the devotees have boarded the bus for the city, is that all his teachings come back to the ashram as they have not been able to absorb anything in their mind. An unconcerned and non-concentrating mind cannot receive anything. *Yoga* occurs when there is vigilant watchfulness of the movement of thought.

Though I have interest in reading and understanding Śaivism, yet being a scientist by profession, I also had a conflict in my mind. Science works on different principles to explain the origin and evolution of life forms. Apparently it seems that the teachings and practice of science and spirituality follow different paths. I brought out this variance in my thoughts before Prabhaji and asked her how Swamiji would have solved this conflict. She said the teachings of Swamiji clearly state that Kashmir Śaiva thought does not interfere with one's own faith or occupations or lifestyle.

She explained that if one goes by the Śaiva philosophy then one does not see the difference. The scientist is looking at the creation of the creator. He analyses and utilizes his creations. He is trying to re-understand his own self through demystifying his own creations. On the other hand, a spiritual person who follows the grammar of Kashmir Śaivism is concentrating on the nature of the Creator, besides His worldly creations. In fact, if one is full of awareness, even by looking at creation one can feel the nature and bliss of the Creator. One is an indirect route to know the Master; the other is a direct route. She told me that while probing and understanding the beauty of life forms created by Śiva through his own free will, be aware that Śiva's *tattva* is in all of them. Enjoy his presence in all forms and actions. The doer in you should always remain in front of you physically and mentally.

Swamiji and His Disciples

The other aspect of Swamiji's personality rare to find was his concern for his disciples and devotees. This part of his godly quality came to the fore at the time of passing away of Sharika Devi. Through his teachings and yogic power, and by her own efforts as a devoted and committed *śiṣyā*, Sharikaji had herself reached the pinnacle of self-realization and had reached the highest state of God-consciousness. On many occasions on his birthday he used to tell Sharikaji to distribute *prasāda*. In fact, at the time of morning prayer on his birthdays, when he was immersed in *samādhi*, he used to ask Sharikaji to sit next to him. In this connection an incident was told to me by Prabha Devi. On one such occasion, some of the persons in the ashram objected to Sharikaji sitting next to Swamiji. They were adamant that this should not be allowed. Though not approving of what was being asked of him, he hesitatingly told Sharikaji if she would mind sitting outside the *maṇḍapa* (open room) that was built near the ashram house, and where Swamiji and Sharikaji and Prabhaji used to sit on the occasion of his birthdays for *Gurustuti pūjā*. She in her gracious way accepted the instructions from her Guru as an order, but was not too happy that he had to do this after having been told by someone! As the preparations for his birthday *pūjā* were going on, during the night it suddenly started raining very heavily. And the rain would not stop. When Swamiji was contacted he said that it is only Sharikaji who could do something. "This is happening since you made me change the sitting place of Sharika." He then went to Sharikaji and told her that we will not alter the traditions of the ashram and we will retain the sitting arrangement as has been the practice. After a moment of silence she said she was happy to sit at the feet of her Guru. Nevertheless, within an hour the rain stopped and the morning *pūjā* was performed as usual. Swamiji knew that Sharikaji has reached a higher state of which he was proud. He used to ask the devotees to celebrate Sharikaji's birthday and he himself used to take part in the celebration.

The legal Will of Swamiji had empowered Sharikaji to take all the decisions about the ashram. She was to be consulted by other trustees for performing the activities of the ashram after he has taken *nirvāṇa*. In an interview with Mother Alice, he told her: "Once I leave this body, I will be able to act and see beyond the limits imposed presently on me by this body." It is not clear, but Sharikaji by her own will probably got an inclination of the wishes of her Guru. Being an inward-looking saint, she would not have liked to take such a responsibility. At the same time, she would always respect any orders from Swamiji. In order to get away from such worldly activities she left her mortal body before Swamiji. In fact, she once asked Swamiji that he must ask for more time from God and continue to bless his devotees and carry on his teachings. This was done so that she would leave this mortal world before him.

On February 2, 1991, I got a call that Deviji was no more and Swamiji would be reaching Jammu from Srinagar. Her body was laid to rest at Gandhi Nagar in the house of Shri Motilal Sopory, my eldest brother. What followed at Srinagar and how Swamiji bade farewell to Sharikaji, who was sick then, has been amply recorded in an article written by Motilalji in *Śraddhārcan*. Before bidding her farewell at Ishber he showed her a mirror and said: "Now look at the real Sharika Bhagavatī!." I was told that when Motilalji, along with his sister, reached Srinagar to bring Deviji to Jammu, he made them fast for three days and then only allowed them to take her. It was a coincidence that at that time Dr Bettina had also reached Srinagar and received Deviji's last blessings.

Along with a few of his devotees I left Delhi in a taxi. However, we reached late by mid-night and by that time the last rites had been performed by Swamiji. Not following the normal protocol Swamiji had delayed taking the body to the burning *ghāṭa* till sunset. Normally the last rites are performed before sunset. When asked, he said that she was a *kanyā*, a virgin and hence the rays of the sun should not fall on her.

We were told that the day Swamiji reached Jammu, he performed *tāṇḍava* dance in front of the body of Sharikaji and did not allow anybody to shed tears. However, he did mention to Asha Sopory that he was now a pauper. While tying a knot on the photograph of Sharika Devi, he said that Sharika never stayed away from him. For the same reason he kept the earthen pots containing the ashes in his own room. Swamiji also went to Hardwar to perform the last rites himself. He had earlier mentioned that he would follow Sharika after six months and that he had sent her early to make preparations for his arrival. That is exactly what happened. He also left his mortal body within six months.

The day after our arrival in Jammu, all of us who had come from Delhi, went to see Swamiji. He was sitting in a *shamiana* (tent) and many persons were sitting around. As we entered and bowed in reverence, on looking at one of his devotees, he said "here comes a big fraud." This is one occasion I felt very bad. I started thinking how come a Master who has reached the glory of Śiva could utter such words towards his close disciple. This thing remained in my mind and I could never give a meaning to his utterance. It is only now after 15 years of those spoken words, that I have realized what he wanted us to know about the personality of the subject. Having followed the events that have taken place in the Īśvara Āśrama since last few years I realize the scanning ability of Swamiji of any person who came before him. His sight was like X-rays which could see all that one was planning and thinking. I myself had experiences of this on many earlier occasions. At one time when he was at Mr Kachru's place, I had taken Sharikaji and Prabhaji to meet him. Not everybody was allowed inside. However, after some time I was called in. He asked me if I had shown the Lotus temple to Sharika. This was something we had discussed only that morning at home. I told him that I was planning to do that. He immediately got up and said: "Let us go now and show the temple to Sharika."

One day at Jammu, when Sharikaji's 11th day *śrāddha pūjā* was going on, he called my brother Suresh, who was then Manager in the Government Printing Press, to get a *śloka* printed and distribute it to all. That was the time he wrote the following *śloka* in his own handwriting for Sharika Devi and later asked one and all to recite.

para-bhairava-līnyai parāśaktyai śrī śārikādevyai namo namaḥ ||

After Sharikaji's passing away, during 1991, Swamiji was once staying at Mr Dhar's house at Vasant Kunj, Delhi. I got a call that Swamiji was looking for Mohanlal, my uncle, who was staying with us at JNU. He had gone out and we frantically tried to contact him. When my uncle came, I took him to see Swamiji. On seeing my uncle he said: "The whole world is after me and here I am trying to meet you, and you are not available!" He asked my uncle to wait for some time. Later he called him and after some time I was also called to his room. That was one of the rare *darśana*s that we had of Swamiji. It was difficult to look at his face that was full of radiating energy. He asked me if I had a photograph of Sharika. I told Him that it is at my residence. He asked me to get it immediately. When I was leaving, Mr Dhar took out a photograph and gave it to him. Swamiji kept that photo with him for some time and then himself framed it and gave it to my uncle and said "Give it to others also and do *pūjā* of Sharika."

I wonder how many Gurus have done this for their *śiṣyā*? Traditionally it is always the *śiṣya* who would compose and recite hymns to worship his or her Guru. This is another facet of our Gurudeva who conferred the highest status to his disciple serving him all her life. In fact, he always bestowed love and affection on all his devotees. He poured His blessings on anyone who sought them with pure mind and devotion. This was irrespective of who the person was; may be a gardener, milkman or the Prime Minister of India. It was so easy to reach him in person. In his presence one could experience the ocean by getting oneself immersed in the ocean. He taught how to get detached from the worldly things by just concentrating on all things as the creation of Lord Śiva. "Find *Śiva-tattva* in everything." In many of his lectures he emphasizes on reaching a vigilant, watchful understanding of thought in the mind. He talks of a stillness of a different kind, a thoughtless state. He always emphasized that to reach such a state one has to constantly keep watch on one's breath — the centre-point of inhaling and exhaling. When asked how long one needs to do this, he replied, only six months. However, he said, if you miss on this point even once, then you have to repeat it for the next six months!

Swamiji also took great care of his other close *śiṣyā*, Prabha Devi. He taught her all the religious texts. He handed her many of his handwritten commentaries and wanted her to bring these to the reach of more and more persons. Today she follows his instructions, long after her Guru is no more, without any signs of moving away from the path he showed to her and to many of his devotees. Anyone who wants to learn about Kashmir Śaivism, she does so in the style of Swamiji. In his legal Will, he gave her all the rights to live in the Srinagar ashram and to use the place. She has been going to the ashram every year since 1991, even during the worst years of militancy in the state, and stays in the ashram to carry on with the teachings of Swamiji. It may be mentioned here that at the time when Sharikaji was not well and was being taken to Jammu, Prabhaji did not accompany her and stayed back with her Gurudeva. She told him: "Someone has to be here to take care of you. At this time I cannot leave you alone."

Then and Now

It was a pleasure those days to go to Srinagar ashram to meet and see Īśvara Svarūpa, the God in flesh and blood. For me he is still there. One has only to feel His presence. He responds to our deepest desires. He guides me wherever I go and whatever I do. I consider Īśvara Āśrama where Swamiji lived and still lives, as one of the most holy places. I hope the sanctity of the place will be maintained and all will be allowed to have access without any strings attached whatsoever.

In my subject of science, I classify two kinds of teachers. Those who read books and teach. Then there is the other class, who conduct the experiments themselves and incorporate their own experience along with the published work. It is the second kind who can communicate the truth much more convincingly. Such teachers in Śaivism are rare now. Those who have not experienced what the *turīya* state is, probably cannot explain it either! In one of his lectures at Varanasi, Swamiji gave a talk on *kuṇḍalinī*. Everybody felt what he was telling was what he had experienced himself. It was not a bookish explanation. It is difficult to find a Master like Swamiji, yet I hope someone will rise to come near that level to keep the philosophy of Kashmir Śaivism alive in the hearts of those willing to get a dip into its oceanic depths. We should look for at least having teachers of Kashmir Śaivism of the first category and encourage them. The second category of teachers with self-realization and self-experimentation will come up only with the grace of God and the Will of Swamiji. Presently I see only Prabhaji in this slot. I may be biased and may be ignorant too!

Swamiji I bow to thee a million times. Shower me with your blessings as always. I am sure you will continue to enlighten many minds through your written and spoken words, and bring peace and prosperity to all your devotees. Lead us into Divine thoughts!

13

My Gurudeva

Motilal Sopory

SWAMI Lakshman Joo was my uncle and my Master. Two peculiar things about Swamiji used to strike me in my early childhood: He was a bachelor, unlike his brothers, and that he did not live in his parental house. This was situated in Fateh Kadal where the rest of Swamiji's family — his parents, brothers, sisters, sisters-in-law, other cousins and their children used to live. For Swamiji there was a separate house, about a quarter of a kilometre away. It was called "Marbal," and it was situated on the banks of some interior water bodies of the famous Dal Lake. The atmosphere at this place was really superb. Even at this stage of my life, when I want to concentrate, I can visualize Swamiji sitting on a folding easy chair, and I sitting in front of him on the plush green grass, gazing at him. The scene becomes so vivid and powerful that, left to myself, I would not like to come out of it.

I recall an event at "Marbal." In 1935-36 my father's sister Prabha Devi and myself, both around ten or eleven years of age, were at "Marbal." Swamiji asked us to memorize some verses of *Saṁgrahastotra* of Utpaladeva's *Śivastotrāvali*, and if we did that, he would give us a *kandi kulcha*, a sort of Kashmiri sweet. Both of us started on the job, without of course disturbing the peaceful atmosphere prevailing there, and did that to the entire satisfaction of Swamiji. We of course got our promised reward, but along with that the realization that Swamiji was not only our maternal uncle, but much more than that. I realized that he was a personality quite different from the others. He appeared to me to be a guide who could lead us from darkness to light and put us on the right path. As time passed, the "Mamu" (maternal uncle) in him faded away, giving place to a divine soul: Swami Īśvara Svarūpa, a name given to him by Devi Sharikaji.

In those days, i.e. in the early 1930s, Swamiji had interaction mainly with the members of his family, who would visit him at "Marbal." His Guru was Sri Swami Mahtab Kak, and Paṇḍit Sri Maheśvara Razdan taught him Sanskrit. He did not have the usual schooling except up to eighth or ninth standard. His eldest sister "Jigri" used to relate anecdotes about Swamiji so graphically that we children would sit around her and listen to her with rapt attention. We would listen to the events such as when Swamiji was born and how Swami Rāma, his *paramaguru*, would shower blessings on the child. Even in his boyhood Swamiji used to tell his sisters and other cousins that he was in search of *Baḍe Bod* — the Overlord of all lords. Even in his cradle he used to get into a trance. On one such occasion, when the mother noticed the infant motionless in his cradle, she rushed to Swami Rāma in her anxiety. Swami Rāma is reported to have smiled it away and instead asked her to apply some butter on the head of the child, instructing her not to get perturbed on such an occasion, nor to disturb the baby.

Swami Rāma was aware of the greatness of the infant. Even when Swamiji's mother was in the family way, Swami Rāma had pronounced that a great soul was coming into this world. It was Swami Rāma who gave the name of "Lakshman" to our Gurudeva — he being Rāma himself! The spiritual relationship between the two was intimate and complete. They knew each other well enough as the subsequent events reveal. These cannot obviously be described here, they would be the subject matter of a full biography of Swamiji.

It was a landmark in the life of Swamiji when Devi Sharikaji became his first disciple. Devi Sharika was the younger sister of my father. It was in the late 1920s that Devi Sharika became the disciple of Swamiji. A young girl in her early teens becoming a saint was not common those days — as it is unusual even today! Deviji's younger brother, Mohanlal Sopory, would accompany her whenever she would visit the cottage of Swamiji. These two, sister and brother, were the earliest disciples who had very close proximity and who received *dīkṣā* from Swamiji. While the sister chose to be a saint, her brother had to become a *gṛhasthī* (householder), as ordered by Swamiji.

My father objected to the encouragement which Devi Sharika received from our Gurudeva, to choose the path of a hermit. He felt that this would jeopardize the prospects of her marriage. My father sent a letter to Swamiji using strong language. I would like to quote from the reply which my father received from Swamiji in 1928:

> Thy respected self does not understand the nowadays situation of blessed Sharika. She should not be advised by thyself in such a way, for her flaming *bhakti* towards the Lord of lords has totally defeated the whole Mayavic universe. Thy respected self may, I fear, commit sin in advising her in future in such a way. I do not mean to say that you should allow her to come to my cottage; that you should never do, but what I mean is that nowadays she is very weak in her physics (Swamiji means "physique") and by marrying her thy respected self may, I fear, prove the end of her precious and devotional life also. Sir, such Devis are rarely found in this world of pains. Her holy existence in your own house will prove the result of thousands of good *karmas* of the past *janmas*, if she lives long. Dear Jawarharlalji, do not get deep into the saying of others.

This letter has been preserved as a treasure, first by my father who received it, and later by me, till date.

My father and his parents had to yield after receiving Swamiji's letter. Devi Sharikaji became the soul of the ashram at Ishber. Along with Swamiji and later Devi Prabhaji they lived in the ashram, severing all worldly ties.

Swamiji was very close to my family, not only because of Deviji, but also because of my grandparents whom Swamiji respected very much. I hardly recall any important event in our family which was not witnessed by Swamiji. He would bestow his blessings on us, either directly or through miracles. He would also restore the emotional balance in our family in the event of a tragedy.

I had the privilege of living in the company of Swamiji and Devi Sharikaji at the ashram at Ishber. During my winter vacation, for about three months or so, from Christmas to the end of February, I used to shift along with all my school books to Ishber and live in the ashram. I was then in my secondary classes. This was in the winters of 1936, 1937 and 1938. It was a great opportunity for me to be so close to Swamiji. There used to be only four of us — Swamiji, Devi Sharikaji, myself and a cook. Devi Prabhaji joined the ashram later. For days together, we would not see any visitor. Those were the days when there was no bus service to Ishber. The only conveyance available were a few *toṅgās* (horse carts) which would ply between Ishber and Srinagar. On some occasions Swamiji would take me to Amirakadal, the main shopping centre of Srinagar, on bicycles, crushing the snow on the boulevard which skirts the Dal Lake. Swamiji would on such occasions often lay down a condition, that I would not insist to visit my parental house in the city. This was an order which was readily accepted. Probably Swamiji wanted to test my endurance to live in seclusion.

I used to enjoy playing with snow. Swamiji would also join me sometimes. A lot of fun would follow when we would throw snow balls on each other without reservation. The time I spent in the ashram in those three winters had a decisive influence to mould my way of thinking and functioning, not only as a student but subsequently as a civil servant. Swamiji's company taught me many a virtue, specially discipline, punctuality, judicious spending and avoiding waste. Moreover it moulded me into a "never-sit-idle type of a person."

As the number of disciples started growing and I joined college and university away from Srinagar, I could not afford to live in the ashram for long durations, as I did in my school days. There were only occasional visits. However, on occasions like the birthday of Swamiji and other *yajñas*, a visit to the ashram was a must. In the later years, four to five thousand people would visit the ashram on the auspicious occasion of Swamiji's birthday. It was a deep joy to see Swamiji himself distributing *prasāda* to his devotees, lined up in devotion for hours.

On Sundays Swamiji would teach his devotees. Regular classes were held. The main theme was Kashmir Śaivism and its basic texts. Entry to the ashram was restricted on other days. Besides, scholars from all over the world would come to learn Kashmir Śaivism from Swamiji. In some cases special classes would be held for them. When the classes would be over, all were supposed to leave the ashram in the evening, barring the permanent residents.

When I look back on the events and activities of the ashram over the last three to four decades, my only regret is that I had to keep myself away, being a very busy civil servant. I had decided in my mind to re-establish my close contact with Swamiji and the ashram activities after my retirement. Somehow I could not venture to attempt anything unless I could do it seriously. But this was a mistake, because by the time I could find myself free and fit enough to be wholeheartedly at the service of my master, it was too late in the day.

When Devi Sharikaji got very ill in January 1991, I was summoned to Srinagar by Swamiji. My sister Sarojani Ganjoo and myself flew to Srinagar from Jammu on 27th of January. Swamiji wanted that Deviji should be taken to Jammu — obviously as things were not normal in Srinagar.[1] We flew back along with Deviji on 29th January. Deviji was made to lie down on the rear seat of the car, to take us to Srinagar Airport. When the car was about to leave, Swamiji asked Deviji to sit up. He opened the door of the Amṛteśvara Bhairava Temple and asked her to have *darśana* of the temple. Deviji, who was as if in a coma, opened her eyes wide and looked at the *Śivaliṅga* as ordered by Swamiji. Swamiji also made her look in a mirror. In a loud voice Swamiji told her to have *darśana* of Shārikā Devī. This also she did. Swamiji then walked out of the ashram in the snow and followed the car slowly for some distance. He then gave us a send-off in a manner which implied that Devi Sharika was never to return.

This is what exactly happened. Deviji achieved *nirvāṇa* in Jammu on second of February, 1991. Swamiji was promptly informed at midnight. He along with Devi Prabhaji and others flew to Jammu in the morning hours. Instructions were communicated in advance by Swamiji that the body of Deviji be kept as it was and that he would supervise all the ceremonies himself. This is what he did. When Swamiji reached Gandhi Nagar, he started with a *tāṇḍava nṛtya*[2] in the room where Deviji was lying. What Swamiji had said about Deviji in 1928, in his letter to my father, was translated into action on this day by Swamiji himself, by his words and deeds, and the manner in which he performed the rituals with the body for the whole day. Everyone around was alert. When the body was being carried to the cremation-ground, Swamiji moved up to the gate and in a loud voice spoke to Deviji that he would also follow soon. This happened, six months later the same year, in September 1991, Swamiji left his mortal body, leaving all of us rudderless.

During the days of Sharika Devi's mourning, Swamiji continued to stay with

---

1. Terrorism had already engulfed Kashmir and medical services were difficult to avail (ed.).
2. Śiva's dance of creation and destruction.

us at Gandhi Nagar, Jammu. I was able to re-establish the close contact with Swamiji and I felt the same warmth as I used to feel at "Marbal." My wife Asha Sopory being a disciple herself carried out the orders of Swamiji meticulously. During that time the place was visited by hundreds of devotees. Due to Swamiji's and Deviji's blessings we were not found wanting. It is only painful to think that the two great souls could not be with us for some more years.

14

I Saw Śiva in Him

Arunditi Raina (Bhabhi)

I WAS very young, only seventeen years, when I got married to Nilkanth Raina, Swami Lakshman Joo's brother, who had lost his first wife. I had to look after his children from the first marriage. "Bhai Sahab" (as everybody called Sri Nilkanthji, being the brother of Swamiji) was only three years younger to his saintly brother who was at the same time his Guru. In the early years of my marriage Swamiji used to live in the old ashram on the slope of Ishvar Parvat, the hill forming the backdrop also of his later Īśvara Āśrama lower down. Whenever we went to see Swamiji, I had only one feeling: we are going to have the *darśana* of Śiva — and I saw only the divinity in Him. Bhai Sahab, my husband, was devoted to his elder brother since childhood, and he became himself a higly elevated soul, who realized the Supreme by grace of his Guru-brother. Although of a shy and silent nature, which was hiding his spiritual greatness from other devotees, he shared with me many memories of his childhood and of the experiences he had with Swamiji. These are some of the recollections from his accounts.

Swami Rāma Joo was the Guru of their parents. When Swamiji's mother was expecting him, he directed her to live in a houseboat. When the time of delivery came, he instructed her to return to the house, along with the nurse who was looking after her. Swami Rāma Joo was in the same house, and he went into deep *samādhi* for two hours, covering his face with a veil. When he came out of his *samādhi* and removed the veil, he asked what had happened. By that time Swamiji was just born and he could hear his first cry. At that moment he got up and started dancing and singing — although his legs had become almost paralysed due to his long hours in *samādhi*. It was then that he declared: "I am Rāma and he is Lakshman!" giving the child the name.

As Swamiji grew up he used to get into states of trance which his parents took as a sign of some disorder, and they got extremely worried. At the age of five, they consulted a doctor who expressed his helplessness in this case. Again they brought the boy to Swami Rāma who exclaimed: "I wish I had the same state of divine absorption — this is a sign of sainthood and not any disease!" He also advised his parents to apply some butter on his head when the trance continued for a long time.

From the time Bhai Sahab could remember, they used to sleep in the same room, but even in childhood Swamiji had a *pūjā* room upstairs where he used to go and sit in meditation. Often, as the children were playing, he would suddenly call his brother to go up for *pūjā* — *pūjā* meaning only silent meditation. He made his brother sit beside him for one hour, and asked him to put his body straight in case he was bending sideways or forward. When Nilkanth asked Swamiji what he was doing during that time, his answer came spontaneously: "I am meeting *Baḍe Bod*" (Kashmiri for "the greatest of the great"). When his younger brother asked who he was? Swamiji answered: "He is my all-in-all, the Greatest of the great, he is also yours and everybody's."

After the death of Swami Rāma, when Swamiji was seven years old, he was sent to Swami Mahtab Kak, a *siddha* and his chief disciple, and he became his devoted disciple. He attended school up to 8th standard, but his heart and mind was with his Guru. When Mahtab Kak was living in Chandpora (near Harwan), Swamiji used to go early morning to him for instruction and for serving him. At that time there was no bus service, and his father had given him a motorcycle, at that time of horse-carts a rarity! so that he could go to his Guru. But he often came late to school, which angered his teacher. Once the teacher beat him seven times with a stick on his hand. After that the teacher became sick and had a severe fever for seven days — he then realized that it was a punishment for beating a saint.

In the early part of the twentieth century Kashmiris used to marry their children at a very young age, even between eight and ten years. Swamiji was about twelve when his parents made an attempt to arrange his marriage. The father of the proposed girl came to see Swamiji and to arrange the marriage of his daughter. Swamiji got so angry at this proposal that he drove the man out of the house with a stick! He sat on his *āsana* and declared to his parents: "I do not want to get married — I am already married — to Lord Śiva!"

During these years before Swamiji left home Bhai Sahab (Nilkanth) used to serve him and follow his instructions faithfully.

At the age of sixteen Swamiji took formal *dīkṣā* from Mahtab Kak. He was disturbed in his *sādhanā* because the family was very big and with many brothers and sisters there were about 25 who took meals together. He needed solitude for his spiritual experiences to unfold. When he could not retain himself from the call of the Absolute — *Baḍe Bod* — he escaped from home at the age of eighteen, seeking solitude (the account of his flight from home and the search for him is given elsewhere).

Brother Nilkanth later took over the responsibilities for their father's houseboat factory which Swamiji did not want to carry on, being totally absorbed in his private studies of Sanskrit and of the Śaiva scriptures, and in his spiritual practice.

After looking after my family duties I also became Swamiji's disciple, and since we had taken a house in Ishber in the vicinity of Swamiji's ashram in the later years, I was fortunate to serve the Master in practical ways, such as ironing his clothes and assisting the Devis in their household work. Thus I was given the chance to be in the divine presence and to observe his power. His one word was powerful enough. Once I had neuralgia in my right hand, due to overwork, and I felt very bad that I would not be able to use the iron to press Swamiji's clothes. I came to him and told him of my trouble. He only looked at me with that piercing glance and said forcefully: "Nothing has happened!" At that very moment my hand got alright and I could continue my service.

My daughter Uma (nicknamed Babli) had two sons, and they lived in Jammu where they attended school. One morning I went to the ashram and Swamiji, seeing me, immediately advised me strongly to go to Jammu, something has happened to my grandchildren. He had seen the accident in which the two boys were almost killed. I was shocked and alarmed, but he reassured me: "I am with you, they will be alright." He arranged for my proceeding to Jammu where I found everything correct as Swamiji had said. Although the boys were unconscious and not out of danger, Swamiji predicted the exact time when they would come out and recover.

There were many instances showing his power, but he used to hide it. The most important power was the divinity radiating from him and transforming us in every action of our life.

Jaya Gurudeva!

15

In Search of Myself

Rajan Khosa

DURING my nomadic life, visiting places of spiritual importance from 1986 to 1990, I stayed beside Īśvara Āśrama, near Nishat, Srinagar. In the year 1987 to 1988, I lived the waking part of my life, for a year with the man known to be the last living legend of Kashmir Śaivism, whose name was formally written by scholars as Swami Lakshman Joo Raina, or simply Swamiji, and who viewed many scholarly conventions with utter contempt and professed practising-philosophy as the only way of being.

It was Dr Kapila Vatsyayan, my mentor in New Delhi, who sensed what I was going through at the time. She thought I was asking her questions that only Lakshman Joo would have the answers to. But then I had to make the journey up to the Himalayas and seek the answers. I am so glad that she at that tender age, opened that window, and also introduced me to Dr Bettina Bäumer in Varanasi who finally became a Guru *bahin* and kept feeding the fire in me with all her knowledge.

Lakshman Joo lived a life that suited someone placed in the ranks of a lineage of "saints." He had a natural persona and dignity to win the place of a leader. I walked up to his door one bleak winter morning. He was 79 years old at the time, and I was arrogant 26. As you know, it is always our first meeting that we remember, and I then ended up spending all my waking hours for that year in his presence.

I sometimes wonder what he really thought about me at that time? "I have come," that is how I had introduced myself, subtly implying that I had visited him in my dreams before, I always imagined him waiting for that perfect disciple at his door, to which I had finally arrived. He flared, "Who are you?" (read, "Who the

HELL are you"?). His tone of voice scared me, I shuddered, "I am an artist," which he seemed to like. He commented, "artists are very spiritual people," at the same time throwing me out of his compound, I imagined he was about to throw his shoe at me.

I don't know what made me just sit at his door for hours until he opened that door again and called me inside. (Fortunately it was snowing and he could see my adamant, lovelorn face from his window.) How I yearned for his acceptance day after day. Even a glance of his on me in the crowd will send me into an epiphany.

Lakshman Joo did not meet people's eyes. No matter who you were, a statesman or a beggar, he did not meet your eyes. His eyes always remained transfixed on another reality; a reality that seemed to be fixed beyond thought. There was that glassiness in his Kashmiri-blue eyes that said he was living at better pastures. He only every now and then disconnected from "it" and attended to the world around him. And when he attended to something or somebody, he was utterly focused. The concentration on his face showed what concentration can possibly be.[1] Well these are just some of the qualities that made you fall in love with that man. Swamiji at 79 was irresistible.

What kind of a *sādhu* was this Swami Lakshman Joo? Everywhere, other *sādhus* that you visited, you dropped some money into the donation box. But when you visited Swami Lakshman Joo, he gave you some pocket money as a gift, crispy currency notes, freshly picked up from the Jammu & Kashmir Bank. It was a big statement he made. He managed his inheritance well, and earned enough from family royalties to survive gracefully. He was well known for his generosity to the majority of poor Muslim neighbours. He was really what you could dream of as a wise king.

His father had been a rich businessman, who is said to have owned 64 houseboats in Dal Lake alone. And not to speak of his family's timber transporting business. There was a lot of goodwill for him in his town, and people looked up to him to be guided and told, like only the legends are looked up at. And on each of his birthdays, 6000 people, mostly from Kashmiri rural areas, descended at his home just to congratulate him, and he responded by promising each one shelter for that night,

1. Swamiji loved the expression "one-pointed awareness."

hence the Indian Army provided the large canvas tents studded around his home for the occasion.

Normal days were slow at his home. Swamiji talked rarely. And when he did, the disciples knew it was time to listen. Specially "open Sundays" was an exercise for him to experience his own *śakti* as he would sit on a pedestal, gazing away from the congregated people in complete silence, while expecting all to remain silent, as if silently saying, in this very silence was the door . . . Has anyone ever forced you to experience silence, think about it, anyone in your life? It was as if this man had integrated the *mauna vrata* (fasting on speech, or vow of silence) in his daily life.

Then people would drop in, they often came with gifts, and richer ones generally showed off their wealth with gifts like fine utilitarian household objects. Swamiji would then painstakingly distribute it all amongst the congregation as *prasāda*. Rich guests often hated to see the very gift that they parted with, passed on to the one they simply could not stand.

In his day-to-day life, gifts were acceptable to him but not cash. If anyone tried to offer Swamiji cash, he or she was simply insulted and thrown out of the house. And this humiliation of the guest that he had become so famous for, no devotee wanted to experience, they better keep small contact with him than lose him. They wanted his individual attention; even his glance falling on them was a blessing.

One man used to bring a Sunday newspaper, and give it as a gift to Swamiji (yes there were disciples who thought they were smarter than him), and Swamiji would never pick up the newspaper for the course of next many hours, and then suddenly to a departing devotee he would give it as *prasāda*. All the onlookers understood his utter silence maintained towards the daily news. It impacted him little. What was Kashmir going through at the time, was never something that interested him.

I remember walking around Srinagar those days, amid grafitti on the walls, calling this land Pakistan. This was a year before Zia-ul-Haq was blown up in a plane in Pakistani skies. And this was much before I saw my Kashmiri Paṇḍit aunts and uncles in the refugee camps of New Delhi, in 1989-90, victims of systematic evacuation.

For Swamiji human behaviour was transitory. He appeared to respect the cosmic laws, and worshipped the energy that animated them. He called it God, without any shame. And that is where Tantra, to my mind, formed the backbone of his Śaivite persona.

I saw him draw Tantric diagrams on people's bodies and heal them, though he did that very rarely, sometimes to sick travellers who came from very far, and whose faith in him was intense. He made them lie down and he drew Tantric diagrams in space four inches above their bodies, reciting a few *mantra*s and gave some *prasāda*. And the recipient would be healed, in due time, sooner or later. He was famous for being able to heal chronic illnesses, in rural parts of Kashmir.

Sometimes I ask myself, what kept me there, in his attractive gaze, as if basking under his sun? The answer is: I do not know.

All I can say — there is a time in one's life when someone else seems to have all the answers to the world's mystery. Someone who could be our strongest ally in this journey called life, and who could appease the various cosmic forces that may act upon us.

We sat at his feet, just in silence. Nothing was ever said for hours at a time. The silence was palpable, it reverberated, as if with a distant *hum*. It was interspersed by daily chores. *Kehwā*, the Kashmiri tea, in brass bowls, and *parāṭhā*s that tasted more than heaven. We would sit there, three of us — like three servants, privileged to bask in the sun. They were Australians and I was a Kashmiri brahmin (whenever, and if, he did speak to us all, it was in English, and sometimes to me in Kashmiri).

First it took some time getting used to this, but soon it became knowledge that such is life at Swamiji's home which turned into an ashram on Sundays — our day of entertainment, when outsiders were allowed to visit and revere our venerated old man.

After my "initiation" took place (which took three months for him to consider me worthy of it), every day was like being in a *gurukula*.[2] My day was spent meditating and chanting, along with long silent walks, and working in Swamiji's orchard, climbing trees and cutting firewood. Or doing the minute nit-picking of grains and herbs that Swamiji would need for his large congregational fire sacrifices.

2. Family of Guru and his disciples.

Even in summers you could see the shining snowy Himalayan peaks that stood proud daring the skies. Being in that space was like a double bite, on the skin and the atmosphere. May I say, all was severe but serene.

Sometimes I would ask Swamiji the meaning of a verse from the *Śivasūtras* (the seminal Śaivite text), and he would say, his teacher sat at it for years, before turning a single page; politely implying *Sūtra*s had deeper meanings, scriptures had to be respected and given their due. I was young and he was shaping my attitudes. And after my initiation, when I started asking him questions about my meditational experiences, he would often ask, did I not feel so and so *cakra*, was there no physical throbbing there, he will ask about the feelings of warmth and cold, colours, and then leave the rest to my good imagination. He knew that I was no scholar, he took every opportunity to discourage me from my enthusiasm for scholarly pursuit.

And I imagined that he implied that all bodily systems were different, each one of us had to find our own tools of assessment in this meditational laboratory. And the first thing you do here is banish fantasy, and stupid vanity of becoming a *sādhu*. Well, at this time, I had not learnt that I am the Reality. Until here, in my life, there still was the searcher and the searched.

As I read the above, what I have just written, it is as if I pull open the lid. . . .

And Swamiji pulled open that lid, completely challenging me, in ways that are just too inexplicable, in ways in which only teachers can transform disciples. Yes, transference of energy happens, even in a glance. . . .

Today I live in Mumbai, overlooking the sea from my window. Even my dawn is punctuated with clothes-beatings of *dhobī*s in the yard below, and I can hear the city's cocks crow. *Yoga* is breathing this city's pollution with salty aroma of the sea, yet humanity wakes up in Mumbai to a hum of positive energy.

But Swamiji's house had a unique silence. Now it belongs to an imaginary silent place in my heart. A place where calmness of the ocean gives rise to all the human grief and expels it. A place where there are no comparisons, no hopes and no regrets, a place of being, archaic and joyfully present.

When life is fragile we can truly laugh. When life is on the edge, we are everything and nothing at the same time, we are alive.

In the fast-changing world of today, two decades later, I am wondering what is the value of such an experience, and why so many of us at some point or the other in life, begin seeking something different. When we run away from gossip, when we get bored of our jobs, when we have the impulse to run away from our families and children; when we suddenly achieve success and witness its futility; when we seek love that is beyond the physical, or when sometimes we touch the same very love through the physical.

It is this inexplicable search that Lakshman Joo was all about. He just became a living mirror for people to see within themselves.

He also fulfilled an archetype of an old wise man in my psyche that I at that young age was irresistibly seeking. Metaphorically, unless we find the wise man, worship and challenge him, and then demolish him, unless we do that we are never reborn as the awakened one.

All awakenings have their price to pay. And here there are million stories of Gurus doing the hard work, bearing blame and pride, to help the caterpillar disciple to break into wings.

Wings of inner propulsions. This unknowable energy, so present, bursts through us like life, to perform our daily acts of worship.

Tomorrow's child will only know the keyboard, and handwriting might be extinct by then. These saints, it can't be helped, will turn into photos, busts and books that warm a million hearts. Yet the life goes on, irresistibly.

16

Sitting Under a Mighty Chinar Tree

Sharad Chandra

THERE are many who are grateful to Paul Reps for helping them to discover great Swami Lakshman Joo and his marvellous hermitage and the splendour of Kashmir Śaivism. I am one of those.

After reading Paul Reps' *Zen Flesh Zen Bones* I was spellbound, not only with the encounter with *Vijñāna Bhairava*, but I had a great wish to meet Swamiji whom Reps described in so few words, yet it left a deep impression. A little later I found an article about him in some magazine with his picture; it was a very unusual photo but then all his photos are unusual because very few people remain so unaffected while facing a camera. Then I came across an introductory book about Kashmir Śaivism. Though the book was somewhat dull one could discern the majestic beauty of the language of that philosophical school, the structural grandeur, depth and the delicate mystery rooted in human existence and the whole creation itself. I then decided to visit Kashmir whenever the opportunity came and also meet the great man at his hermitage.

Some time later one night I woke up with a marvellous dream: A friend gave me a very exquisitely carved gift box and asked me to carry it to a friend but warned me that it was to be a most difficult journey. I had to traverse the entire length of the Himalayas, run from peak to peak and do it in a single day. I had to start at sunrise and complete the journey at sunset. There I was to meet a friend of his to whom I should deliver the gift box.

I set out the very next morning and by the evening I had traversed the entire Himalayan ranges. At the end of the journey I found nobody waiting there. After the sunset and much waiting I decided to open the gift box and found the message — "you yourself are that friend and this Himalayan journey was the gift meant for you." It was in 1977.

Well, within a week I received a letter from Katyayani asking if I could plan a journey to Amarnath. I was overjoyed. After our Amarnath pilgrimage we went to Srinagar, and the very next day we rushed to the hermitage of Swamiji. Luckily it was the day of his weekly public audience.

We learnt that he was at the Gupta Gaṅga Centre, so we went there and there we learnt that he had just gone back. Probably he was to give classes at Guptagaṅgā but the previous night there was a big storm and a great giant of a *chinar* tree had fallen, covering a large part of the garden. It seems that Swamiji had organized the small crowd of the regular visitors and engaged them into a cleaning up operation that was a delight to see.

Different groups were doing different things. A group was busy sawing thick branches, another group was axing down smaller branches, still another group was busy chopping off still smaller branches with garden choppers. Some were breaking off tender branches.

Women had formed separate groups, they were taking off leaves and breaking stems and tender branches and arranging them in separate heaps. It was a swift operation, a clean job and they were doing it smilingly with dexterity and devotion, the job had to be finished on time. We could see that Swamiji had a sense of urgency and order.

There were other groups of ladies busy with cooking and serving the workers by turn. They offered us a meal but our help was refused.

In the afternoon we went to the hermitage. Sharikaji sat near the gate brooding, upon enquiring she silently pointed the way without looking up. In the spacious clearing in the garden we found Swamiji sitting on a chair facing a small crowd of 150 or so visitors. Here he was "Lakshman Joo, tall and shining" as described by Paul Reps. One could see he was majestic like a king, he had a certain innate authority. There was a certain elegance and depth in his presence and a totally unaffected air. His calm gaze followed us. We saluted him and sat down behind the crowd. One thing about his gaze, it was deep and steady, his expression never changed even slightly when total strangers arrived, he just calmly observed them.

He looked at us a few times, then looked at other visitors, he talked gently and graciously with some, with others he joked and laughed like a child. Then suddenly he would look away from all, then he had a solitary and distant gaze. There was deep melancholy in it. Did it come from much solitude or from a certain visionary richness of which he was able to share very little because there were so few takers?

Then suddenly he turned his attention towards us and shot a couple of perplexing and indiscreet questions over the heads of the crowd; it was very unpleasant to hear personal questions publicly! Instead of being angry I looked at Katyayani and laughed, a mildly angry retort came from Swamiji: "you need not laugh!" He had a sonorous voice. He looked away, then after some time he looked again and asked: "what brings you here"? I: "We thought it would be nice to have your *darśana* and always waited for this opportunity."

Swamiji very seriously said: "It is not like other *āśrama*s, we don't sing *bhajana*s here, it is a place of serious studies." (I had known great Dr Nataraja Guru saying this to people to discourage unwanted visitors.)

"We knew this."

"How do you know about this place?"

"Through the book of Paul Reps and an article about you we came across somewhere."

A little silence: "Do you find here what was described there?"

I: "Yes Swamiji, we do." The talk was between me and Swamiji, gentle Katyayani was silent all the time.

A little later the crowd thinned but not before everyone was served delicious tea and *parāṭhā*s. Then Swamiji asked us to go near him. In the meanwhile he talked to a few other people by turn; it seemed, everyone received his attention by turn with a gaze, a smile or a few words or a joke, all with a completely unaffected manner.

Then one young man got up, he was the sole Western visitor in the crowd apart from Katyayani. He had to shout as he was at the other end: "Swamiji, I have a question." Swamiji just looked and waited. The gentleman recited a Sanskrit verse and asked: "What does this verse mean?"

Swamiji: "This verse contains the whole of Kashmir Śaivism. I shall explain it later in a class. We don't have enough time today."

Then Swamiji said: "He is my student Mark Dyczkowski."

Then I broached the subject of Kashmir Śaivism: "I realize how little I would really know about this subject, this magnificent philosophy since I don't know Sanskrit."

He calmly looked at me for some time and then said: "You will have this knowledge, you will get there!"

Finding me puzzled, he said: "Trust my words, you will get there."

Then he took out five cardamoms, counted five and gave them to me. Seeing this, some other people also asked for it, he laughed and said: "No, no, you cannot have it by asking for it." But one man just won't go away empty-handed so he gave him a fruit but he insisted on having cardamoms. "No, no, not that," and laughed like a child again.

He then asked me: "Do you know something about Kashmir Śaivism? Have you read something?"

"Very little and that too through translations only."

Then I told him about a few things I had read and when I mentioned *Abhinavagupta* by K.C. Pandey he smiled: "Oh, you have read that too, good!" Then knitting his eyebrows: "My advice to you is, don't read too much, try to understand it." I: "Anyway, I cannot read Sanskrit and I am not ready to give many years of studies to it."

He: "That is not necessary, you need not worry about that."

By then he had become very affectionate and asked: "Where do you live?"

"Swamiji, at present we are staying at Brindaban."

He smiled and said: "It is a very pure and beautiful place, I have been there once." Then he was very fatherly and very seriously said: "I would like to advise you to stay away from *guru*s, there are many wicked *guru*s there. Both of you are very innocent and young, don't ever fall into traps. You may also meet some real saints if you are lucky."

I: "We have no wish to associate with *guru*s. It is the peace and beauty of the place that attracts us there."

It was then truly the most beautiful oasis in the world. Like many other places which have been damaged seriously by unplanned growth, this place is no exception, alas!

Then there appeared Denise Hughes, we were not introduced that time, that came during the second visit a few months later. She was carrying a basket filled with peaches. She bent low to show it to Swamiji, she had a shy and fearful look of a little girl. Swamiji examined each fruit carefully then said: "I sent you to pluck fruits carefully, not too many not too fast. Some of the fruits could have stayed on the trees for some more time, what was the hurry?" There was mild pain in his voice.

Then again: "I sent you not only to pluck fruit but also to become aware of the divinity of the trees, you must do it with respect and awareness." She was slightly sad and silent after the gentle rebuke. She just nodded and withdrew.

The crowd had mostly dispersed, the twilight hour was fading fast, there was silence for a long time. Then Swamiji spoke: "Won't you be coming again? I think you will."

Then we took our leave. There was a feeling that this most unusual human being belonged so much to the sublime landscape of the valley like a great *chinar* tree.

II

Very soon in the following season of autumn we were back in the Valley. This time the mother of Katyayani wanted to visit the famed Valley, so we accompanied her. The beauty of the place in autumn was exhilarating, it was all clear, shining and so fresh.

After settling down in a wonderful houseboat the very next morning we went to the hermitage of Swamiji. We found him along with two very elderly visitors with charcoal fire on the verandah, talking in very low tones. All dressed up in winter robes looked very ancient. After offering our salutations we sat down. He didn't say a word for quite some time. He just looked at us without any change of expression, then looked away at the fire and then at the Kashmiri visitors and said very few words to them, they looked at him with such a reverence as if they were in presence of a living god. Then after some time he turned towards us: "How did you come? you didn't inform me!"

I: "We did but not getting any reply we decided to check if the letter reached."

Then he remembered: "Yes, yes, I received it, can you come tomorrow afternoon?"

As we were leaving, Katyayani's mother was saying audibly: "I don't understand people like this" She was furious. Swamiji exchanged no pleasantries, didn't even reply to our greetings, didn't even give us a pleasant look.

One may ask if he was a gentleman? To this I would say, yes, he was a gentleman very gracious and charming and a very delightful conversationalist, and entertaining host. But was he a regular gentleman as social conventions demand every time? No, despite all his very rare refinement, elegance and cosmopolitan qualities, which was amazing when one thinks that he grew up and lived in solitude, he was not a gentleman on all occasions as some would have liked with their particular demands. His moods were governed by his profound and unpredictable inner nature, he had no time for pleasantries or affected mannerism. For a newcomer it could be a real disaster sometimes.

The next day we were back, on the way we stopped at a shop specializing in lotus honey, the honey seller was a Kashmiri gentleman, he was more than 100 years old. He asked us where we were going, when we told him he raised his arms and exclaimed: "Lakshman Joo is such a splendid human being!"

We found Swamiji resting, his back turned towards us, Denise Hughes was massaging his legs, he asked her: "Did they inform me before coming?" She told him "yes, they did." He jumped up and sat down comfortably and smiling like a mischievous little boy fixed his gaze upon us and asked us the same, very personal questions he had asked a couple of months back! Hearing this, I roared with laughter and told him: "I have now caught you with your game and this time you will not succeed in upsetting me, sir! you had precisely asked these very questions last time, no?" Hearing this, he too began to laugh and we all laughed.

He was silent for a long time, then: "You look like a saint with your white *kurtā*, *luṅgī*, hair and beard.

"No, sir, I am not a saint as far as I know and have no wish to be one. I have adopted this dress since I lived in south India and it is very comfortable.

"Do you wear this kind of dress when abroad?"

"No Swamiji, there I wear trousers like everybody else."

"Why?"

"There I wear Western dress so I don't invite unnecessary attention."

"You are so right, why invite unnecessary attention?"

Conversation continued like this with intermittent silences.

"You must have met many spiritual personalities, can you tell me about them?" He asked.

"One I am meeting right now."

Smilingly he asked: "And others?"

"Well, some I met are completely unknown, some are known only to small groups and some others are widely known. . . . Among the famous J. Krishnamurti, Ānandamayī Mā, Vinoba Bhave, Gopinath Kavirajji. . . ."

When I mentioned J. Krishnamurti he appeared very pleased, his eyes shone. Later I learnt that Swamiji went to the cottage of Dr Karan Singh in Srinagar to the group meetings of Krishnamurti a few times and had told Mrs Jayakar that on hearing Krishnamurti's words he was in "ecstasy."

Then he asked me about my readings into Kashmir Śaivism in translations. I told him of the very little that I knew but when I told him about a very old translation of *Spanda Nirṇaya* in English published by the Government of Maharaja of Kashmir, he frowned: "That is a useless translation. Just a word-to-word translation . . . without understanding and experience one cannot translate such profound texts."

Then again he asked about the mystics I had met: "When you met these mystics and saints, did you ask them for teachings? What did they teach you?"

"When I met them, I asked very few questions, I preferred to remain silent and just feel their presence."

"You have a right attitude, one shouldn't ask many questions to such people."

After some time I said: "When I see you I feel I am sitting with a very ancient personage, who has seen many centuries passing before him."

With a very serious but very gracious look he pointed towards the mountain slope converging into his garden: "You know the whole of Kashmir Śaivism took shape right here!" Then he went into deep thought and remained like this for quite some time.

Katyayani asked only one question, it was about Lilian Silburn. Swamiji smiled broadly: "You know she loves me very much and treats me like a child, she is so funny, such a delightful person, not just a wonderful scholar. She visits fun-shops in Paris to find funny gifts for me. Last time she sent a big parcel, when I opened it a paper fist sprang up into my face!" Then he giggled.

Then there was a rather long spell of silence. We all were still. The whole landscape shone with an exceptional light. Everything was magical and distinct, every sound was clear. It appeared that awareness had extended to greater distances. I later wondered, how was it possible to hear rustling of faraway lotus leaves and gently creaking sounds of boats swaying in their moorings at a considerable distance and sounds of faraway mountain-streams. All of a sudden a veil had been removed from the whole creation for some time.

The long spell was broken as someone came to deliver a large steel food box wrapped up very nicely in a cloth from a friend.

"Hum, let us see what it is" Swamiji observed and with great curiosity opened the box. "Oh, we have something very nice here to go with our tea, an apple pie!" Then looking at us: "See, you chose the right day to come." "How did they know that I had guests here?" It was always like this with him, deeply serious, then suddenly like a child, playful.

Then tea came, Kashmiri tea, very delicious, served in bronze bowls. Swamiji cut the pie in precisely equal portions, then tasted from each piece, savoured and contemplated then, "yes it is well cooked, each side tastes the same." Then he gave each of us our share.

After tea, after such a happy day an unpleasant and very ridiculous drama unfolded. A young American with beard and long hair, dressed in a funny way appeared on the scene, followed by a younger man and a very young woman. The young couple looked gentle and innocent, perhaps they were following their "master" who looked very arrogant and silly and had an unfriendly, wicked look and a sarcastic smile. He probably was full of undigested "paperback mysticism."

They sat down in the furtherest corners. Swamiji just ignored them.

In the meanwhile I asked Swamiji a question: "Is it possible to enter a certain state where one would touch upon the source of all languages and know them all?"

"Yes, it is called *Parā Vāc*, I sometimes enter that state."

"Then you know all languages in that state?"

"Yes, I can, but when in that state I have no wish to know any of the languages. But I don't stay in that state for very long time. I enter into it then the door closes and I am out again."

At this stage the visiting American "master" took over the discussion. "Is there someone who throws you out?"

"No one throws me out, I am thrown out because of my inabilities."

Again the intruder asked: "Why do you wear the sacred tuft of hair on your head?"

"It is my tradition, I respect my tradition."

Then again: "Do you eat meat?"

"No, I stay away from it."

"Why? Can't you get clean meat?"

Swamiji: "I abhor it, can't you understand it?"

Then he asked: "May I sit on your seat for some time?"

"No, you can't."

"Why not? It is just a seat!"

Prabha Deviji had come, she sat down, Swamiji laughingly turned to her: "Look, he wants to sit on my seat!" All of us laughed. Again the visitor: "What is so funny? Why all of you are laughing? It is just a seat."

Then he asked if he could sit near Swamiji, when this was granted he tried to go closer by a few inches with each move and tried to share the seat even if only on the edges. This time though with a smile Swamiji was physically pushing him away. The visitor tried to force his way still closer. Now Swamiji gave him a very stern look and told him: "Behave, go back!" The fool was scared out of his wits and peevishly retreated at once and went back to the corner, his young followers had a very painful expression, they were almost in tears to see their idol come crashing down, the idol too looked pathetic and humbled, then quietly left.

It took some time before we again started from where we were earlier.

He introduced Prabhaji to us, then another elderly lady Kamlaji, then finally he introduced Denise Hughes: "She is Mrs Denise Hughes. She and her husband are my students. They have a very nice house, they have money and they have their personal Swamiji!"

Then Kamlaji and Prabhaji got up, Prabha gave me her Hindi translation of *Parā Praveśikā* and Kamlaji gave me her translation of *Pratyabhijñā Hṛdayam*. Then Swamiji sent for another book, it was his own commentary on *Krama Stotram* called *Kramanaya Dīpikā* also in Hindi. He gave me saying: "*Krama Stotram* is said to be by Abhinavagupta. It is my commentary but you have to pay for it."

It was a ridiculously cheap print, just as I was getting ready to pay he said: "You need not pay, you can have it." Then he signed it with "with my warm blessings."

I was grateful for all these gifts.

Then I asked: "Why so little is known about this profoundly beautiful philosophy?"

"It is my misfortune" was his reply. Then I told him: "However much I love the grandeur and beauty of Kashmir Śaivism, I would have to rely solely on a few translations available[1] and my knowledge will amount to a few glimpses only."

He assured me: "No, you can have this knowledge, you don't have to know Sanskrit, there is also direct teaching." Then he turned to Denise Hughes: "She and her husband don't know Sanskrit, they are receiving direct teachings from me."

Then he told her: "Please give your address and take his and you should both always stay in touch and please share with him whatever I teach you."

1. At that time; since then many translations and studies have come out.

She looked at me somewhat surprised and nodded in affirmation.

Perhaps it was too much to ask of her. If a father gives nice toys to his child then asks to share them with a visiting child, the child wouldn't like it though agreeing. I wrote her a couple of times and she never replied. However, I am glad that after many years they are letting some of those precious teachings go public.

I then asked: "Are there any other *ācārya*s besides you, in this tradition in Kashmir?" Suddenly there was a profound sadness in his gaze, he sighed and then: "None that I know of, as far as I know I am the only one, the last one." Then laughingly added: "I wish there are some and even better than me, if I come to know about them I would go to them to pay my respects."

Then I asked: "What happens after you Swamiji?"

"Well, the philosophy would be always there, I have done all I could do to the best of my abilities, the future is in the womb of the future, no use pondering about it," and laughed again.

At this point a gentleman walked in, I learnt soon, as he introduced himself, that he was a disciple of a very famous and popular *guru* whom I always regarded unworthy of notice and considered him a charlatan. He would draw from many sources and market vulgarized versions of everything he could lay his hands on, to indiscreet, uncultured and uninformed or misinformed crowds; usually his followers were noisy, arrogant, deluded and shallow, but this gentleman was extremely humble and polite. When Swamiji finally looked at him questioningly he very timidly said — "Swamiji, I am a disciple of . . . he has explained *Vijñāna Bhairava* many times, I was never satisfied, but when I read your version (he was referring to Paul Reps' version with Swamiji's help) I decided to make a pilgrimage to this place." Then Swamiji looked very graciously at him, then pointing to a spot in the garden: "Come on such and such day if you are staying for some time, I will take you there and I shall personally speak to you on this text, you will be the only student to sit with me that day."

Then: "Paul Reps was a wonderful person, he truly was a wonderful person."

"Now, I have these visitors but later we shall find enough time to sit together. You have made a long journey, I won't let you go empty-handed." Then gently laughed. The gentleman left after bowing, smiling with gratitude.

Then I think it was my last question: "Where can one find *Rudra Yāmala*?" He looked surprised: "Why are you looking for this lost text, only a fragment of it survives."

It was actually a request from a friend in Delhi, when I told him this he said gravely: "Don't search for any text for other people, search only for yourself if it is necessary." Katyayani said "Swamiji is right!" These were the very few words among others she uttered that day, the talk was mostly between Swamiji and myself, but, the whole conversation had intervals of long silences and this made it a richer experience. Later Katyayani told me: "Now I know what the word *ṛṣi* means, we had been sitting in the presence of a very great *ṛṣi* today."

The evening was turning into twilight hour and Swamiji appeared to be withdrawing into himself. Soon the last glow of twilight was fading fast. We got ready to take our leave but Swamiji was lost in deep thought. We waited but Swamiji wasn't coming out of his contemplative mood. He had a remote inward gaze but I also discerned a certain sadness and some worry, as if listening to rumblings of a distant storm that had not yet stirred. We bowed down and left silently.

It was such a wonderful day, like "Pastoral Symphony" of Beethoven, only a storm was missing but it was coming.

The evening sky was clear, the weather was peaceful when we boarded a very small and light boat. It was very pleasant, we were enjoying moving upon the tranquil waters. Suddenly the waters became choppy, at first it was windy, then very soon it was growing into a powerful storm. The sky was quickly dark. The last glow of the twilight and stars were blotted out. The storm let out terrible screams. Violent waves rose, ready to pour into the boat, the little boat appeared helplessly adrift.

Later when I read Swami Vivekananda's poem "Kali the Mother" he wrote in his houseboat on Dal Lake after a terrible storm, I could see how true was his image: "The winds howled as if 1,000 lunatics were let loose."

Then came thunders and lightning and the little boat appeared so fragile between the dark sky and the angry waves of the dark lake. Suddenly the boatman used exceptionally powerful strokes and cut across the riotous waters and brought us underwater willows growing around a very long beaten mud road going deep into the water body towards the floating vegetable gardens. The floating vegetable gardens were tossed about violently and loudly clashed in their moorings.

Then came showers and a few hailstorms. The boatman said:"If showers and hailstorm continue we are in a very serious trouble, these trees cannot protect us." He loudly prayed to Allah. Suddenly the storm vanished and there were no more showers or hailstorms after initial start. It was very cold but the sky was absolutely clear and filled with stars. The lake was still again as if nothing had happened! The boat sailed smoothly again. My thoughts went to Katyayani's mother who must have been so worried, and to Swamiji whose serene and smiling visage I could now almost see clearly. Upon reaching our houseboat we were welcomed by poor mother with great joy but emotions were choking her, she had gone through terrible worry during the storm.

III

Many years have gone since we visited Swamiji. Neither C.O. Katyayani nor I again visited Kashmir since then. Kashmir was far away. The famed haven of tourists was too expensive a place. It continues to amaze me that those three visits to the hermitage of Swamiji are still so fresh in my mind as if it was only yesterday! It is rare that so few and such brief encounters leave such a lasting impression.

But there has been a certain continuity unbroken since then and this partly I would like to share with those who revere his memory and with those who would continue to discover this most unusual phenomenon of a great human being. I would also like to add a few reflections.

Over the years I have continued to meet him though not regularly and always with some years' intervals, I am talking about dreams. Some may call it blessing, others would like to call it teachings. For me I would use words of Hölderlin: "How do we know the mystery? By guarding it we know it." Therefore I shall make only a few references.

Once I was travelling by air and I dozed off and dreamt that I was in Swamiji's hermitage, we talked a little, he told me about his heart problems and also said that he was wondering where I was. Later I learnt that it was around that time he fell ill.

Another time Katyayani was up early writing a review on a book sent to her. It was a book about dreams in classical Indian literature by Wendy O'Flaherty. I took my bath, had breakfast, got ready and went out for my walk, a little bit of daily shopping, etc. I was buoyant and fresh but as I was rushing down the stairs I felt a sudden spell of great sleep. I immediately went up again. She asked "what? You just left and are back! did you forget something?"

"No" I said "I must have a little more sleep." She was worried — "Are you unwell! you just woke up only sometime back." I told her not to worry and to continue writing her review. I went into deep sleep which lasted only a few minutes then I walked up to her writing table, she was surprised: "But you said you were going to sleep?" "I did! Actually I made a dream journey to Kashmir to meet Swami Lakshman Joo. What time is it in India now?"

"May be 6 a.m. or so."

"Perfect, it was early morning hour, I had made the dream journey. Swamiji had something important to tell me."

Another time when in Korea I wanted to show some friends a photograph of Swamiji I thought I had brought with me from India. I couldn't find it, I was sad, perhaps I had lost it. Then on the eve of the Easter Sunday, the day of resurrection I had a dream that I entered a cave. There was a picture of Swamiji there, with many fresh flowers placed around it, many lamps were burning. It was understood that he was no more and I shed tears and regretted that I did not visit him again after our last visit to Kashmir. Then suddenly I saw him emerging from the dark inner recess of the cave, shining and smiling broadly: "Who told you I was dead? Look, I am still very much alive in this world."

A day later a letter arrived from Katyayani with two photographs of Swamiji, one taken by herself during our last visit and another by a friend who had just been there.

Some more years passed and during the last phase of his life I began to search for his news. I phoned Dr Karan Singh, he told me that Swamiji was in Delhi but in complete seclusion at some location unknown even to him. The place remained secret because Swamiji did not want people to flock there. The people closest to him had brought him to Delhi, they thought he was not safe because of the violent events taking place in the valley.

Some time later again I phoned Dr Karan Singh, this time he told me that

Swamiji, unmindful of his safety, had returned to his hermitage saying that he was already 80 or so years old and he feared no death.

Then much later after he had passed away I learnt that he was very ill so they brought him back to Delhi and that he breathed his last somewhere in the environs of Delhi but somehow I knew it that very day he passed away.

Nature has a way of celebrating all events of human life cycle and her own way to announce them. She did it that day again, in a dream.

In a dream I saw a multitude of celestial figures as one sees in the faded Central Asian Buddhist frescoes. They were not clear but still luminous, the sky was lit by a vague light though no source was visible. The figures were still, full of expectation and reverence. Then the scene disappeared and I heard a voice: "And thousands of gods gathered to welcome great Lakshman Joo to his true abode, and thousands of *dundubhi*s resounded in the sky." (It was somewhat like this — *"aur ākāśa meiṅ hazāron dundubhiyoṅ kā nād gūñja uṭhā"* referring to the sound of hourglass drums).

So the knowledge was swift but the news was late by several months.

IV

I am now going to add a few reflections, then a few suggestions.

After meeting such a rare, phenomenal human being with most excellent qualities I have wondered a few times if it was a great tradition that created such a magnificent human being or the human beings like him created such a great tradition. Though it is true both ways, I like to emphasize that it is human beings like him that created such a great tradition.

The heydays of Kashmir Śaivism were over long ago but though fewer and fewer in number there were always some scholars and sometimes some *ācārya*s, otherwise such a big body of scriptures could not have been preserved. But two stars shine with peculiar intensity in the whole history of Kashmir Śaivism. One is Abhinavagupta who embodied the entire tradition and added many new dimensions to it. The other is Swami Lakshman Joo who also embodied the whole tradition and was its last blazing light, its final summary, and he liberated this great tradition from its traditional isolation and obscurity. It was his genius that manifested such excellent human qualities which drew wonderful scholars and other people to his place.

The traditional lineage ended with him but before that he threw a whole new light on this tradition and the study of Kashmir Śaivism spread to many far-flung places among the scholarly communities, and also among people who are not scholars — it found an ever-growing audience.

Though the tradition was known to some extent to some serious Sanskrit scholars, the studies were limited. It remained largely confined to some *paṇḍit*s in the Valley. Its was also one of the causes of its decay.

During the time of Maharaja Hari Singh's rule there was an attempt to rescue it from the fast vanishing old manuscripts, and many texts were printed, but soon even these forgotten texts were, though now in print, gathering dust, yellowed leaves were falling apart, moisture was spreading through them.

It was the genius of Swami Lakshman Joo that gave it a new life and also liberated it from the traditional and personal domain of the *paṇḍit*s and opened its doors wide to all those who would be interested in it, without distinction of caste, creed and nationality. It was a big change. It was late by quite a few centuries but finally when it came through him the world received a lasting and magnificent gift.

One saw sometimes a profound sadness in his eyes, it could have been because of his being alone with such an abundant knowledge and the fact that he was the last *ācārya* of this great tradition. It came to the end with him but it is also true that "the Hīnayāna" of Kashmir Śaivism was transformed into "the Mahāyāna" of Kashmir Śaivism because of him.

Teilhard de Chardin, when he came across Tibetan Buddhism, spoke of it as "a strange and mysterious beauty whose time has yet not come." The time had since then come. Similarly Kashmir Śaivism's forgotten beauty too is now being discovered by the world. A band of dedicated scholars has made the task of great, lone Swami Lakshman Joo easier and the world is richer by their efforts.

Having written an account of my few meetings with Swamiji, I still feel that I have not paid sufficient tribute to him, hence I am adding a few more words here.

Once Swamiji told a student the story of Macchandanāth and his 12 disciples who had renounced their kingdoms to follow him. Of these 12 princes six went to teach in different directions and the other six went into great wilderness forever, each living a solitary life away from the world. Then Swamiji told his student that he himself would have preferred the life in wilderness.

But then is it not true that he integrated both these aspects in his life? It was all too evident that he did. While he generously shared his rare gifts with all those who were receptive, his true domain was still the wilderness of solitude. He would wander off into that region in an instant and then would suddenly return. While sitting with people he would be suddenly absent and then suddenly be wholly present as a great teacher and as a most benevolent, affectionate and generous human being. It was this touch of wilderness that shone through his personality and gave it such a mysterious depth, power and luminosity.

Having known that vast wilderness he had no inclination or use for personal glorification, fame, great crowds and accumulation of wealth. Had he made a slightest move towards the stage of worldly fame, he would have been most likely the most famous and wealthiest *guru* of all the twentieth-century *guru*s. Who else had such manifold qualities?

He had all he needed to live a life of beautiful simplicity, elegance, contentment and generosity. He only gave and took nothing from the materialistic world. Once I was talking to Dr Karan Singh and told him: "If I had ever decided to choose a *guru*, I would have made a request to Swamiji to take me as a disciple."

"Why don't you still do it?" he asked. I replied: "I sometimes like to sit under a great tree as a traveller but don't wish to build a house there."

I once sat for a while under the generous shade of that mighty tree and I am grateful for the rest of my life.

Appendix

Lastly a few suggestions for scholars. There may be already some works that I have not come across. In that case I can blame only my ignorance:

1. A good biography, a true human biography of Swami Lakshman Joo is missing. Research into that field may yield rich material while many memories are still very fresh. If all of it is not gathered we shall be left only with hagiographies.

It is very likely that it may soon all turn into legends. I have already come across two different versions about his birth, about Swami Rāma celebrating his birth and different stories about his leaving his home. And it all happened in such a short time!

2. Before Kashmir Śaivism fully took shape, Kashmir was a great cradle of Buddhism with all its different manifestations. At one time Buddhism and Śaivism were well intertwined in an open twilight zone as even today one sees in Nepal. A good study of that period is needed. One may also have to consult Tibetan travelogues still awaiting translation.

3. There is another curious period of socio-cultural history, the history of Kashmir's Sūfī movement which had some good interaction with Śaivism of the Valley. A thorough study is needed.

4. The non-Sanskritic tradition of Śaivism that circulated among common people also had some most unusual personalities. The most celebrated case is Lal Dêd but there were others too who survive in diverse legends. Some manifestations had continued till recent times.

   Now, Swami Lakshman Joo too has become a part of that other tradition prevalent among people who have no philosophical interest. Legends about him and worship of his image are growing within the Kashmiri *paṇḍit* community. This too may interest some scholars.

5. Socio-economic-political-cultural history of the times during which Kashmir Śaivism flourished and declined would be a very interesting contribution and complementary addition to the study of Kashmir Śaivism.[2]

IV.
The Presence Continues

दुःखान्यपि सुखायन्ते विषमप्यमृतायते ।
मोक्षायते च संसारो यत्र मार्गः स शांकरः ॥
— शिवस्तोत्रावली २०.१२

duḥkhānyapi sukhāyante viṣam-apyamṛtāyate ।
mokṣāyate ca saṁsāro yatra mārgaḥ sa śāṁkaraḥ ॥
— *Śivastotrāvalī* 20.12

Where even suffering is transformed into joy,
Where even poison becomes nectar,
Where the world itself leads to liberation:
That is the path of Śaṅkara.

47. Iśvara Svarūpa.

48. In absorption.

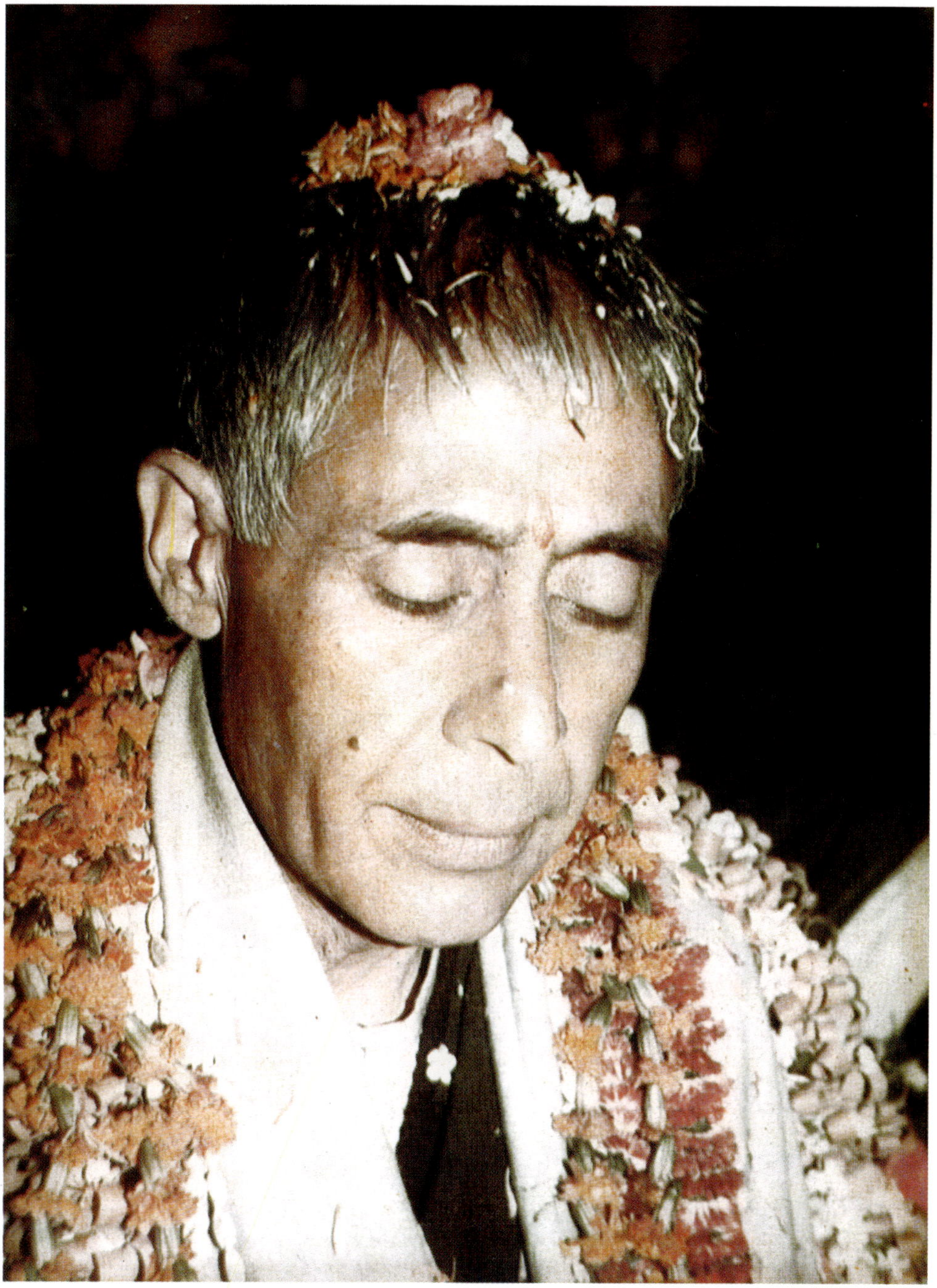

49. In *samādhi* on his Birthday (c. late 1970s).

50. Emerging from *samādhi*, 1985 (still from a video of Swamiji's Birthday).

51. Absorbed in study.

52. Iśvara Āśrama, Nishat, Srinagar.

17

A Transforming Meeting

Ernst Fürlinger[1]

I NEVER met Swami Lakshman Joo in his lifetime. Yet to meet him changed my life. In retrospect I realize that this was the turning-point of my life which now started afresh.

In spring 1999, eight years after his death, I was engaged by a prestigious institution of the Catholic church in Austria, responsible for the section "Interreligious Dialogue and Meditation," organizing courses, conferences and seminars in this field. There was a weekend seminar on "Hindu Forms of Meditation" at the institution in co-operation with the University, guided by an Austrian disciple of Swami Lakshman Joo, Bettina Bäumer. She herself did not mention him, but I found his name in the dedication of her book on Abhinavagupta. I was curious about him, and so, during lunch hour I searched in the internet for entries on "Swami Lakshman Joo," finding some photos of his on an American website. At the end of this day of the seminar in the late afternoon, I told her about this and she suggested showing me the video of his Birthday celebration. At this time I knew nothing about him or his tradition, hardly anything about Hinduism in general. At that time I was mainly interested in Buddhism, especially Zen.

On the screen I saw a tall, handsome man, Swami Lakshman Joo, who seemed to have an absolutely natural authority. He, in the first part of the video, walks through the ashram in Nishat, personally checking the preparations for the festivities of his birthday celebration. Everybody seemed to blossom when he came near — all the people cutting vegetables, cooking, cleaning, etc. started to smile, laugh and shine when he came and talked to them. Then, in the second part of the

1. I want to thank Claude Wampler for editing the English of this text.

video one could see him leaving the house in the early morning of his birthday and entering the *maṇḍapa*[2] where he remained in meditation, only on this day in public view. For the first time in my life I saw a person in *samādhi*, in deep absorption. It was breathtaking to watch his face, when he tried to come out of this state, opening his eyes half-way, then falling back again into the depths of his own nature. It seemed difficult for him to surface again, to come back to the dimension of differentiation. Seeing that was a moment of recognition for me — a recognition of the highest possibilities of man, of myself.

The video was very touching, but nothing special happened. I must clarify: subjectively nothing happened — because Dr Bäumer told me later that I could not walk straight after watching the video, I staggered.

After my experience of seeing Swami Lakshman Joo on video I left my work, as I did everyday, in the early evening and went to an old coffee house in the centre of the city. This was part of my daily ritual. Being single, I liked to spend the early evening in this atmosphere where one could be alone in the midst of many people. While I was reading the newspaper and drinking hot chocolate, I became disquieted. I was somehow moved and had to leave the coffee house. I realized a certain feeling, like a winding pillar right inside myself, reaching above my head, which was rotating in such a way that it sometimes felt as if there were two pillars which rotated into each other, like the Double-helix. I did not know what was going on. I could not even fathom what it could be. I was deeply touched, and I was inspired to go to the top of a mountain near the city. I wanted to be alone.

In the summer, maybe three months later, I attended a meditation week guided by Bettina Bäumer, in an old farmhouse in the Alps. This retreat was like an inner explosion for me. I had practised Zen-meditation some years before — it was unavoidable, since I was organizing meditation courses. But I had given it up, in fact, I couldn't meditate. There was no progress at all. But in that week I experienced what is meant by: "The stages of *yoga* are full of astonishment."[3] An inner sound occurred, a vibration in the upper part of the body. To meditate became easy (at least in this beginning stage!), a pleasure. When the participants were asked to

2. Wooden structure in the garden, open on all four sides, where he used to sit.

3. *Śivasūtra* I.12.

give a feedback at the end of the week, I said: "For me it is very fitting that we got a type of pap for breakfast, like baby-food, because I feel like newborn."

The first time I was able to talk to someone about these experiences was with Bettina Bäumer. From her I heard for the first time the "labels" connected with my experiences, according to the Tantric traditions which were at that time completely unknown to me. But still I could not grasp what was going on. I continued to meditate and, in an almost unconscious way, to accept Swami Lakshman Joo as my master. I hadn't even been searching for a master. At the time I was mainly involved in political activities as the co-founder of an anti-poverty network NGO in Austria. "Accept" is a very dry notion, actually I fell in love with him — as you are suddenly in love with a woman, and you don't know how it really started and why. You just *are* in love.

In winter I travelled to Varanasi, the "city of Lord Śiva," for the first time, and was overwhelmed by the atmosphere there. I only thought, "I want to come back." When I returned home from India, I immediately re-arranged my whole flat to create a free space and a better place for meditation. I remember I was so charged with energy that I carried a heavy chest of drawers from one room to the other all by myself. I think this re-arranging was symbolic of what would soon happen in my life.

In the spring a phase lasting several weeks began where all my energy was turned inwards. Externally I functioned, did my duties, but like a robot. I was wrestling deep within myself: "Should I do it?" After some weeks there was a clear decision. In fact, after this whole inner process the decision was crystal clear, and it was an absolute necessity. When I told my friends and the superiors in my institution that I wanted to quit my job, leave my flat and go to India to learn Sanskrit and study the texts of Abhinavagupta — there was a storm of opposition. I had not even revealed the real reason, to be free to follow this inner path — nobody would have understood. Some warned me not to give up all the securities of a good job, a flat, career, social securities. . . . But this is exactly what I wanted to do. I had the feeling it was necessary for me to lose these securities, to interrupt the routine of my life and to throw myself into the Unknown. It sounds more heroic than it was. I had saved money, had the moral support of my sisters and some friends, and I had the clear feeling of guidance by Swamiji.

This insecurity is sometimes hard for me. It is like the people of Israel who started their exodus from their exile in Egypt into the desert, and there dreamt of all the food and comforts which they had left in their imprisonment. I had a childish wish to hear the voice of Swamiji inwardly or in a dream, that would tell me what to do. This never happened to me. But a disciple of Swamiji in Delhi, Dr Sarla Kumar, told me of a dream she had about me. I was wandering in the fog but Swamiji was guiding me from behind. When I went back to Europe for the summer, I went through a crisis — I was unable to integrate my inner path and my recent experiences in India with my life at home. Afterwards, when I overcame this confusion, I remembered Sarla's dream. Swamiji really guided me, not visibly, but from behind.

Since that time I have been living in Varanasi. I found a Paṇḍit with whom I could study the richness of the Kashmir Śaiva texts, Paṇḍit Hemendra Nath Chakravarty, the foremost disciple of MM Gopinath Kaviraj. Slowly I was able to understand better what had happened to me. It was the touch of grace — the grace of "that," the unnameable Mystery, which for me has a face now, the face of Swamiji. "Grace" means: unexpected, not earned, not the result of any effort, qualities or merits. This is absolutely obvious in my case. "Grace" means: to be thrown off track.

In September 2003 I visited the ashram of Swami Lakshman Joo in Srinagar for the first time, on the occasion of the *yajña* on his death anniversary. I expected it to be pure joy for me, but in fact I was also saddened. I realized concretely that he had lived here and I had never met him, that I would never meet him in his body. Among his former disciples, I was the only person who had never met him. But the atmosphere there is still filled with his presence, full of his traces: beauty, simplicity, clarity, transparency, joy, lightness, peace — qualities of the Divine. He was also present in even the smallest details of the daily routine in the ashram and in the people themselves. One detail I liked especially: the birds too had a place to receive *prasāda*, they too were not forgotten — a beautiful practice of Advaita.

What does it mean that this place exists in Kashmir, in the midst of extreme violence, and has to be guarded by armed soldiers? For me this place is a seed of hope.

I am writing all this to bear witness that Swami Lakshman Joo is still acting as a master, performing the five acts of Śiva, and the foremost act: to show grace. Therefore there is no reason to be worried about the continuity of the tradition after his death, leaving behind the community without a successor. Once he himself said in an interview: "Who cares for the empty sky? It is not up to us to take care of it. The same is the case with this spiritual tradition. . . ." It reminds me of a crucial moment in the history of the tradition in which I was born: When Jesus died, his devotees remained desperate. What should happen after the death of the master? Then they were touched by his Spirit, from above, by his living presence, and they could bear witness: He is alive, he is not dead.

18

An "Icon" of the Divine

Borghild Baldauf

It was in the late evening of June 27, 1997. I was sitting in the small quiet backroom of my home, listening to a monthly radio programme on different world religions. I had always found this broadcast interesting but this time it was specially recommended by Dr Bettina Bäumer whose lectures on "Language and Mysticism in Hinduism and Christianity" I was attending at Vienna University during the current summer semester. It was there that I heard names like Abhinavagupta and Utpaladeva for the first time, and I was fascinated by Dr Bäumer's interpretation of a few verses from the *Śivasūtras* and *Vijñānabhairava*.

The tradition to which these great masters and texts belonged was also the theme of the radio programme: "The whole of reality is one with me: meeting with Kashmir Śaivism." I expected some kind of general introduction or survey — and it was that too — but it was more. To my surprise the whole broadcast revolved around the life-changing experience of initiation which was granted more than forty years ago to an Indian woman, Dr Sarla Kumar, by the last Guru, scholar and saint of non-dualistic Kashmir Śaivism, Swami Lakshman Joo. Both what she said and how she said it touched me deeply. Although my spiritual quest goes back to the time when I was still at school and finally led me to study Catholic theology, and despite the fact that I had already visited India in 1984, I was far from the glittering world of the so-called masters or Gurus. Not only that I had always been sceptical of any personality cult, I was neither interested in those exotic figures travelling through Europe and USA, selling their wisdom like fast-food for high amounts of money and "initiating" hundreds of people in the big town halls of our cities — nor was I convinced by the often strange and esoteric behaviour of some of my friends who followed a Guru in India and visited him or her regularly. Though they thought they knew many things about *cakra*s, the power of *kuṇḍalinī* and the practice of *mantra*s, they seemed to be more unstable in life and sometimes even more egocentric than other people.

However, listening to Sarla Kumar's words in all their sincerity, simplicity, devotion and joy was something completely different. Yet at the same time I felt a little wistful, if not sad, because experiences like hers have always been a rare gift, and also the great master was no longer living and there was no one to be his successor. So what remained was the vague wish at least to meet this privileged disciple of Swami Lakshman Joo. To my great pleasure this happened totally unexpectedly six years later in Varanasi, where she and I were both participating in the "First International Workshop on Kashmir Śaivism" held there.

During the years between these two events, important changes had taken place in my life. There was the sudden death of my parents, the necessity to look for a new job and the outbreak of a serious and extremely painful disease which conventional medicine considers to be incurable and would possibly result in my spending the rest of my life in a wheelchair. As I was passionately fond of dancing, and teaching dance contributed to my earnings, this diagnosis sounded like a death sentence. But I refused to give up, and attempted what seemed impossible. And after three years the diabolical process of my illness slowly started to reverse, so that step by step I could return to normal life. This new life I owe mainly to India, as it was — among a number of treatments including a two months' stay at an Āyurvedic hospital in Kerala — the experience of healing powers which are still alive in this country and which finally not only led to a full recovery but completely changed my way of thinking and way of life.

As far as possible in the course of these difficult years and even more so afterwards, I continued to make use of every opportunity to learn about Kashmir Śaivism, attending Bettina's university lectures in Austria and her annual meditation weeks in the mountains there. Increasingly I was captivated by what I discovered and experienced in practising this tradition as well as by the intellectual challenge of its clear and subtle philosophy in which content and linguistic expression — full of beauty and power — form an inseparable unity where not a single word seems to be redundant. Intuitively I felt that here I could find that final kind of fulfilment I had been longing and searching in my own religion for vain for so long, that here I could go "beyond" to an extent and to a depth which was limitless and where nothing had to be excluded. But there was something which held me back from throwing myself unreservedly into this adventure. There was, first of all, a great respect for this tradition which one could not just "taste" from time to time if one wanted to practise it in a serious way. This is true of any involvement with a different religious tradition as I already knew from many years of being closely connected to a Sufi Tarīqa in Turkey. It requires, in a certain way, the dedication of one's whole life. I was lacking an Indological background, I did not know Sanskrit, and because of my professional duties I saw little chance to extend my daily meditation time to the degree I considered necessary for making real progress. Secondly, as it was emphasized by the texts, I would have needed to be initiated and guided by an authentic master of the tradition without which it would be almost impossible to enter into it in any real sense. So how should I approach the desired goal when already at the beginning of the journey I knew that I could get only halfway?

This was discouraging, especially for someone like me who cannot bear doing things by halves. So, travelling to Varanasi in 2003 in order to take part in the workshop on Kashmir Śaivism was not merely a valuable opportunity to study and practise this school in its Indian context but was to help me come to a decision as whether to continue, and if so, how?

It became quickly quite clear that I should continue. Still there and even more back home again I realized increasingly that I wished to stay for a longer time in India, for at least one year, to continue my studies there which meanwhile had taken shape in my intention to write a thesis in the field of Kashmir Śaivism. The following summer I started to learn Sanskrit, first on my own for lack of an alternative near my home town.

In the spring of 2004 I returned to Varanasi for a short time, for another workshop, and it was at the end of the week that Bettina showed me a photograph of Swami Lakshman Joo which she had recently received. In it the master was sitting in *samādhi* and something indescribable radiated from his appearance. Spontaneously I uttered my wish to have a copy from it and Bettina agreed to get one for me. By chance in this year both our birthdays were at the festival of Easter which we celebrated at the German monastery of Niederaltaich, famous for its beautiful Russian-orthodox Liturgy. It was there that Bettina handed me Swamiji's photo, carefully framed, as a birthday present. She did so, saying simply: "It is an icon!"

Icons have always played an important role in the theology, liturgy and individual worship of the Eastern Churches. I myself had a deep relationship to these "windows on eternity" or "windows to the Absolute" and had studied their theology and art for several years. Icons are the locus of an immaterial presence and as such they invite the contemplative beholder to develop an inner, immaterial vision of looking. The saints, or subjects of the icon, look out at him, or rather, they look straight through him, as if to reveal his true nature, transforming him into what they themselves represent. They are pure transparency, transparent for the light which is neither artificially produced nor projected into them from outside, but shines forth from them, as indicated by their golden background, a symbol for the uncreated Divine light. In addition — according to Orthodox belief — icons are the locus of grace, of purifying grace, and the saint depicted in them is filled with grace (cf. Bulgakov S.N., L'Orthodoxie, Lausanne 1980, quoted in Quenot M., Die Ikone. Fenster zum Absoluten, Würzburg 1992, p. 119). Because of his participation in the Divine life, he sanctifies space, time and his whole environment. Free from passion he stands there in the fullness of his divinized nature which means to be the goal of the entire creation, comprising man and the cosmos.

I do not know whether it was right to do so or not, but with all this in mind I started to live with the "icon," which from now on had its place in my meditation room. Sitting and meditating before the upright serene figure, which was nothing but pure presence and merged into the One, I felt that something started to change in me. There was not only a silent communication with this "icon," a communication beyond words and thoughts, but I was pulled into a powerful process in which new dimensions of my inner life opened up and where I was more and more bereft of false securities and at the same time filled with wonder, a new intensity and joy. Often I found myself in tears. But again I did not want to make it too easy for me, did not want to get into the trap of the slightest illusion or projection. Who really was this saint? What could he, being no longer in his physical body, ever mean for me? And how far was I allowed to go in this constantly growing inner relationship with him?

The response came soon and it was a surprising one. It reached me at the end of the same year when I was already in India and had taken up my studies. One early morning I had just got up from an intense time of meditation and, crossing the room to come to the place where I prepared my breakfast, I glanced at Swamij's photo which I had brought with me from Austria and put into a niche in the wall.

What I saw was no more the familiar shape of the master but someone Divine, totally Divine. It was, as if he were bodily present, sitting in perfect absorption, his eyes closed. Spellbound I stood before him, like frozen, unable to move anymore. Suddenly, after a long time, he slowly opened his eyes and he looked at me. Then his eyelids closed again and for a short while that process of opening and closing continued. About fifteen or twenty minutes passed, then the picture went back to its original appearance. I was awestruck, asking myself what this could signify and, like Mary in the Gospel, I kept the incident in my heart.

As if to confirm it, another experience was granted to me soon afterwards. Again it took place at the end of a period of meditation, when suddenly Swamiji appeared before me, standing erect, tall, awe-inspiring. This was so unexpected, so full of power, that my only reaction was to be terribly frightened, to be shocked. But immediately he was transformed into light and then the light dissolved into something indescribable which was beyond light. I still felt stunned. What was it that Swamiji wanted to teach me through this? Was it not a similar experience to that of the three disciples of Jesus on Mount Tabor, the "Transfiguration," the "Metamorphosis," where their master revealed to them his true Divine nature which was no less than their own nature? And were the three disciples not similarly shocked and fearful?

Getting in touch with Reality is never innocuous. It shakes up one's whole being and involves undergoing a kind of death which is inevitable in order to give birth to a new, transformed life, in which everything is perceived in its essence: neither matter, nor light, but something "beyond. . . ."

At first, my time in India was not easy. Nothing seemed to work; bureaucracy, health problems, and the usual difficulties in the daily routine made life wearisome. Several times I felt that I was at the end of my tether, but obviously this was a necessary phase of putting to the test my motivations and intentions.

But there were two more important occasions of clarification, highlights of my sojourn in India. First there was the unforeseen opportunity to spend an unforgettable week in Kashmir together with Bettina, which meant not only the fulfilment of a long-cherished dream but put me in touch with the origin of the living tradition, which can never be achieved by the mere study of texts. Visiting Swamiji's ashram in Srinagar, feeling the still dense and concentrated atmosphere there, that peace and intensity which is always a sign of authenticity, sitting for meditation in the small *maṇḍapa*, where his presence seemed condensed to the utmost, participating in the great annual *yajña*, celebrated on the day of his *mahāsamādhi*, listening to the fervent recitation of the ancient hymns, all this was connected with deep inner experiences and it was like seeds, falling on a soil which increasingly was open and ready to receive.

Next there was a ten days' retreat when Bettina and Sarla took me to their ashram in Phulchatti in March 2005. I was quite happy to escape Varanasi for a while, busy and noisy as it was, longing for a more suitable environment in which to practise regular meditation than my room near the kitchen of a constantly vociferously quarrelling Indian extended family, as well as two enthusiastic singing and Sitar-playing room neighbours, could offer me. Here I could only hear the rush of my beloved Gaṅgā merging in the outer and inner silence, and the hours of intense meditation I was allowed to spend together with Bettina in her inspiring meditation room as well as listening to the recollections of their Guru which the two disciples of Swami Lakshman Joo often exchanged during dinner were rare and precious gifts.

Yet on the last day of this enriching time, a strange thing occurred. I started weeping and for hours there was no end of my tears. Fortunately I was alone that day because it was as if — maybe for the first time in my life — I had lost control of myself. Completely helpless I was unable to form a clear idea, lost in a welter of disparate emotions and the vain attempt to get the rudder back into my hands again. There was nothing I could do except going to the meditation room, prostrate myself there and let go of everything. In the evening a long and heavy thunderstorm broke off, like the cosmic counterpart to my explosive inner state.

The morning of the following day was particularly bright and fresh. The nightly shower had cleared the air and freshened all of nature and in the same way something had become obvious to me. What had happened? During the night my former life had passed by like in a flash. It was the glimpse of a rich and busy, if not always easy, life which had brought me a lot of satisfaction. Still there was something else too. Grown up in an atheistic-agnostic family there was a call, an inner attraction going back to my early childhood. I remembered the intensity of my first communion where in a childlike way I devoted myself to the Lord. For a while I had the rather obscure idea of becoming a hermit and I gobbled up a large number of religious books, given to me by my God-mother, my only ally during this time.

After finishing school I studied music and, two years later theology, the latter against the will of my parents whom I confronted with the *fait accompli* not before I had already completed the first two semesters. We were a group of committed and critical students and shared a number of different spiritual activities and practice too. I wondered if I should become a member of a religious order and for years I spent parts of my holidays in a small community. But it was not only my family which held me back; I soon discovered that this way of living was too narrow for me and certainly not my final vocation. Anyhow, I was missing something, something essential, and the question as to where I could find a place where I could lead a life deeply rooted in the silence of the mystery and penetrated by it in all its aspects, remained still open. The dilemma increased during ten years of working as an assistant and lecturer in the department of Old Testament Studies in the theological faculty of my home town, where I rubbed myself sore on the limits of Christian theology and exegesis and the arrogance of a mostly smug and boring academic society which had itself cut off from the source and thereby lost its credibility, dynamism and creativity.

But all this was a thing of the past now, and getting to know Indian philosophy and Interreligious Dialogue, first in the books of R. Panikkar and then in Kashmir Śaivism, had opened up a new and exciting world. Gradually I realized the treasures embedded in this tradition till eventually it was to become "my path." During that night full of rain, storm and tears the original desire burst open again in a vehemence which comprised and combined all the different, sometimes also desperate, periods of my inner quest. It was as if my whole life focused into one single moment, and I understood that I had come home. I also realized that I had reached the point when I was called to answer and that this opportunity would never come again in the same way. The time was ripe to throw myself into the abyss of the all-devouring Divine, to give everything, to lose everything in the pull of the One whose irresistible attraction had come to an extent that I could no longer escape. Too long I had hesitated, too long held back, but now at that moment there was no more choice, there was no return. And — was it not Swamiji's hidden guidance which had brought me to this extraordinary path that changed my life and increasingly filled my days and nights with indescribable bliss? Was it not he who had brought me to India, to this particular situation here?

More than one year has passed since then. I had to come back to Austria but I was able to return to India for a second longer period. As always in this country I had to maintain a balancing act between extremes. Life and death, beauty and ugliness, the highest and the meanest are inextricably interwoven here and sometimes functioned like a mirror to reflect my own strengths and weaknesses. Living in Varanasi — fascinating as the town can be — is a harsh school and I had to learn my lessons. How easily it is said that everything is Divine, "from Śiva down to the earth," down to the tiniest particle of dust! Would I be able to realize this when walking in the street, covered in clouds of dust, coughing and eyes burning? How beautiful it is to read some of Utpaladeva's *stotras*, praising the "lake of infinite bliss" in the Sanskrit class. Would I be able to discover this lake on my way home too, hopelessly stuck in the mud and dirty water on the road I cycled on day after day? The occasions to practise in the simplest contexts of daily life were endless — and complete. And now and then it actually happened that even the muddy road became translucent for the ocean of never-ending joy. . . .

My last month in India brought me back to Phulchatti to spend some time in silence there and finally to go on pilgrimage to Gaṅgotrī and the source of the Gaṅgā, which had been my wish for many years. It turned out to be a wonderful, unburdened week and I was overwhelmed by the beauty and power of the Himalayas and the atmosphere on the way which I shared with people from almost all parts of India. Besides, the symbol of the source is so rich and seemed especially apt for this period of my life. I do not know why, but mainly it appeared to me as a symbol of grace, and was it not grace alone that had led me during all these last years?

Climbing up and down the stony path was not difficult as I was more or less born with mountain-boots on my feet, but the low temperatures during the night and the permanent wind gave me a heavy cold and nearly unbearable headache. So I spent most of my last day in Gaṅgotrī in bed, hoping that I could manage the long bus ride back to Rishikesh the next morning. Around 4 o'clock in the afternoon I woke up from a short sleep after having had a strange dream. My head still raged. Yet I decided to go out for a while. I had already unlocked the door and put on my shoes when a sudden force held me back. There was an inner urge pressing me not to leave the room but to stay there, sit down and meditate. It was an unusual time for meditation and how should I be able to concentrate with a head like a swarm of bees? But the urge was so intense that immediately I took off my sandals and placed myself on the dirty bed. The room was filled with a presence and it was immensely strong. Just a few seconds passed and I felt that something had opened in me, completely opened and nothing was more "in between." I left everything, ascending to the source, returning to the source and there was nothing but the source, the life-giving source of everything, the pure *aham*.

Slowly returning to my body I found myself bathed in tears. But this time each tear was a pearl of immeasurable bliss and peace. My head was clear, the pains had disappeared. Opening my eyes I saw the "icon," Swamiji's photograph. His face was shining from within, with an indescribable light that does not exist in this world. When, if not now, would I accept that the path the Guru opens by his grace is not only for those few who had the chance to meet him in his physical body? It was a long journey, starting with a radio-broadcast in Austria nine years before and ending in a tiny, cold and smelly room in Gaṅgotrī, hard and wearisome, wonderful and full of surprises. Its end will be a new beginning, just as the constantly flowing Gaṅgā reminds the pilgrim never to stop and stand still.

Words are so poor and insufficient. What I have found in Kashmir Śaivism transcends all I ever expected to receive in my life. It is fulfilment, and as such leaves nothing to be desired. So what verse would be more suitable than the following one by Utpaladeva?

> *garjāmi bata nṛtyāmi pūrṇā mama manorathāḥ* |
> *svāmī mamaiṣa ghaṭito yattvamatyantarocanaḥ* ||
>
> I shout, O I dance! My desires are fulfilled
> because this my Lord has come to me,
> you, who are infinitely shining
> and bestowing everlasting contentment!
>
> — *Śivastotrāvalī* 3,11

This hymn of the great Kashmiri philosopher, mystic and poet has flown out of a heart which was full of amazement and gratitude. Immense gratitude I also want to express to Bettinaji and Sarlaji who opened their door and their hearts to me, and were the bridge without which I could never have approached Swami Lakshman Joo, the master.

19

Love Song to the Master

Ariane Hentsch Cisneros

MASTER, Lakshman Joo, my Gurudeva, I salute you and bow before your might.

For some time now, you have been my guide, Śiva incarnate, a harbinger of the real Self. You first made your presence felt to me about eight years after that powerful flash of grace, and nearly fifteen years after you had entered *mahāsamādhi*. Ever since, your subtle teachings have come as many boons to treasure on the way to Bhairava-consciousness.[1] I have received your infinite love and kindness as an invitation to tread the golden path towards the highest realization. You have been strong where I was weak, you have been awake when I was asleep, you have stayed close to me even when I did not see you. This love song is a humble sign of gratitude to you.

My Master, I am not sure of my origins. Was I born in the cave of the heart where your own Master, Abhinavagupta, is said to have vanished? In that cave for the first time I sensed an adorable presence — though I did not know you then. Black-skinned, red-eyed Kālī ushered me to my Master. Tall and mighty, he was standing at the entrance of the cave, where he taught me the secret of transparency. Śiva was already extending His shadow over us, and high in the sky, a dazzling star was radiating as a witness of our meeting.

On the way to *pratyabhijñā*[2] I came to know you as my father. Each and everyone of your moves was stirring the universe. You were so immersed in Śiva that Pārvatī all around you was absorbed in total worship. Your call was too strong to resist — I

1. Today these teachings are still imparted through some of his most fervent disciples such as Prabha Devi, Bettina Bäumer and Sarla Kumar in India, and others.
2. Self-recognition as recognition of the Lord.

could only surrender and fall into the sweetest bondage. There you were, deep inside, totally transparent and in command, defeating all resistance to love.

From that moment on, your breath has been nurturing my breath. You have taken me to worlds of light and darkness, void and fullness, and you have taught me the mysteries. We have danced together in the ethereal spaces of the heart, playing with time and form. We have listened to your great Master. On the endless grey plain, in the midst of the night, I have seen guarding a great pillar of fire. In *rudrasamāveśa*,[3] you taught me the name of the magnificent swan perched on a five-pointed star, and explained the everlasting mighty foundation of the world. I knew that when you would have imparted your knowledge to me, and I would have recognized you as Śiva, I would be liberated.

Slowly, your presence bent the course of my life. You inhabited my dreams, you stirred my psychic structures, purifying my perception of reality. Your heart proved an open door to a wider, greater reality, beyond space and time, going back to your beloved Master Abhinavagupta.

When you open your eyes, you are like a corpse; when you close them, I am like a corpse. When you are facing me, you make me breathe freely.

When you teach me in the great space of the heart, you are at my sides. But at other times you are much closer. Then I miss your mountains in Kashmir, your room at Īśvara Āśrama. When you are close, my ego looks so entangled with itself, in spite of its enthusiasm. But in the end, does it matter if I am you or her?

> Svāmijī — my Master
> He who has seen you will recognize me,
> He who errs has never seen you.

O Lakshman, how terribly I miss you! You are here and there and everywhere, but I just lack the clarity to see you. When will we be united in eternity? With your help I rose from among the creatures. I am nothing without your love. You are in me, and in the world. I am you, you are me, we are everything. Īśvara created us. Our love is the vestibule of infinite space and time.

Our hearts are one, and you slowly pour your knowledge into the various

3. Union with Śiva/Rudra.

regions of my consciousness. The touch of your hand once unveiled the *axis mundi*. In tears, I discovered how I could, with great simplicity, wander in my wonderful garden. A slight touch of my fingertips caused the flowers to bloom suddenly.

Once I went to a mountain high above the plains. It was empty, warm, quiet, and peaceful, beautiful, wholesome, good, and eternal. And of the utmost simplicity. You were there, and your Master, too. I recognized you as a great man in the eyes of God — my little self was so small in comparison! I leaned with great love over you. For the first time we were not corpses to each other. I was so content with you — you had been my Master! And you were so close again, while my love was flowing into the entire world.

When you sat in Bhairava state at Īśvara Āśrama, you pervaded all and everyone around you. But some of your devotees did not see the reality of your state. I could feel your pain and the beauty.

> The sight of a child, or that of a flame,
> The sight of the ocean, or that of a glance
> of the Guru. See that transparent brilliance!

In your great generosity, you showed me how Śiva rests at the depth of the heart and everywhere around me, behind the thin surface of appearances. With closed eyes and great mastery, you reveal yourself as Śiva with neither a gross nor subtle mediator. If only my perception could be reabsorbed so that undivided consciousness dawns unto me as a new day! When you invite me into the great column of fire, I blow a sweet wind of life unto the world.

Your play is amazing — you are you playing to be me. You are one and many. You are Śiva, and you inhabit me. My body can only perform physical devotion, but your communication is so subtle; it causes Śiva's great magnificence, supreme beatitude, and mighty power to awaken. When will I get rid of the dross that keeps me away from Śiva's infinite glory? Trinity, transfiguration, one and many, this is the secret of life, death, eternity, here and now.

My father, my Master, once your shadow was sitting close, and with great love, you put your left hand on my head. Your love was so strong that I could again offer no resistance.

How many times have I cried, longing for your presence until my heart opened up? Tearfully I wanted to let you fully live in me. You are a great, magnificent king — your glory shines, dazzling, under your *phiran* (tunic).

You are a sure guide: you lead me to the real treasures of the soul. When the great column of fire is made mine, over and over again, you are still at my side, and my ego is a little further on the great grey plain. When I am firmly established in the great fire, in total humility you let me take control of my journey in the inner space. I am in command, but you are there, seeing that I take leave of the world smoothly.

I would still collect the petal of your lotus heart to purify mine, and in your company, caress the serpent of light. You would know when I needed you again. Then you would take command again and let me be you, and anything and anyone again. In moments of great intensity, how indeed would I safely reach my destination without you?

There was a great chaos on the way to the abode of *khecarī*, the golden goddess of the heart. You helped me sail through the apocalypse and keep course into the great, dark, infinite emptiness. Since then you have been a warden of the union, and then again a leader into fullness at the origin of thought. From there, you have helped me when I turned around to look at the world again. Coming home is a great bliss and it is a gift that you repeatedly bestow unto me.

I bow before you, you bow before Śiva, Śiva before His Śakti, and Śakti before Him.

And again and again, I missed you terribly. Every time I was distracted with the multitude, you breathed your wisdom into me.

O my Master, it is the universe that shines within you! A high atomic energy, Śiva-Bhairava just below the thin surface. At each moment, you were just born into this world and discovered it as if for the first time. Dying to yourself, you are the foundation of the world. You have truly sacrificed your life to Śiva and you have made me a part of this sacrifice. All and everything around is plunged into the deepest worship.

And deep inside my heart, Śiva is contemplating His kingdom. The Masters, Jesus and Siddhārtha, and other awakened beings are standing before Him in total devotion. And their devotion is my life. I am so content with you Lakshman Joo.

You have loved and accepted me so perfectly and so humbly that my glory has shone through you.

And there was void, and there was a lotus, and there was bliss. Then you took me to the open space above the mountain before leaving again. The masters and the devotees disappeared. I was a little frightened of the unknown, and I felt alone, but I was me as I never had been, and everything was mine. Void and fullness, calm and omnipresent. The goddess opened her eyes. With great astonishment she discovered the limitations of the world — she was the dogs, she was the birds, she was a man, she was a woman, she was the humid soil!

Once in our play you asked whether I could be the corpse. I was wary — was I ready? But so much love emanated from you, I could only let you in, and our hearts were one. And lo and behold, the sight of Śiva in you was stupendous! I recognized you — Śiva! My true Father. You had always been there, but had given yourself a face so that I could find a way to you. You had always been there, hidden only because I did not see you. You have found me just when I found you. Because of your love only, I truly recognized myself as who I am. I recognized the world, the universe, the ether of consciousness as my kingdom. There is infinite bliss. We are a perfect triad: you my Gurudeva, Śiva, and myself — my Guru, Śiva and Me. Recitation is the world engaged in the deepest worship, designed to bring Śiva to Self-recognition. Verily, nothing is more moving. O, the great ploy to find myself! How grand, intense and genuine is that love which has shattered the path of unconsciousness which leads to Śiva.

Lakshman Joo, Gurudeva! You feed me. In your presence, I will never, ever be hungry anymore. You are the open door to the light of the world. If I stay close to you, all my fears will be shattered, albeit in dire pain.

My Gurudeva, soon I must take leave of you, with immense gratitude and nostalgia. Already, your image inexorably breaks and let Śiva shine gloriously. But you will stay with me forever, Lakshman Joo, for your true nature is Śiva, who dwells at the depth of my heart.

Everything remains. In my heart, in the great void, in the fullest of plenitudes. Calm, peace and plenitude, where in the end all and everything is reabsorbed.

Now I shun every experience, and tire of all forms — texts, concentration, meditation, visions, bliss, even *samādhi* or my own presence. I long for supreme peacefulness, the repose of Paramaśiva in His unfathomable immensity, the ineffable solitude of His state. And again, you lead me, showing me the way of love through devotion. Only your presence is bearable: love to the Guru, love from the Guru, is this *bhakti*?

And coming back from the multitude again I have been waiting for you with an open heart. When you heard my silent call, you came to me, and your intense love knocked at the door of my heart. O, the emotion of receiving this powerful love, that only aims at invading the bottom of the heart! And there you were, within and without. Your presence was so strong that I hardly dared opening my eyes, lest I be crushed by the powerful love that emanated from all things. You were in me, and I let you be entirely. I was you. I was there. Seeing through these eyes, existing through this body.

My Master, you have found me again, you have taken great care of me, showed me the way, and consoled me.

Now when we meet, I can only withdraw and let you be in me. When I am you, I am me, my Master. I am filled with light, void, plenitude. Only Śiva is my Master: He exceeds the limits of my ego and fills the entire universe. O, the play between *nara*, Śakti and Śiva along a thinning breath! I am so far away, or rather, the world seems so far away. Śiva, let me stay with You, in You. Now, I am returning from such a distant region. My adorable, unfathomable, wonderful solitude. . . .

Whatever the world, it is contingent. Śiva is universal consciousness, stable in itself, so remote and yet so close. Master, it is by your most delicate touch that I have found the way to Śiva. The great consoling marvel: I am me, I am the Guru, and the Guru is Śiva.

It is the Guru, it is you, my Master, who takes me to Śiva, who gives me Śiva, immediately and unconditionally. I long to love you, I long to come to you. And you accept me completely. "Come! I will give you Śiva" is your powerful invitation to love. As soon as I embrace you, you withdraw and give way to Śiva. Your essence is Śiva, you are the door to Śiva. Again and again, I respond to your invitation, finding myself at the depth of your heart, which is none else than Śiva — infinite, empty space that fills and transcends the world, which is only a region of his infinite glory.

Once I was in the mountains, perched on a pine tree high above an abyss where a river flows down from melting snows. You were all around me. You reiterated your invitation, and again we were one. You gave me Śiva immediately. Your generosity appeared boundless — as is your humility: you disappeared as soon as I had found you. As you were in me, all around me was Śiva — and could only be Śiva. When you withdrew, you gave me the world as the most precious wedding present. All was mine, and I was in everything. All around me was bathed in endless, perfect devotion. The majestic mountain stands enthroned, high above me — yet how much higher I was! I was the only one left. Perfect bliss, profound peace. What intense delight: I was immersed in myself, in everything around me, in full adoration of Śiva. Every thought was born and dead before getting ripe, reabsorbed in the plain, perfect, luminous sphere of consciousness, so massively present as a plain background from which every thought, sensation, etc. detached before it returned to it and died. You, my Guru, have revealed your place in me. Gurudeva!

How immensely moved did I remain, still overwhelmed by your presence. I was feeling short of adequate emotions, contemplating my present, the world, entirely absorbed in my heart. O, the universal touch!

I devoured everything, returning the world to universal consciousness. Anger, envy, infatuation were all ephemeral, of no consequence, unproblematic. There was total freedom, lightness of being.

I was in tears in the middle of the night when I again beseeched you to take me with you. You invited me again and again you took me to Śiva. But lo, the night was suddenly enchanted and hollow! As we took possession of the void, you were also purified by it. And after dark, the great grace! There was light. In the void light was revealed. In everything, and you and me. Lakshman Joo, Gurudeva, stay in my heart, always !

Only in the end, I knew I must call you with my whole heart to hear your eternal invitation, again and again: "Come! I am here." Gurudeva, you are here, you are here.

Appendix

Published Works of Swami Lakshman Joo

1933 Pandit Lakshman Raina, ed. Śrīmad Bhagavad Gītā with commentary by Mahāmaheshvara Rājānaka Abhinava Gupta, Srinagar: Kashmir, Pratap Steam Press.

1958 Rājānaka Lakṣmaṇa, ed. Śrīkramanayapradīpikā, Srinagar: Ishwar Ashram Trust. Reprint : Varanasi 2004.

1964 Rājānaka Lakṣmaṇa, ed. (Hindi Translation), Śivastotrāvalī of Utpaladevācārya with Sanskrit commentary of Kṣemarāja, Varanasi: Chowkhamba Sanskrit Series Office.

1965 Brahmacārī Śrīrājānakalakṣmaṇa, *Kuṇḍalinīvijñānarahasyam*, in *Sarasvatī Suṣamā*, Varanasi, Saṁvat 2022 (CE 1965), pp. 57-62.

1976 Sri Swami Īśvarasvarūpa Jī, ed. Sāmbapañcāśikā with Bhāṣā Ṭīkā, Srinagar: Ishwar Ashram Trust.

1982 Swami Lakṣmana Joo Raina, Lectures on Practice & Discipline in Kashmir Śaivism, Kashmir: Universal Shaiva Trust.

1985 Swami Lakshman Joo, Kashmir Śaivism: The Secret Supreme, Srinagar: Universal Shaiva Trust.

1987 Śrī Dharmācāryakṛtā Pañcastavī, Hindi translation by Śaivācārya Mahātmā Śrī Lakṣmaṇa Jī Mahārāja, Delhi: Sarika Publishing.

1993 Īśvarasvarūpa Lakṣhmaṇa Jī Mahārāja, ed. Śrī Amṛteśvara-Bhairava Mahimnastotram, Kashmir: Ishwar Ashram Trust.

1994 Īśvarasvarūpa Laksmaṇa Jī Mahārāja, Kāśmīra Śaivadarśana meṅ sādhanā aur yama-niyama, Kashmir: Ishwara Ashram Trust.

1994 Shivācārya Swami Lakshman ji Mahārāja, Trikaśāstra-rahasya-prakriyā, Delhi: Sarika Publishing.

1995 Īśvarasvarūpa Swami Lakṣmaṇa Joo, Śrī Tantrāloka, (First Āhnika), Srinagar: Ishwara Ashram Trust.

1996 Swāmī Lakṣmaṇa Joo Mahārāj, *Vātūlanātha Sūtra, with an Exposition of Aphorisms in English*, ed. by N.K. Gurtoo, M.L. Kukiloo, Ishber (Nishat), Ishwar Ashram Trust.

1998 Jankinath Kaul, ed. The Awakening of Supreme Consciousness. Lectures of Swami Lakshman Joo, Srinagar: Ishwar Ashram Trust, and Delhi: Utpal Publications.

2002 Swami Lakshmanjoo, Shiva Sutras: The Supreme Awakening, with the Commentary of Kshemaraja, U.S.A.: Universal Shaiva Fellowship.

2002 Swami Lakshmanjoo, Vijñāna Bhairava: The Practice of Centring Awareness, Varanasi: Indica Books.

The Contributors

Borghild Baldauf, born in Linz, 1956, had intense liking for music since childhood which led to the study of music in Salzburg, followed by Catholic Theology, training in international folk dance and sacred dance (with emphasis on the tradition of Mevlevi-dervishes in Turkey). She has been working in various fields like teaching music and dance, adult education, assistant and lecturer for Old Testament Studies, Hebrew language, and dance in liturgy at the Theological department of Linz, and as spiritual assistant for theological lay students. At present, she is teaching Old Testament and religions at the College of Education, Linz. Her interest in interreligious dialogue, Indian philosophy and finally Kashmir Śaivism gave her life not only personally a new direction but brought her to India for two longer periods to study Sanskrit and to start writing a thesis in this field.

Dr Bettina Bäumer was born in Salzburg, Austria, in 1940. She studied Philosophy, Indology (Sanskrit) and Religious Studies in various universities and completed her PhD from Munich University in 1967. After her post-doctoral studies she remained as a Lecturer at the Banaras Hindu University, Varanasi (India), from 1967–1974; thereafter she was assistant and Lecturer in Indology, University of Vienna (1975–1980), Director Research of the Alice Boner Institute, Varanasi, and Hon. Coordinator of the Indira Gandhi National Centre for the Arts (1986-1995). She has been Visiting Professor in the Universities of Vienna, Berne, Salzburg, since 1975, and obtained "Habilitation" (Professorship) in Religious Studies at the University of Vienna in 1997. She received an Honorary Doctorate from the University of Salzburg. At present she is a Fellow, Indian Institute of Advanced Study, Shimla. Her main fields of research and publication are: Non-dualist Śaivism of Kashmir, Indian Aesthetics, Temple Architecture and Religious Traditions of Orissa, comparative mysticism. She translated important Sanskrit texts into German (Upaniṣads, Yogasūtras, Abhinavagupta, *Vijñāna Bhairava*) and English (*Vāstusūtra Upaniṣad*, *Śilparatnakośa*, etc.) and edited three volumes of *Kalātattvakośa*, A

Lexicon of Fundamental Concepts of the Indian Arts. Her articles on Kashmir Śaivism have been published in German (Trika, Grundthemen des kaschmirischen Śivaismus). She met Swami Lakshman Joo in 1986 and became his disciple.

Madame Jacqueline Chambron is the chief disciple of Lilian Silburn. She is a specialist in mysticism of different traditions. She has contributed articles on mystical themes in volumes of "Hermes," edited by Lilian Silburn. She met Swami Lakshman Joo in 1975 in the company of Lilian Silburn. After the death of the latter she continues to guide spiritual aspirants.

Dr Ernst Fürlinger born in 1962 in Austria, studied catholic theology. From 1991 till 2001, he was Director of Studies, Bildungshaus Salzburg. From 2001 till 2005 he studied in Varanasi (BHU). In spring 2006, he returned to Austria and since then he has been Lecturer at the Institute for Religious Studies, University of Vienna. He is also a member of Department of Intercultural Studies, Danube University, Krems.

Ariane Hentsch Cisneros was born in Switzerland in 1972. She studied international relations and interreligious dialogue at the University of Geneva, and the spiritualities of Native North Americans at Smith College (USA). Ariane has volunteered and worked in the field of interreligious dialogue since 1999, for institutions including the Council for a Parliament of the World's Religions, the University of Geneva's Faculty of Theology and the World Council of Churches' Unit for Interreligious Relations and Dialogue. She first entered into contact with Kashmir Śaivism in 1996 through a commentary of the *Vijñāna Bhairava Tantra*. Basic concentration practices induced a powerful opening to the tradition. Seven years after, she met Bettina Bäumer in Brussels, and soon started to benefit from Swami Lakshman Joo's subtle teachings.

Ācārya Rameshvar Jha (1906–1981) was born in a traditional brahmin family of Bihar. He studied Sanskrit and practised yoga from an early age and became a foremost scholar of Sanskrit grammar. He founded some Sanskrit schools in Bihar and Varanasi. He was a follower of Vedānta, but it did not satisfy him spiritually. Through Pandit Gopinath Kaviraj he came in contact with Swami Lakshman Joo in Kashmir, and became an ardent follower of Pratyabhijñā. He received the title Mahāmahopadhyāya from Banaras Hindu University. He was a prolific writer in Sanskrit, and his Sanskrit text *Pūrṇatā-Pratyabhijñā* is a modern work on the philosophy of Pratyabhijñā. He taught some important scholars, especially Bhartṛhari's *Vākyapadīya*, and texts of Kashmir Śaivism.

PANDIT JANKINATH KAUL 'KAMAL' (1914–1997) was a Sanskrit scholar specialized in Vedānta and Kashmir Śaivism. He was one of the early disciples of Swami Lakshman Joo. By profession he has been a teacher, but his spiritual quest brought him near to a number of highly elevated souls. Besides his scholarly works in Kaśmīrī, Sanskrit and Hindi, he was also a poet in these three languages. He has authored twelve books in Kaśmīrī, Sanskrit, Hindi and English, including translations and critical editions of the *Bhavānīnāmasahasrastuti* and *Pañcastavī*, besides contributing a number of research papers and articles in various journals. He received the President's award for his contribution in the field of Sanskrit studies, and was also honoured by the Dharmārtha Trust of Kashmir, as well as by the Uttar Pradesh Government for his Hindi poetry.

His foremost contribution was to disseminate the knowledge of the rich cultural and spiritual heritage of Kashmir during the times of exile of the Kashmiri Pandit community.

RAJAN KHOSA belongs to a family of Kashmiri Pandits and artists (his grandfather Somnath Khosa painted portraits of Swami Rāma, Mahtab Kak and Swami Lakshman Joo. His father K. Khosa is a well-known modern Indian painter dealing with philosophical themes). Rajan is a writer, director and film producer who has worked between Europe, UK and India. He has won several national and international awards for his films: "Wisdom Tree", "Dance of the Wind", "Flower Girl", besides installations and multimedia projects. His films are celebrated for exploring the spiritual essence of their subjects. He was trained at Film and Television Institute of India and at the Royal College of Arts, London. His formative years were spent at the National Institute of Design, Ahmedabad. (www.rajankhosa.com)

DR SARLA KUMAR was born in 1928 in Lahore. Her studies were interrupted due to the Partition in 1947, when her family migrated to Delhi. Married to Datt Kumar, she moved with him to Europe from 1951–1958; upon returning to India she resumed her academic pursuits. After serving as Lecturer in English in several colleges, she completed her PhD in 1981. She taught for 16 years as Lecturer and Reader in Delhi University colleges. She came in contact with Swami Lakshman Joo in 1969 through her sister who was his disciple. She remained in close contact with her Master till his *samādhi* in 1991. After her retirement, she has devoted her time to the study and practice of Kashmir Śaivism, as well as to classical music.

PRABHA DEVI was born in Srinagar in 1924, the younger sister of Sharika Devi, Swami Lakshman Joo's chief disciple. She was associated with Swami Lakshman Joo from her early childhood, and from the age of ten, she studied with him texts such as *Śivastotrāvalī* and *Tantrāloka*. She studied Hindi and Sanskrit at Panjab University and at Srinagar. She married Moti Lal Mattoo in 1942, but he passed away just one year after their marriage. After the death of her husband, Swamiji asked her to join her sister and to live in the ashram, which she did from 1944. When the ashram moved down from the hill to the present Ishvar Ashram in 1962, she lived there with Sharika Devi and served Swamiji until his *nirvāṇa* in 1991. Prabha Devi and Sharika Devi studied a number of texts with their Master, and she edited and translated several texts with Swamiji's commentaries into Hindi, e.g. *Kramanayapradīpikā* (1959), *Parāpraveśikā* (1973), *Sāmbapañcāśikā* (1976), *Paramārthasāra* (1977), *Pañcastavī* (1987), and Abhinavagupta's commentary on the *Bhagavad-Gītā* (1987). She edited Swami Lakshman Joo's book *Trikaśāstrarahasyaprakriyā* (in Hindi, 1994). She also released Swami Lakshman Joo's commentary on the *Vijñāna Bhairava* (2003). She edited a commemoration volume for Swami Lakshman Joo in Hindi (with sections in English), *Śraddhārcana* (1998), and a volume on Sharika Devi in Hindi, called *Bhāvārcana* (1998). Prabha Devi lives in Ishvar Ashram, Srinagar, during the summer months and teaches texts of the tradition to seekers.

SRIMATI ARUNDITI RAINA was born in Srinagar in 1929. At the age of eighteen she married Sri Nilkanth Raina, Swamiji's younger brother. Ten years after her marriage, when they were staying in Bombay for some years, she received initiation from Swamiji and became a fervent disciple. They spent the years after retirement in Ishber, near Swamiji's ashram, in close contact with him.

RAM CHANDRA RAINA (1904–1992) started his career in 1924 as a revenue officer in undivided Punjab, where he also served as an electoral officer. In 1949 he was appointed as Land Reforms Officer and he was entirely dedicated to the implementation of land reforms. He was subsequently appointed as Settlement Commissioner, Jammu and Kashmir. His books on Land Reforms and Settlement Operations became guidelines for the Government. It was under his guidance that the "Jammu and Kashmir Agrarian Reforms Act" and the State's policy of "Land to the tiller" was enacted.

Sri Raina was a disciple of Swami Rāma Joo and Swami Mahtab Kak, and before his death he started writing a book on Kashmir Śaivism which he could not complete.

ALEXIS SANDERSON (1948–): A Spalding Professor of Eastern Religions and Ethics, University of Oxford, Fellow of All Souls College, Oxford, since 1992. He was a University Lecturer in Sanskrit, University of Oxford, 1977-92. He has conducted and guided research in the fields of Indian Śaivism, Khmer Śaivism, and the influence of Śaivism on other religious traditions, beginning his work in Kashmir as a pupil of the late Swami Lakshman Joo from 1971 to 1977.

His recent articles are: "Śaiva Religion Among the Khmers (Part I)," *Bulletin de lòcole française d'Extrême-Orient* 90-91, pp. 349-462 (2003-04); "A Commentary on the Opening Verses of the Tantrasāra of Abhinavagupta," in: Sadananda Das and Ernst Fürlinger (eds.), *Sāmarasya: Studies in Indian Arts, Philosophy, and Interreligious Dialogue*, pp. 89-148 (2005); "Religion and the State: Śaiva Officiants in the Territory of the King's Brahmanical Chaplain," *Indo-Iranian Journal* 47, pp. 229-300 (2004); "The Lākulas: New Evidence of a System Intermediate Between Pāñcāthika Pāśupatism" and "Āgamic Śaivism," *Indian Philosophical Annual* 24, pp. 143-217 (2003-05); "The Śaiva Exegesis of Kashmir," in Dominic Goodall and André Padoux (eds.), *Mélanges tantriques à la mémoire d'Hélène Brunner*, Pondicherry: Institut français d'Indologie / òcole française d'Extrême-Orient, pp. 233-442 (2007).

DR LILIAN SILBURN (1908–1993) was born in Paris in 1908, where she studied philosophy and indology (Sanskrit) with the great masters like Louis Renou, S. Levi and P. Masson-Oursel. Her thesis "Instant et Cause," a path-breaking work, has been published in Paris (1955). Her complementary thesis was a translation and study of Abhinavagupta's *Paramārthasāra*. Having discovered the non-dualist Śaivism of Kashmir, she became one of the foremost scholars who made this tradition known in Europe through her excellent translations and studies. She came to India and Kashmir after her Doctorate in 1948 where she met Swami Lakshman Joo with whom she studied the major texts of the tradition for many years. Her last visit to Kashmir was in 1975. She translated the following texts into French: *Stavacināmaṇi, Vijñāna Bhairava, Mahārthamañjarī, Śivasūtra* with Kṣemarāja's *Vimarśiṇī, Vātūlanātha-Sūtra*, Hymns of Abhinavagupta, Hymns to the Kālīs,

Spandakārikā, and five chapters of the *Tantrāloka*. She was Director of Research at the CNRS (the French Council of Scientific Research, Paris) from 1962–1970. Being a realized spiritual person, she gave guidance to many seekers on the spiritual path.

Dr Jaideva Singh (1893–1986), respectfully called "Thakur Sahab," was born in 1893 in Shoratgarh, in what is now Bihar. He studied philosophy, Sanskrit and music, and he became lecturer and principal of a college in Lakhimpur Kheri (U.P.). Later he was appointed Chief Producer of Hindustani Music in All-India Radio in Delhi. He was one of the foremost scholars of musicology and wrote on Indian music in Hindi and English. However, deeply drawn by the tradition of non-dualist Kashmir Śaivism, he settled in Varanasi in 1962 to be near his Guru Pandit Gopinath Kaviraj with whom he studied until the latter's passing away in 1976. He went to Kashmir where he became a disciple of Swami Lakshman Joo with whom he studied a number of texts which he translated into English for the first time: *Pratyabhijñā Hṛdaya* by Kṣemarāja, *Śivasūtra* with *Vimarśini*, *Vijñāna Bhairava*, *Spanda Kārikā*, and (published posthumously) Abhinavagupta's *Parātrīśikā Vivaraṇa*. He was awarded the Padma Bhushan by the Government of India in 1974. He passed away in Varanasi in 1986.

Mohan Lal Sopory (1916–1998) was the younger brother of Devi Sharika, and he was closely associated with both, Swami Lakshman Joo and Sharikaji. Being one of the earliest disciples of Swamiji, he was a lone witness to the important episodes connected with the Guru-*śiṣya* relationship between the two great saints. Though he wished to renounce the world, he was advised by Swamiji to marry and carry out a job. He, thereafter, worked in the transport business.

On 15th of October 1998, when he was already ailing, he told his family that the next day would be the last day of his earthly journey, and the same came true.

Motilal Sopory was born in 1925. Swami Lakshman Joo was the younger brother of his mother, and Devi Sharika was the younger sister of his father. Being closely associated with both these great saints since early childhood, his life was deeply influenced by them.

After having worked in the State Bank of India in Rawalpindi (now in Pakistan) he had to give up this position due to the Partition of India in 1947. He later joined the Jammu and Kashmir Government and retired as an Indian Administrative Service officer in 1984.

S.K. SOPORY is working at the International Centre for Genetic Engineering and Biotechnology, New Delhi. He had his early education in Srinagar, Jammu and Kashmir, and did his PhD in Science at the University of Delhi. He later joined the Jawaharlal Nehru University as a Faculty member and became full Professor in 1985. He has visited many countries and did his post-doctoral research. He was a visiting scientist at Max Planck Institut, Koeln, Germany, at the University of Texas, Austin, USA; United States Department of Agriculture, Beltsville, Maryland, USA; and also at the University of Munich, Germany. He is a Fellow of all the National Science Academies of the country, and also Fellow of the World Academy of Sciences (TWAS). Prof. Sopory is recipient of Shanti Swarup Bhatnagar Award of CSIR and the Birbal Sahni Award. He was awarded Padma Shree by the Government in 2007. He has published over 200 papers and edited seven books.

DR KAPILA VATSYAYAN was born in 1928. She began to learn classical dance at an early age and became the greatest authority on Indian dance forms. She studied at Delhi University and obtained a Master's degree in English Literature, continued her studies at Ann Arbor University, Michigan (USA), and received her PhD in Indology and Indian Art from Banaras Hindu University in 1982. Her postings included Lecturer at Delhi University, Visiting Professor in various universities in India and the USA, later Adviser to the Ministry of Education, and Additional Secretary, Dept. of Culture, Government of India. She held important posts in the fields of Art and Culture; as Secretary, Dept. of Arts, she made the conceptual plan for the Indira Gandhi National Centre for the Arts, New Delhi, of which she was also the Academic Director (1985–2000), and of which she is presently Chairperson. She also helped in building up several institutions, such as the Central Institute of Higher Tibetan Studies, Sarnath. Her vast knowledge and experience in all fields of Indian Art and Culture make her an invaluable reference for scholars in India and abroad. Some of her important publications include: 1. Classical Indian Dance in Literature and Arts, 2. The Square and the Circle of the Indian Arts, 3. Several publications on the Gīta Govinda. She also edited such important volumes as: "Concepts of Space, Ancient and Modern," "Concepts of Time, Ancient and Modern," among others.

SHARAD CHANDRA is a creative writer, poet and painter, based in Vrindaban.

Glossary of Sanskrit Terms

advaita	:	non-duality / aduality
advaitācāra	:	the practice of non-duality
anākhyācakra	:	cycle of the Nameless (in the Krama system)
antaryogi bahiḥ saṅgī	:	being a *yogi* within and living in society externally
anupāya	:	means without a means, wayless way to liberation (described by Abhinavagupta in Tantrāloka II)
aṇu	:	lit. atom, the individual soul
ācārya	:	teacher, master
āsana	:	seat, place where a *yogi* or spiritual practitioner sits for meditation
ātmā	:	the innermost Self
ātmasaṁskāra	:	transformation of the self (effected by initiation)
bhajana	:	devotional song
bhakti	:	devotion, love of the Divine or of the Guru
bimba-pratibimba	:	theory of reflection according to which everything in the universe is a reflection of the Divine Consciousness
bodhisattva	:	in Mahāyāna Buddhism: a Buddha who renounces *nirvāṇa* for the sake of liberating all living beings
brahmacārin	:	celibate, monk
Brahman	:	the all-pervading Absolute
brahmarandhra	:	'opening of *Brahman*', yogic centre at the top of the head
cit	:	consciousness
dīkṣā	:	initiation
darśana	:	vision, view, mainly seeing the deity or the Guru

devī	:	goddess; female saint
dhāraṇā	:	practice of concentration, spiritual practice
dhobī (Hindi)	:	washerman
guru-dakṣiṇā	:	gift to the Guru
guru-paramparā	:	tradition of Masters
gurubhāī (Hindi)	:	guru-brother, disciple of the same Guru
gurudeva	:	Divine Master
havana-śālā	:	hall for performing fire-sacrifice
icchā	:	will, impulse; one of the energies of Śiva
Īśvara Svarūpa	:	embodiment of the Lord; title given to Swami Lakshman Joo by his disciple Sharika Devi
iṣṭadeva	:	the chosen or beloved deity
jñāna	:	knowledge, gnosis; one of the energies of Śiva
jñānī	:	sage, wise man
jagadānanda	:	cosmic, universal bliss, the highest of all the stages of *ānanda*
jīvanmukti	:	liberation in life
kalaśa	:	earthen pot, here in the context of *śrāddha* or ritual to the departed souls
khecarī	:	moving in the sky of consciousness; Divine Energy (Śakti); also a mystical *mudrā*
kīrtana	:	religious songs
kramamudrā	:	spiritual state integrating the internal and external awareness
kriyā	:	activity, ritual; one of the energies of Śiva
kuṇḍalinī	:	Divine Energy residing in the body which can be awakened and made to rise by spiritual practice and by Divine Grace
liṅga, Śivaliṅga	:	conical and phallic symbol of Śiva
loṭā (Hindi)	:	water vessel, jar
mahāpuruṣa	:	great person, Saint
mahāsamādhi	:	great absorption; death of a saint or *yogi*
maṅgala śloka	:	benediction or invocation, introductory verse given at the beginning of a work invoking the deity or asking for blessing, etc.

mala	:	impurity, three types of defilements, according to the Āgamas
mūlādhāra	:	lowest yogic centre (*cakra*) situated at the bottom of the spine
maṇḍapa	:	pavilion
mantra	:	sacred word or syllable, expressing the power of the deity
mauna	:	silence, vow of silence
mudrā	:	gesture, attitude, mystical state
nara	:	man, human being and created reality; the third of the categories of Trika (also called *aṇu*)
nimitta-kāraṇa	:	instrumental or formal cause
nirākāradhyāna	:	meditation on the formless aspect of the Divine
paddhati	:	manual, ritual manual
pūjā	:	worship
Parā-Parāparā-Aparā	:	the three goddesses of Trika: the supreme, the intermediate, the non-supreme
Paramaśiva	:	supreme Śiva, Lord
paramādvaita	:	supreme non-duality, name of the tradition of Kashmir Śaivism which does not exclude or reject anything, since all things partake in Divine Consciousness
pūrṇāhantā	:	"full I-consciousness," the fullness of the Absolute "I" (*aham*)
pūrṇāhuti	:	final offering in the sacrificial fire
pralaya	:	dissolution, apocalypse
pramā	:	pure awareness
pramāṇa	:	knowledge, instrument of cognition
pramātā	:	knower, subject
prameya	:	object of cognition
prāṇa	:	vital breath, life-energy; specifically the outgoing breath in the yoga of Kashmir Śaivism
praṇāma	:	prostration, salutation by touching the feet; *sāṣṭāṅgapraṇāma* complete prostration with all the (6) limbs
prāṇāpāna	:	practice with in-breath and out-breath

prasāda	:	grace; blessed food distributed after any ritual, or blessed by the Guru
pratyabhijñā	:	(Divine) recognition; name of the philosophical school of Kashmir Śaivism, founded by Somānanda and developed by Utpaladeva (9th–10th centuries)
puṇya bhūmi	:	sacred land, auspicious place
rahasya	:	secret, mystical, esoteric
rājānaka	:	title given to a learned Paṇḍit
sādhanā	:	spiritual practice
sūtra	:	aphorism, short authoritative text
Śakti	:	power, Divine Energy
śaktipāta	:	descent of Divine Energy, grace
śaktipīṭha	:	sacred place of the goddess
samādhi	:	yogic state of absorption or deep meditation
samāveśa	:	state of absorption, penetration or union with the Divine (Śiva)
śāmbhavāveśa	:	state of union with the Divine (Śambhu = Śiva)
Śambhu	:	Śiva, the bestower of grace and peace
saṁvid	:	Consciousness, Absolute / Divine Consciousness
śāstraguru	:	teacher of the scriptures
sauḥ	:	seed mantra of the goddess Parā, also called *hṛdayabīja* (seed of the heart) in the Parātrīśikā Tantra and Vivaraṇa
siddha	:	perfected being, saint, in the tradition of Tantra
siddhi	:	yogic power, extraordinary powers attained through yoga
śiṣya/śiṣyā (f)	:	disciple
Śivasvarūpa	:	embodiment of Śiva
śrāddha	:	ritual for the departed souls
stotra	:	hymn, praise
suṣumnā	:	central channel, also called *madhyanāḍī*, through which the *kuṇḍalinī* energy rises in the body
svātantrya	:	freedom, autonomy; the fundamental energy of Śiva

Ṭīkā	:	word by word commentary
tīrtha	:	sacred place of pilgrimage
Trika	:	triad, trinity; name of the triadic school embodying the three principles — Śiva–Śakti–Nara, or the three energies — Parā–Parāparā–Aparā
turīya	:	the fourth, transcendental state of consciousness
ullāsa	:	joyful radiance, manifestation
upādāna-kāraṇa	:	material cause
upāya	:	spiritual means, way to liberation; three ways are mentioned in the *Mālinīvijayottara Tantra*, to which Abhinavagupta adds a fourth one: *anupāya*, in his *Tantrāloka*
vāk	:	the Word
yajña	:	sacrifice, Vedic fire-sacrifice, modified in the tradition of Kashmir Śaivism
yajñopavīta	:	investiture with the sacred thread, Vedic initiation ceremony bestowing the sacred thread and the Gāyatrī mantra to boys
yama, niyama	:	basic internal and external disciplines of yoga according to Patañjali, such as non-violence, purity, non-attachment, etc.; the moral basis for spiritual life
yoga-bhūmi	:	sacred land for performing spiritual practice or yoga
yoginī	:	perfected female saint, often deified

Index
for the article by Alexis Sanderson

admission of ignorance, 103
Aghoramantra, 107
Amṛteśabhairava, 106
Amṛteśvaradhyānavivṛti, 107
Ānandaśāstra, 104
Anantaśakti, 108
Aparārka, 113
Arimalla, 102
Atharvaśiropaniṣad, 108
Ātmabodha of Śaṅkarācārya, 108
bāca-baṭh, 120
Bāch-bhaṭṭas, 106
Bhagavadgītā, 108
Bhagavadgītārthasaṁgraha, 115
Bhagavadgītātattvaprakāśikā, 107
Bhairavakula, 104
Bhairavastotra, 96
bhāṣābhaṭṭaḥ, 120
Bhṛṅgīśasaṁhitā, 118, 119
Bühler, Georg, 105, 111, 113
Bodhapañcadaśikā, 108
Brahmayāmala, 98, 99, 114
Caṇḍā Kāpālinī, 114
chummāḥ, 108
Chummāsaṁketaprakāśa, 108, 111
creative exegesis, 104
Devīpañcaśataka, 102
Devyāyāmala, 108
Dharmakīrti, 113
Dhvanyāloka, 93
Dīkṣottara, 97, 98
figurative initiation, 117
Gamaśāsana, 104
Gāyatrīmantravivṛti, 110
intellectual dishonesty, 103
Īśvarapratyabhijñāvivṛtivimarśinī, 95
Jayaratha, 96
jñānamārgaḥ, 121
Kaivalyopaniṣad, 108
Kalādīkṣā[paddhati], 111
Kālīkulakramārcana, 102
Kāmika, 104
Kārkun, 120
karmamārgaḥ, 120
Kaul, Jiya Lal, 113
Keshav Bhaṭṭ Jyotishī, 112
Khan, Saif, 105
kôrkun, 120
Krama, 95, 108, 111, 114, 123
Kramanayapradīpikā, 123
Kramasadbhāva, 101
Kramastotra, 95
Kṣemarāja, 113
Kuṇḍalinīvijñānarahasya, 123
Lasa Kāka, 107
Lawrence, Walter, Sir, 104
Mādhavakula, 108
Mahānayaprakāśa of Śitikaṇṭha, 108
Mahārthamañjarī, 108
Mahopaniṣad, 108
Mālinīvijayottara, 95, 97, 106, 117, 118, 121, 122
Manodadatta, 111
mantropadeśaḥ, 112
marginal annotations, 106
Mataṅga, 106
Mṛgendra, 106
Mṛtitattvānusmaraṇa, 118, 119, 120, 121, 122
mundane religion, 113
Muslim rule, 104
Nīlakaṇṭhadīkṣita, 94
Netra, 106, 111
Niṣkalasvacchandadhyānavivaraṇa, 107

Niṣkriyānandanātha, 108
Niśvāsa corpus, 96
Niśvāsakārikā, 96
paramādvayavādaḥ, 95
Paramārthasāra, 108
Parātrīśikā, 106, 117
Parātrīśikāvivṛti, 107
persecution, 104
Persian, 106, 120
Picumata, 98
population, 105
Pramāṇavārttikakārikā, 113
Rājānaka Lakṣmīrāma, 107
Rājānaka Maheśvara, 115
Rājānaka Ratnakaṇṭha, 111
Rājarāja, 96
Rāzdān, Maheshvarnāth, 115
Saiddhāntika Śaiva exegesis, 116
samāveśaḥ, 117
sañĕ pŏṭul, 109
sauḥ, 107
Śaiva Gurus, 105
Śaiva initiation, 111, 113
Śaiva post-mortuary rituals, 113
Śaivism, decline of, 112
Śambhukṛpāmanoharastava, 111
Shāh, Hasan (Maulavi), 105
Singh, Jaidev, Thakur, 123
Śiṣyasaṁskāra[paddhati], 112
Śiva[svāmin] Upādhyāya, 109
śivakriyā, 106
śivanirvāṇavidhiḥ, 106
Śivapañcāyatanapūjā, 121
Śivarāma Upādhyāya, 110
Śivarātripūjāpaddhati, 110
Śivarātrirahasya, 109
śivaśrāddham, 106
Śivastotrāvalī, 108, 115
Śivopādhyāya, 109
sixteen Kālīs, 101
Smārta, 114, 118, 121
Spandakārikā, 108
Śrīpādukāstuti, 115
Svacchanda, 106, 111
Svacchandabhairava, 106
Svacchandoddyota, 113
Svāyambhuvasūtrasaṁgraha, 97
Tantrāloka, 94, 95, 98, 99, 100, 114
Tantrālokaviveka, 96
Tantrasadbhāva, 97
Tikku, 109
tolerance, 104
Trika, 111, 114, 116
Trika-Krama synthesis, 101
Trikeśvara, 109
Tripurasundarī, 107
Triśirobhairavatantra, 96
twelve Kālīs, 102
Upādhyāya, 109
upāyaḥ, 117
Vāmakeśvarīmata, 107
Vātūlanāthasūtra, 108
Vijñānabhairava, 106, 108
Vijñānabhairavavivṛti, 109
Vimalaprabodha, 102
Vitastāmāhātmya, 119
Viṣṇupañcāyatanapūjāvidhi, 121
yogamārgaḥ, 121
Yogasaṁcāra, 100, 123